PARTNERS IN COMMAND

PARTNERS IN COMMAND

The Relationships Between Leaders in the Civil War

Joseph T. Glatthaar

THE FREE PRESS
NEW YORK   LONDON   TORONTO   TOKYO   SINGAPORE

The Free Press
A Division of Simon & Schuster Inc.
1230 Avenue of the Americas
New York, N.Y. 10020

Printed in the United States of America

printing number

10 9 8 7 6 5 4 3 2

Library of Congress Cataloging-in-Publication Data

Glatthaar, Joseph T.
  Partners in command: the relationships between leaders in the Civil War/Joseph T. Glatthaar.
      p.   cm.
  Includes bibliographical references and index.
  ISBN 0-68-486363-4
  1. United States—History—Civil War, 1861–1865—Campaigns.
2. Command of troops—History—19th century. 3. United States.
Army—History—Civil War, 1861–1865. 4. Confederate States of
America. Army—History.   I. Title.
E470.G53   1994
973.7'3—dc20   93–25954
                                                              CIP

FOR DANIELLE

the finest that ever was

CONTENTS

PREFACE AND ACKNOWLEDGMENTS

> Fools say that they learn by experience.
> I prefer to learn by other people's experience.
> —*Otto von Bismark*

As American military history has demonstrated, an abundance of war resources does not guarantee success. Political and military leaders must generate power from those resources and direct and sustain it at what the Prussian military theorist Karl von Clausewitz called the enemy's center of gravity, its critical source of strength, to achieve victory.

Even before the Civil War, nationalism and industrialization had magnified the scope of war exponentially. No longer could a single individual supervise mobilization, oversee policies, plan strategy, administer the forces, and direct field operations. Warfare had become too complicated for that. Political and military leaders had to collaborate, to establish effective partnerships that could translate strategic vision into battlefield execution. They needed to learn how to join with others to harness and employ their resources most efficiently in order to triumph in the war.

This book is about those command relationships. It focuses on how commanders in chief interact with top field generals, and how those officers work with critical subordinates.

The study grew out of a course at the U.S. Army War College and focuses on six of those command relationships: Robert E. Lee and

Thomas J. Jackson; Abraham Lincoln and George B. McClellan; Jefferson Davis and Joseph E. Johnston; Ulysses S. Grant and William Tecumseh Sherman; Grant and Sherman and David Dixon Porter; and Lincoln and Grant. I selected these six because of the critical effect of each partnership on the success or failure of its armed forces. Interesting and sometimes colorful personalities individually, together they either offer a unique perspective on or provide distinctive insights into the varied forms of command relationships. All mightily influenced the course of the war, shaping its conduct and affecting its outcome.

Certainly these are not all the significant command relationships in the war. As to the Confederacy, one can build a strong case for the inclusion of chapters on Davis and Lee; Davis and Braxton Bragg; Lee and James Longstreet; even Davis and his secretaries of war. From the Union standpoint, Lincoln and Henry Wager Halleck; Grant and Halleck; Lincoln and Edwin M. Stanton; and Grant and George G. Meade would make wonderful grist for the analytical mill. Several of these emerge in the chapters on other crucial command relationships, albeit in abbreviated form. Civilian and military leaders did not function in a vacuum; these alternative figures drift in and out of these pages as they influence or affect specific associations. One cannot analyze the Davis–Johnston relationship, for example, without delving into the Confederate president's dealings with Lee. Likewise, Halleck's exchanges with Lincoln and Grant come to the fore in several chapters.

Since this book deals with the highest levels of command, it devotes scant attention to battlefield tactics. Instead, the study concentrates on the operational and strategic levels of war, with particular emphasis on the operational art and military strategy. Some definitions, therefore, may be appropriate. The *operational art* is the use of military forces to attain strategic goals in a theater of war through the conduct of campaigns or major operations. *Military strategy* is the art and science of using the armed forces of a nation or an alliance to achieve policy objectives by the application or the threat of force. *National strategy* is the art and science of developing and using the political, military, economic, and psychological powers of a nation during peace and war to further national interests, priorities, and policies. The *operational level* fulfills military strategy, which in turn helps to accomplish national strategy. Strategy, as COL (Ret) Art Lykke at the Army War College explains, is a composite of ends (what one hopes to accomplish), ways (how one intends to accomplish it), and means (with what resources one intends to accomplish it). Colonel Lykke employs a three-legged stool to symbolize the concept. There must be a delicate balance among all three legs—ends, ways, and means—for the stool, strategy, to work properly. Alter one of the legs, and the others must also be adjusted.[1]

My thanks go to Jay Luvaas. Not only was Jay instrumental in the course selection, but I also had the great privilege of spending countless hours discussing military history and the course with him. He served as a continual source of inspiration, friendship, and good humor.

To the people of the U.S. Army Military History Institute, I owe a debt of gratitude for offering me the Harold Keith Johnson Professorship and making the year the most enjoyable professional experience of my life. COL (Ret) Thomas W. Sweeney, LTC (Ret) Martin Andresen, Kathryn Davis, and Al Farris, all friends, deserve special gratitude for their assistance over the year.

My fellow instructors in Seminar 2, COL John Connolly, now Deputy Commandant, COL Bill Eckhardt, and COL (Ret) Greg Snelgrove, along with both modules of Seminar 2, exposed me to all sorts of fresh ideas and information in and out of the classroom.

The War College students from "Command Relationships in the U.S. Civil War" deserve singular praise for their wonderful insights and the excellent learning environment they helped to create. Every class was, without doubt, an exhilarating educational event. Our relationship was symbiotic. These men and women, all officers in the armed forces or civilians in the defense world with over twenty years of professional service apiece, offered most stimulating and penetrating comments, based on the readings and their own experiences. They exposed me to entirely new perspectives. In turn, the reading assignments and seminar discussions unveiled a fresh world to most of them. Through the use of history, they gained insights into political–military relations, strategic planning and execution, the impact of leadership personalities and styles on the conduct of war, and the complex world of interservice cooperation and joint operations. Rather than draw exclusively from their own observations and experiences, they learned to benefit from those of others. After all, who could teach senior officers and Defense Department officials better than Lincoln, Grant, Sherman, Lee, Jackson, and Porter, to name just a few?

My deepest gratitude goes to COL Al Cantrell, USA; LTC (P) Fred Channels, USANG; COL Mike Corbell, USA; CDR (P) Dirk Deverill, USN; CDR (P) Conrad Divis, USN; Ms. Jean Ann Feneis; COL Jack Fox, USA; COL Gary Goff, USA; COL Roslyn Goff, USA; LTC (P) Rich Green, USAR; LTC Bob Grider, USMC; COL Robert Griffin, USA; COL Mel Heritage, USA; LTC (P) J.P. Hogan, USA; LTC (P) Bill Jones, USA; COL Bill Kennedy, USA; COL Al Marple, USA; CDR (P) Gary McKinley, USN; COL Howard McMillan, USA; COL Terry Nienhouse, USA; COL Billy Orr, USA; CPT Bob Payne, USN; Mr. Jerry Peacock, DIA; COL Jake Simmons, USA; Ms. Maria Spring; COL Jon Swanson, USAF; and COL John Welch, USA. Each one opened my mind in ways I had never imagined.

Friends Edward M. Coffman and Gary Gallagher read the entire manuscript, and Jim Jones, Archer Jones, and William C. "Jack" Davis, perused chapters. All provided astute comments. Lynda Crist, Mary Dix, and Ken Williams, who are both editors of the Jefferson Davis Papers and personal friends, provided me with access to their holdings and directed me in my readings on Davis and Civil War Montgomery. LTC Johnston Beach, Professor of Behavioral Sciences and Leadership at the United States Military Academy at West Point and a War College student, gave me an hour from his busy schedule to advise me and provide readings for the chapter on George B. McClellan. Psychiatrist and friend Norman Decker, M.D., read the completed chapter and provided astute comments on my interpretation of McClellan. Dr. Richard Kohn, another great friend, commented on the Grant–Sherman essay.

Longtime buddies Keith, Erin, Caitlyn, and Meredith Cotton in Philadelphia; Stephen, Marlin, Sam, and Lucia Perkins in Maryland; and most of all, Niels C. Holch in Arlington, Virginia, aided me in my travels. Dr. Russell Weigley shared some time and ideas over lunch in Philadelphia. Agent Gerry McCauley and History Editor at The Free Press, Joyce Seltzer, helped to make this all possible. Thanks to Kim Jetton and William Clipson for the maps and Tom Hughes for the index.

I take full responsibility for any errors in this work.

The chapter on Grant and Sherman was delivered originally in a slightly different version at a conference in honor of Dr. Edward M. Coffman at Carlisle Barracks, Pennsylvania, and sponsored by the United States Army Military History Institute. Everyone who knows "Mac" Coffman realizes that a conference pays an inadequate tribute for his friendship, professionalism, and contributions to the study of military history. To me, as to many others, he has been an invaluable friend, mentor, and source of inspiration.

J. T. G.
Houston, Texas
April 1993

1

The Fabric of War

No event has so captivated the interest of the American public as the Civil War. It was the pivotal experience in the history of the United States, pitting brother against brother, section against section, and abolitionist against slaveholder. Northerners rallied around the flag to preserve the Union, and later to destroy slavery, while Confederates took up arms to protect their liberties and to defend their homes. At stake were not only the Union, the "peculiar institution" of slavery, and the rights of individuals under the Constitution but also the direction of this budding nation. The war erupted at a time when America was teetering on the brink of economic and societal transition. Industrialization, the transportation revolution, and burgeoning urban sprawl had begun to challenge the country's rural, community-oriented roots that predated its most articulate spokesman, Thomas Jefferson. Tentacles of the federal government were extending deeply into the domain of state and local governments for the first time, commencing a long and drawn-out process of wresting from them much of their traditional might and influence. In a strange way, a complex debate between concentrated and dispersed power lay near the war's epicenter.

The conflict shook the very foundations of both Northern and Southern society. Families reordered their priorities and responsibilities as adult males marched off to war and parents, spouses, siblings, and children filled the labor gap to maintain productivity. Manufacturers, artisans, and agriculturists churned out fabulous quantities of goods and foodstuffs to equip and sustain colossal armies. Politicians articulated wartime objectives and instituted controversial, sometimes revolutionary policies—conscription, income taxes, the wholesale confiscation or destruction of enemy property, including slaves, and the employment of men of African descent as soldiers and sailors, among others—to marshal sectional resources and convert them into military muscle. And army and navy leaders then attempted to organize and focus that power at the enemy. From the lowliest civilian or private to the commander in chief, they combined to weave an intricate fabric of interrelationships in quest of victory.

The personalities and interactions of civilian and military leadership, too, are an integral component of the enduring appeal of the Civil War. Never before or since has an American event brought forward such a rich and intriguing assortment of prominent individuals. Abraham Lincoln, who camouflaged a razor-like and visionary mind in rural trappings; the silent, directed, unrelenting Ulysses S. Grant; William Tecumseh Sherman, both brilliant and mercurial; David Dixon Porter, ribald in humor, innovative in warfare; and George B. McClellan, a mammoth intellect paralyzed by personal foibles, all rallied to the Union cause. Figures like the knowledgeable, distant, and temperamental Jefferson Davis; Robert E. Lee, an unusual blend of dignified gentleman and audacious warrior; the charismatic commander Joseph E. Johnston, who never measured up to the high expectations of others; and the quirky crusader Thomas Jonathan "Stonewall" Jackson drew the sword for the Confederacy. They served as the vital stitching in that cloak of war. The capability of these leaders to utilize their own skills and draw on the strengths of others, to employ the resources at their disposal most expeditiously, no doubt directly affected the war's outcome.

Never before had the United States engaged in warfare on such a massive scale. During the clash of arms with Mexico fourteen years earlier, Maj. Gen. Winfield Scott commanded an army of only 10,000 men on a decisive campaign against Mexico City. Just prior to the outbreak of hostilities between the states, the nation boasted a puny defense establishment of 16,000 soldiers and 23 active ships. Within a few years, both belligerents had transformed elements of that Regular Army and Navy into a gargantuan fighting machine, with a total of over 3 million servicemen and 700 combat vessels. Indeed, various segments of society had pulled together in uncounted ways to support the martial undertaking.

This staggering endeavor placed enormous burdens on both the political and the military heads. Microscopic peacetime duties had prepared no one for the monumental responsibilities of wartime, as they grappled with an extraordinary array of perplexing problems that none could have fathomed just two years earlier. Civilian and military leaders soon realized that the complex nature of raising, arming, planning, and employing so many soldiers in combat exceeded the capacity of solitary persons. They had to discard outmoded notions of individual dominance in warfare and draw on the unusual talents of others to resolve these issues and supervise their armies. Only through cooperation could they devise strategies, oversee mobilization, and direct operations effectively. Constructive collaboration, top civilian and military officials learned, multiplied power on the strategic and operational level.

Although leaders on both sides possessed immense resources to accomplish their pronounced goals of secession or reunion and the end of slavery, advantages, at least on paper, tipped the scales heavily toward the Northern camp. The Federal states boasted a population of 22 million, most of whom championed a resort to arms. The Union possessed a stable, secure financial house, and its states included 90 percent of the United States's prewar manufacturing and a huge, productive agricultural base. The extensive railroad network facilitated land transportation; the Regular Navy, along with an industrial capacity to expand it readily, could project forces along rivers and coastal areas. The Union also retained the small Regular Army and the bulk of its officer corps. While these professional soldiers calculated how to focus that strength on the enemy, a wealth of experienced Northern political leaders pondered the process of converting resources into military power.

To win the war, Federals must subdue the secessionists, no mean task. Some nine million people resided in the over 700,000 square miles that comprised the Confederate States of America. Most of the 5.5 million whites supported the defense of the homeland, although their 3.5 million slaves committed themselves halfheartedly at best, and indeed many opposed secessionist success. Like the North, the South was a land of agricultural splendor. Its industrial base was weak, but a sound manufacturing infrastructure, and a population with enough know-how to expand it, promised adequate productivity. Although the huge Confederate coastline enabled its mariners to evade the blockade, it served as an avenue of invasion as well. The Southern railroad system lacked effective integration; this inhibited Confederate efficiency while they held it and the Yankees once they seized it. Fortunately, a host of Regular Army and Navy officers resigned their commissions to join hands with their Southern brethren, and seasoned politicians abounded within its vast borders.

Most importantly, the Confederacy did not need to win the war, just to keep from losing it. By contrast, the Union had to conquer the seceding states and break the will of the Confederate populace to resist Federal authority. Anything less would result in Rebel triumph and an independent Confederacy.

Nothing about the war's outcome, then, was inevitable. Victory would crown the side whose leadership best tapped and retained the support of its populace, whose civilian and uniformed commanders harnessed its resources and directed and sustained its power against the enemy's source of strength. How successfully those political and military leaders forged partnerships to exploit their resources most effectively, therefore, would translate into ultimate success or failure in the war.

Robert E. Lee
(National Arcives)

Thomas "Stonewall" Jackson
(National Archives)

2

"He has lost his left arm, but I have lost my right"

Lee, Jackson, and Confederate Success in the East

On the night of May 1, 1863, among a cluster of pines about one mile south of the crossroads tavern called Chancellorsville, Gen. Robert E. Lee and Lt. Gen. Thomas Jonathan "Stonewall" Jackson gathered to formulate a plan. A massive Union army, over double the size of the Confederate defenders, had cleverly slipped its way across the Rapidan and Rappahannock Rivers above and below Lee's forces and converged on them. In response, Lee too had divided his command, checking one portion of the Federals at Fredericksburg with 10,000 troops, while the bulk of his army wrestled with the lion's share of bluecoats in a densely wooded area known as the Wilderness. That day, Jackson had probed the left flank of the primary Union wing and discovered no openings. Lee and Jackson were now convening to plot the next logical step, a blow to the extreme Federal right.

Armed with reconnaissance reports that the western flank of Mr. Lincoln's army lacked a proper anchor and possessed no cavalry screen, Lee and Jackson scrutinized a map to devise a route that would conceal the Rebel columns as they swung around the central

7

Union force. It would be tricky, but it could be done. Then the question arose: How many men did Jackson intend to take with him on this circuitous march? He wanted 26,000; this would leave Lee with a mere 17,000 veterans to hold the immense Yankee command of over 90,000 in place for the better part of a day, perhaps even longer.

Neither Lee nor Jackson flinched at these prospects. After twenty-four months at war, the two Confederate generals had forged a strong military relationship, based on an audacious, aggressive approach to warfare that compensated splendidly for their dearth of manpower and resources. There was no debate, no expressed doubts. Lee the planner, Jackson the executor, they fell into the boldest operational scheme of the Civil War almost matter-of-factly.

Since their days of service in Mexico some fifteen years earlier, Lee and Jackson had known and respected one another. No doubt Jackson came to Lee's attention as a daring artillery officer from Lee's home state. Every West Pointer in the Regular Army was familiar with Lee, the jewel of Maj. Gen. Winfield Scott's elite staff. In 1854, Jackson had sought and received Lee's recommendation for a professorship at the University of Virginia, and the two probably chatted in 1860 at the hanging of John Brown for his raid on Harpers Ferry. When Governor John Letcher appointed Lee military commander of Virginia Forces in April 1861, Jackson rejoiced. "This I regard as of more value to us than to have General Scott as commander," he announced to his wife, insisting that Lee was "a better officer than General Scott."[1]

Jackson was right about Lee. An exquisite-looking man in his younger days, at the midpoint of his sixth decade Lee had aged gracefully. He stood five feet ten inches tall, and weighed about 170 pounds. His thick chest and long trunk conveyed the appearance of robust health; on horseback, he looked impressively powerful for a man of his years. His eyes were deep brown, almost black to casual glances. When the war broke out, Lee had black hair speckled with a touch of grey and sported a black mustache. By 1862, the black had yielded swiftly to gray and then to white, and the facial ornament had blossomed into a full beard, also of white.

The Lee name provided him with one of the premier pedigrees in Virginia, with ancestral ties to all the best families in the dominion. His father, "Light Horse" Harry Lee, had won an excellent reputation in the American Revolution, but he never seemed to adjust to life in peacetime. Although Harry married well, and his son Robert lived for a time in magnificence at Stratford on the Potomac River, Harry's profligate ways had scandalized the family and dissipated its wealth. Perhaps young Robert entered the army with an eye to reviving the family name and restoring the fallen reputation of the Lees as military men.

Throughout his long military career, Lee had punched all the right tickets. Graduating second in his West Point class, Lee entered the prestigious Corps of Engineers, where he performed well and caught the eye of his superiors. In the Mexican War, he campaigned under General Zachary Taylor and then served valiantly on Commanding General Winfield Scott's staff. After a stint as superintendent of West Point, Lee left the engineers for field duty, specifically a lieutenant colonelcy in the cavalry. He resigned his Federal commission in April 1861, holding the rank of colonel in the First Cavalry Regiment. Just two days before, Scott had arranged for him to command the major field army of the United States. Even in his dotage, Scott recognized Lee as the preeminent officer in the U.S. Army. Many others in the service concurred with Scott's assessment, as did informed people in the Southern states, Governor Letcher among them.

"You will direct Col. T. J. Jackson to proceed to Harper's Ferry," Letcher enjoined Major General Lee in April 1861, "to organize into regiments the volunteer forces which have been called into the service of the state, and which may be assembled in the neighborhood." After consolidating the various companies into battalions and regiments, Letcher specified that Jackson should prepare the town's defenses and determine the sentiments in northwest Virginia toward the Confederacy. "Promptness in all these matters is indispensable," concluded the governor's letter. That same day Lee reworked the governor's directive for Jackson's eyes, incorporating fresh details while retaining the original intent. But Lee also included his own twist to Jackson's instructions, insisting that he expedite the dismantling and shipping of the arms manufactory there to the more secure location of Richmond, a most vital task. In the cases of both Jackson and Lee, the governor of Virginia had chosen wisely.[2]

Lee no doubt took comfort in the thought that such an accomplished officer as Jackson lay at his disposal as secession evolved into war. Jackson, a peacetime professor at Virginia Military

Institute, held the rank of major in the state militia. A West Point graduate with an outstanding combat record in the Mexican War, Jackson had resigned his commission in the U.S. Army at the height of a dispute and joined the faculty in 1851. Cadets at V.M.I. played pranks on Professor Jackson and ridiculed him behind his back. In this crisis, though, they gravitated toward him, his reputation for extraordinary achievements in battle and his cool levelheadedness amid turmoil drawing them near. Jackson marched the corps of cadets to Richmond in defense of their beloved Virginia, and less than one week later he received a commission as colonel in the state forces.

Nearly six feet tall and solidly built, Jackson resembled a plow jogger rather than an officer. His large hands and huge feet conveyed an ungainly appearance, and a gaunt, weathered face, high cheekbones, and a bushy brown beard augmented his bucolic looks. Only a military uniform and sparkling steel-blue eyes that suggested clear, penetrating thought belied his seeming rusticity.

By nature an overachiever, Jackson was a man in perpetual conflict with himself. An intense interest in resuscitating his declining family name certainly drove him to attack his personal inadequacies. And experiences in his first two decades of life reinforced this penchant for self-improvement. Orphaned at a young age, Jackson managed to fall under the care of an uncle, who worked his nephew hard, instilled good values, and gained him an appointment to the U.S. Military Academy. With coaching and cramming, Jackson barely squeaked through the admissions examination. But on the lofty cliffs that bordered the Hudson River, Cadet Jackson learned to improve his scholastic performance by sheer strength of will. To compensate for his shortcomings he simply forced himself to work harder than his peers; he rose in class rank from the bottom after the first year to the top one third by graduation. The lesson never deserted him. A tireless worker, he never seemed to stray from the chosen path. Whatever Jackson needed, he drew from deep within himself. During the Mexican War, for example, Jackson brazenly exposed himself to enemy fire on sundry occasions. He simply willed away fear.

Once Jackson had accepted Jesus Christ into his life in 1849, the battle took on even greater meaning. He harnessed that keenly developed discipline and channeled it inwardly, struggling to control all vestiges of human flaw and life's temptations. Every day Jackson fought a war to lead a Godly existence, poring over the Bible, reflecting deeply on its insights, boiling its messages down to precepts, and forcing himself to adhere strictly to them. In his own mind, he was conquering evil, but he paid a dear price for victory. Already awkward in the presence of others, Jackson's intensified internal focus seemed to heighten his eccentricities and distance him further from most people. He felt at ease only with God, his wife, and a handful of friends. Ceaseless strife with sin had sucked the youth from him. To strangers, Thomas Jackson appeared much older than his thirty-seven years.[3]

In those frenetic first months of the war, Lee was delighted to have a subordinate like Colonel Jackson. While military and political officials and civilians bombarded Lee with demands, requests, and pleas, Jackson managed his own affairs at Harpers Ferry. Every day countless problems, large and small, fell to Lee, as he struggled to bring order to chaos. Refreshingly, Jackson eased the general's burden by making intelligent decisions independently.

At Harpers Ferry, Jackson immediately took hold of the situation. He mustered into service available manpower and laid out defensive positions in the area. "Should Federal troops advance in this direction," he vowed to Lee, "I shall no longer stand on ceremony." On his own initiative, he elected to dismantle the musket factory first while continuing production of the more prized rifles; to ensure enough transportation to ship the equipment to Richmond he impounded railroad cars and supplies. All this he reported to Lee, along with the manpower strength and equipment needs that Lee had requested. When Lee instructed Jackson to offer local patriots five dollars per musket taken from the arsenal, Jackson replied that, "Previous to receiving your letter I had authorized the payment of $5 for the best arms, and graded pieces below that." Jackson was one step ahead of his commander.[4]

In one instance, the zealous Jackson exceeded the bounds of his authority and committed a mistake that could have resulted in serious repercussions for the Confederacy. Yet Lee immediately rushed to his aid. To protect Harpers Ferry, Jackson occupied the heights north of the Potomac River, technically an invasion of the Northern states. Lee promptly alerted Jackson that "In the preparation of the defense of your position it is considered advisable not to intrude upon the soil of Maryland, unless compelled by the necessities of war." The following day, he again hammered on the same theme. "Your intention to fortify the heights of Maryland may interrupt our friendly arrangements with that State," and he urged Jackson to employ Marylanders in its occupation. "At all events," Lee counseled, "do not move until actually necessary and under stern necessity." The enterprising colonel obeyed Lee's directives, and the crisis passed without consequences. To be sure, he had erred, but Lee could endure such mistakes. Most importantly, he had not failed through omission or inaction. Nothing rankled the overburdened Lee more than the reluctance or unwillingness of subordinates to act. This fellow Jackson made decisions.[5]

In late May 1861, Joseph E. Johnston arrived to assume command of all forces in the area on behalf of the Confederate government. Jackson, scrupulous to a fault, politely declined to observe the order. His authority came not from the Confederate States of America but from the State of Virginia. "Until I receive further instructions from Governor Letcher or General Lee, I do not feel at liberty to transfer my command to another," he explained to Johnston. Unperturbed, Johnston submitted verification, and Jackson yielded.[6]

Although the ascendancy of Johnston removed Jackson from Lee's watchful eye, he continued to thrive in service under his new commander. Johnston recognized Jackson as one of his finest officers and assigned him to command the First Brigade. In early July, at a place called Falling Waters, Jackson and a dynamic cavalryman named James Ewell Brown Stuart conducted a skillful probe and retreat against overwhelming Federal numbers, winning high praise from Johnston. Better yet, Johnston recommended Jackson for promotion to brigadier general, not in the Virginia state forces but the Provisional Army of the Confederacy. In forwarding the commission, Lee noted his "pleasure" at Jackson's well-earned elevation to higher rank. "May your advancement increase your usefulness to the state," Lee applauded.[7]

Meanwhile, Jackson, the stern disciplinarian, trained his soldiers rigorously, drilling them, marching them, pounding into them a con-

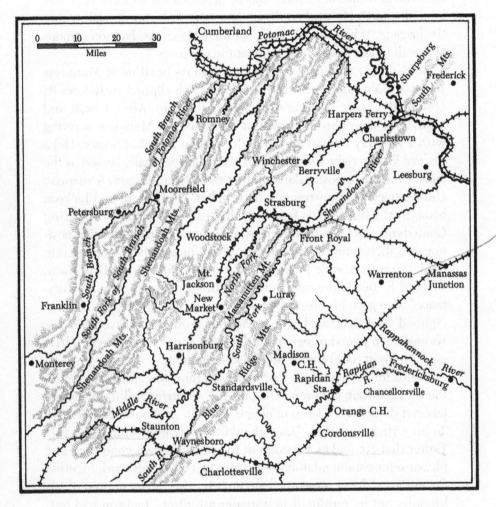

THE SHENANDOAH VALLEY

fidence to stand firm in battle. Jackson knew from personal experience the demands of combat, and he prepared his men the only way he understood: He worked them vigorously, fostering an elan within the brigade. When the test came, at First Manassas, Jackson's troops above all others were ready to meet the challenge.[8]

As Federals advanced on the Confederate position at Manassas Junction, Johnston's Army of the Shenandoah slipped away from its Union adversary, Jackson's brigade in the lead. After a swift and wearisome march to Piedmont, it entrained for Manassas arriving with a full day to spare before the Union attack. Designated a reserve for the right wing, Jackson's brigade eventually served as the anchor for the opposite flank on that eventful afternoon. A surprise Union attack from upstream rolled back the Rebel left, and Jackson brought the bulk of his forces to the rescue. Through retreating Confederates his troops advanced, securing a strong defensive position and then acting as the rallying point for a revived Confederate flank. "Yonder stands Jackson like a stone wall," cried Brig. Gen. Barnard E. Bee to the remnants of his brigade. "Let's go to his assistance!" Bee gave his life, and Jackson a portion of his finger. The disciplined First Brigade, however, held its ground and saved the day. Its men then joined in sweeping the field, at point of glistening bayonet. Nothing could have made Jackson prouder.[9]

Kudos for the victory fell primarily to Johnston and Beauregard, the commanding generals. Despite the powerful ambition that he labored diligently to keep in check, Jackson graciously acquiesced. To his wife he penned, "I am thankful to my ever-kind Heavenly Father that He makes me content to await His own good time and pleasure for commendation—knowing that all things work together for my good." He measured success by the performance of his brigade, not by public or newspaper attention. Jackson had out-trained, out-disciplined, and out-worked the other Confederate units, which explained why his brigade stood firm when others faltered. In a battle with many heroes, his superior officers knew full well the critical contributions that Jackson and his soldiers made in the victory. As he commented to a patron, "the First Brigade was to our army what the Imperial Guard was to the First Napoleon—that, through the blessing of God, it met the thus far victorious enemy and turned the fortunes of the day." Its achievement vindicated Jackson's leadership.[10]

Ever the indefatigable commander, Jackson refused to rest on his laurels. He again embarked on a rigid program of drill and discipline, tempered with personal attention to details that assured the good health and comfort of his men. Furloughs were out of the question. The Confederacy needed to augment its soldiers in the field, not reduce its effective strength. "Every officer and soldier who is able to do duty ought to be busily engaged in military preparation by hard drilling," Jackson noted to his wife, "in order that, through the blessing of God, we may be victorious in the battles which in His all-wise providence may await us." A good campsite with proximity to fresh water, proper tentage, pay, and clothing allotments offset the rigors of service in Jackson's brigade.[11]

The tranquility of camp life did not last long. In early October 1861, the War Department promoted Jackson to major general, followed two weeks later by an order to assume a new command, the Valley District, still under the overall authority of Johnston. His old troops, the famous Stonewall Brigade, would remain behind. In a tearful farewell Jackson saluted his men with affectionate words, doffed his forage cap, and charged off on horseback to their raucous cheers.

Now headquartered at Winchester, Jackson began the laborious process of cobbling together disparate elements to form a bona fide command. Militiamen and some scattered horsemen formed the core of his soldiery. That would not do. He needed a substantial mass of infantrymen around which to build his force. To fulfill Jackson's request, authorities in Richmond assigned him a veteran unit, familiar with the region and Jackson himself. The War Department restored the Stonewall Brigade to its old commander.

Not long afterward, Jackson undertook his first major independent operation. The plan, excessively ambitious in the winter season, called for troops under Brig. Gen. W. W. Loring to reinforce Jackson for a campaign against Federal troops at Romney. The movement would clear out Union forces in the northernmost sections of the Shenandoah and South Branch Valleys, thus gaining access to valuable supplies in the area, and would perhaps compel the Yankees to pull back from the northern banks of the Potomac River in Maryland. If McClellan interpreted the venture as a sign of weakness in the Manassas area and launched an offensive against the Confederates, Jackson's columns would drive on to aid Johnston.

Otherwise, he would crush the Romney garrison, push through the mountain passes into northwest Virginia, and clear out the Kanawha Valley. Military officials toned down the expansive scheme by striking the Kanawha operation, yet endorsed the remainder of the plan, if Loring agreed.[12]

Execution proved far more difficult than Jackson anticipated. Loring willingly cooperated, but it took him longer to join with Jackson than he expected, and operations did not commence until New Year's Day. By indirect march, a practice that soon became Jackson's trademark, his gray-clad column trudged northward to Bath, near the Potomac River, to drive back some Federals and isolate the Union garrison at Romney. Biting cold, sleet and slush, and icy-slick roads taxed the campaigners horribly. By the time they descended on Romney, the Union prey had slipped away. Pursuit by the exhausted Confederates was out of the question. Instead, Jackson divided his forces into small garrisons for easier supply and enemy observation, and then settled into occupation duty for the winter. The campaign, he admitted, had succeeded only partially. His army had forced the Union troops from a substantial chunk of northwestern Virginia, but he failed to deliver a decisive blow to the Federals at Romney.

In the end, Jackson had demanded more than the troops could give, and they reacted with hostility toward him. Grumbling in Loring's army percolated from the bottom ranks up to regimental commanders, who petitioned him to remove the troops from the Romney area. Two colonels appealed directly to politicians for intercession, and brigade commander Col. William B. Taliaferro blamed Jackson for the dreadful condition of the troops, accusing him of depleting "The best army I ever saw of its strength" through "bad marches and bad management." Jackson himself recognized the problem, commenting to Johnston that "Since leaving Winchester General Loring's command has become very much demoralized." Eventually, the complaints and petition landed on the desk of Secretary of War Judah P. Benjamin, who directly intervened. Bypassing Johnston and Jackson, Benjamin withdrew Loring's men from Romney. Jackson responded by requesting reassignment to V.M.I. or acceptance of his resignation. Intercession by Governor Letcher and others kept Jackson in field command, but Benjamin's order stood. Jackson then levied charges of insubordination and neglect of duty against Loring.[13]

Lost in the controversy lay a critical insight into Jackson's command and leadership style. Only the Stonewall Brigade fully met the challenges of the campaign. Through forceful discipline and extensive training, Jackson had prepared his old troops for just such an operation. At an early stage in the war, he had established an exacting regimen as his training standard, one more severe than that of any other commander. The fight at First Manassas proved the commander's practices right. There was genius to Jackson's madness. Troops in the Stonewall Brigade realized that Jackson had been hard on them in camp and in the field to save their lives in battle. By contrast, Loring's men were unaccustomed to Jackson's mode of warfare, lacked the training for it, and never grasped its utility. Whereas the Stonewall Brigade evinced confidence in Jackson's leadership, Loring's troops balked at their new commander and his methods.

During the next two months, Jackson's troops rested and refitted in the Winchester area for the upcoming spring campaign. Although drill and firm discipline remained standard fare, Jackson attended to the welfare of his soldiers, providing clothing, ample amounts of food, and adequate protection from the elements, as he had done after First Manassas. Loring and his men did not stay long. The War Department, fearful of insurrection, transferred Loring from Virginia and broke up his command, shipping several regiments into Tennessee and scattering others throughout Johnston's department.

By early March 1862, though, renewed Federal activity destroyed the tranquility of camp life. McClellan's massive army began gearing up for a long-awaited offensive, which stirred Johnston to life. In the Valley, reinforcements increased the strength of Jackson's opponents to approximately 35,000; he commanded barely 4,600 troops. On March 12, the last of Jackson's soldiers evacuated Winchester in the face of a Union advance, which marked the opening of his spring campaign. The following day, President Davis signaled his grave concern for the plight of the Confederacy when he formally entrusted Gen. Robert E. Lee with "the conduct of military operations in the armies of the Confederacy." For the past four months Lee had directed the defenses of South Carolina and Georgia, and on March 2 he received a terse telegram from Davis: "If circumstances will, in your judgment, warrant your leaving, I wish to see you here with the least delay." The recall to Richmond brought a valued military advisor to the president's side and rekindled the Lee–Jackson relationship.[14]

If Jackson had been the Confederacy's great overachiever, Lee had become its most pronounced underachiever. While Jackson's fame soared, Lee's reputation sank into the abyss. Military fortune, it seemed, had bypassed Lee during the first ten months of the war. His service alongside Davis in organizing the defense of Virginia had been excellent. Above all others, Lee had foreseen the struggle for Manassas Junction and had assembled a substantial force in northern Virginia to defend the valuable railroad intersection. Yet his contributions in a staff position had been relatively invisible to the public and the press. In his first command assignment, Lee's standing as a skillful officer plummeted when he attempted to coordinate a sloppy campaign in northwestern Virginia. Caught between officers who lacked competence to lead men in battle, rough terrain, and bad weather, Lee attempted to converge too many independent columns on the enemy position. The scheme failed and Lee withdrew without delivering a major blow to the Federals. The news media and the public suddenly lambasted Lee as an officer lacking in the necessary strength of will to command men to victory. Gossip of Lee's indecisiveness swirled throughout the capital city. Davis then sent him south, away from the hostile public's eye and where his engineering skills could aid the Confederacy significantly in the preparation of defenses in Georgia and South Carolina. In those first ten months Lee may not have lived up to the expectations of most Confederates in and out of uniform, but neither Davis nor Jackson lost faith in him.[15]

At first, Lee did not intrude on affairs in the Shenandoah Valley. While his position required him to oversee all military operations in the Confederacy, in the chain of command Jackson reported directly to Johnston. Absent from the seat of power for over four months, Lee needed some time to familiarize himself with the situations of the various armies in the field. And military crises to the southeast, north, and east demanded Lee's immediate attention. A Union invasion of North Carolina, Johnston's clumsy retreat from Manassas to the Fredericksburg area, a substantial accumulation of manpower at the Yorktown Peninsula that signalled the first wave of George B. McClellan's campaign for Richmond, and a large force to the north that threatened Johnston's army below the Rappahannock River— all these greeted Lee in rapid succession.

Strangely enough, what tempted Lee to divert attention to the Valley was a bungled attack on March 23 by Jackson at Kernstown, just south of Winchester. Confederate cavalry had misreported that the Federals had withdrawn northward, leaving behind a small rear guard ripe for Jackson's picking. Since Jackson's instructions called for him to defend the Valley against Union incursions and cover Johnston's left flank, he thought that an attack now might scramble Federal plans and draw off substantial forces that would otherwise oppose Johnston's beleaguered numbers. After a demanding march of forty miles, Jackson boldly hurled two brigades at the Federals, who held Kernstown in much larger force than the Confederates had anticipated. At first Jackson's troops drove the Yankees, but soon an extension of the Union line enveloped his left flank. Men from the Stonewall Brigade resisted until their ammunition ran out. Jackson expected them to defend their advanced position with the cold steel of bayonets. Instead, their line collapsed, as soldiers rushed pell-mell to the rear.

Through faulty intelligence and impetuosity, Jackson blundered tactically at Kernstown. He struck a force twice his size, was out-flanked, and had his line shattered, suffering heavier losses than his opponent. He then shifted blame for the entire failure onto the Stonewall Brigade commander, Brig. Gen. Richard B. Garnett. With no information from the secretive Jackson on the general battle plan, Garnett had retreated without authorization in order to save his troops from capture. Jackson levied charges against him, and it took Garnett months to shake the weak accusations and return to field duty.

Yet the implications of Jackson's attack far exceeded the disap-pointment of defeat. Jackson's boldness prompted Lincoln to inquire whether McClellan actually intended to leave behind enough troops to protect Washington and northern Virginia as his forces pushed up the Peninsula. On paper, McClellan claimed a defensive strength of 73,000; in point of fact, he lumped the 35,000 Federals operating in the Valley area among those defenders and stripped much of the rest for his operations east of Richmond. It appeared that McClellan had failed to live up to his promises. Lee observed with amazement how the Lincoln government reacted to Jackson's band of 4,500 by withholding large numbers of reinforcements from McClellan's army.

To deal with the overwhelming Union numbers, Lee concluded on a powerful diversion. McClellan's army on the Peninsula totalled approximately 100,000, and smaller commands—Maj. Gen. Irvin McDowell at Aquia with 40,000, Brig. Gen. C. C. Augur commanding 5,000 near Fredericksburg, Banks in the Valley at 35,000, and Maj. Gen. John C. Fremont west of the Valley in charge of 19,000—placed the Confederacy in a precarious position. Armed resistance to the Federal hordes consisted of Johnston on the Peninsula with about one-half McClellan's strength; Jackson in the Valley now augmented to approximately 6,000; Maj. Gen. Richard S. Ewell, a bald-headed, long-nosed, witty veteran whose penchant for indecision sometimes paralyzed him, between Brandy Station and Gordonsville with 8,500; rough-and-tumble Brig. Gen. Edward "Allegheny" Johnson guarding the Staunton area with 2,800; and athletic and intelligent Brig. Gen. Charles W. Field heading 2,500 men at Fredericksburg. But reinforcements could by no means offset the staggering manpower disadvantages. Jackson was Lee's great hope to distract the Lincoln government and prevent further increases to McClellan's army.[16]

From active duty in Mexico and the Confederacy, readings on Napoleon's campaigns, and mature reflection, Lee had honed his skills in the operational art of war. Simply stated, the *operational art* is the use of military forces to achieve strategic objectives in a theater of war. Often accomplished through a campaign or series of campaigns, it seeks to concentrate military power against the enemy's center of gravity, its source of strength. Lee certainly possessed a powerful sense of vision and a firm grasp of the complex interrelationship of ends, ways, and means. Both qualities lay at the heart of effective thought on the operational level. Yet Lee also had an uncanny talent for anticipating the movements of the enemy. As a trained engineer and student of war for more than thirty years, Lee understood the possibilities that confronted his opponents, and by studying their decisions and courses of action, he gained great insight into the minds of the enemy leaders. He understood how they reacted to particular circumstances and used that information to predict how they would respond to specific situations that he created.[17]

In this instance, Lee most likely perceived Northern public opinion as the enemy's true source of strength. If he could convince the populace that the price for victory was too high, or that the Union could not conquer the Confederacy, the Federal war effort would collapse. He also surmised that Lincoln, a politician with limited military knowledge, believed above all else that the Union could least afford to lose Washington to the Confederacy. The North could replace manpower; but shock waves from Washington's capture could collapse public support for the Union war effort. The Federal president, then, took excessive precautions to defend the city, and Lee, sensitive to his opponent's decisions, intuited this fear and intended on exploiting it.

Jackson, too, began to see his army as a means of influencing Federal strategy in the Eastern Theater. Lacking Lee's muscular intellect and knack for understanding human behavior, Jackson nonetheless possessed an unusual brilliance that made him one of the truly formidable commanders in the war. A weak tactician, and untested as a strategist, Jackson's true genius lay in his development as an operational commander. Just as he reduced God's teachings to fundamental tenets with which to assess his own conduct and feelings, so he boiled down war-making to precepts that he employed time and again. Seizing the initiative, skillfully maneuvering troops, massing forces at the decisive time and place, and employing the element of surprise lay at the heart of Jackson's style of fighting. When he engaged the enemy, Jackson turned those inward tensions outward, striking with unbridled ferocity. His two previous independent campaigns, against Romney and at Kernstown, exhibited his promise as a military planner and executor on the operational level. With counsel from Lee and maps prepared by topographical engineer Jed Hotchkiss, which enabled him to visualize the Valley and its features as never before, Jackson blossomed into an outstanding operational commander.[18]

Military activities in other areas preoccupied Lee for his first month, but once the War Department charged Johnston with command on the Peninsula, Lee became much more acquainted with

Jackson's predicament. All correspondence between Johnston and Jackson passed through the Adjutant and Inspector General's Office in Richmond, where Lee could peruse its contents. And with Johnston engrossed in everyday operations near Richmond, Lee stepped into the void and opened a frequent exchange with Jackson.

Professionally, Lee and Jackson meshed splendidly. Unlike many Civil War commanders, Lee did not feel compelled to control all aspects of campaigns personally. Far to the rear in Richmond, he defined his job as one of coordination, support, and general supervision. Commanders on the scene had to decide many issues for themselves. Lee could lay out the options, provide viable alternatives, and offer recommendations, but he refused to micromanage the war. Circumstances in the field changed on a daily, sometimes hourly basis. A good field commander understood his army and its morale, the capabilities of his subordinate officers, the terrain, the weather, and a host of other factors that influenced planning and execution. From a distance, Lee knew none of this. Thus, the officer entrusted with command, the individual in charge at the scene, was the person best poised to judge for himself. If that officer lacked the capacity to formulate and implement decisions, then he must be replaced. Jackson suffered no such problems. He had long exhibited a willingness to make hard choices and carry them out.

Three weeks after his defeat at Kernstown, Jackson began lobbying for reinforcements. A victory over Banks in the Valley "may greatly retard McClellan's movements," he asserted. If the Confederacy could amass a force of 17,000 and twelve artillery pieces to join him, he could threaten Banks's rear, drive that army back, and strike it in flight. The request fell on deaf ears.[19]

Then, on April 21, Lee intruded in the process by initiating an exchange with Jackson and Ewell. The Union and Confederacy had scattered their forces from the Peninsula to the Valley. Everywhere the Confederates were hard pressed, and Jackson had to use Ewell's 8,500 as reinforcements to attack Banks or yield them to Fields at the Fredericksburg area. Four days later, Lee exposed Jackson to his own assessment of the operational level in the Virginia Theater. He explained the entire military situation to Jackson, who some weeks earlier had complained to Ewell of his isolated state. Then Lee spelled out his agenda. "I have hoped in the present divided condition of the enemy's forces that a successful blow may be dealt them by a rapid combination of our troops before they can be strength-ened themselves either in their position or by re-enforcements." He intimated a preference for an advance on Banks, but a Jackson–Ewell attack on Federals around Warrenton, northwest of Fredericksburg, offered a viable second option. Both plans would relieve the pressure on the defenders near Fredericksburg, which Lee had just bolstered with 8,000 fresh troops. "The blow, wherever struck, must be successful, be sudden and heavy," Lee insisted. "The troops used must be efficient and light," an ideal mission for Jackson's command. Finally, Lee concluded by confessing, "I cannot pretend at this distance to direct operations depending on circum-stances unknown to me and requiring the exercise of discretion and judgment as to time and execution, but submit these suggestions for your consideration." He had skillfully established the context for their relationship. Lee would offer aid and advice; Jackson would decide and execute.[20]

The final days of April marked the genesis of the Valley Campaign. After two meetings with Ewell and messages back and forth to Lee, Jackson laid out three courses of action. He could unite with "Allegheny" Johnson's small band of men near Staunton and drive back a Federal advance from the west there, leaving Ewell behind at Swift Run Gap to threaten Banks's army if it pursued Jackson. A second alternative called for Jackson to link with Ewell and swing around Banks's main columns near Harrisonburg, employing the Massanutton Mountains as a shield, and attack detachments in his rear around New Market. With Jackson sitting on his line of communication, Banks would most certainly retreat. The third possibility was to slip through a gap in the Blue Ridge and march on Warrenton. Again, Jackson's army would turn Banks's position and perhaps cause mayhem among the Federals in the Fredericksburg area. His preference fell with the plan to merge with Johnson near Staunton and eliminate the threat to his supply base. Then, if Lee could provide reinforcements, the combined com-mands of "Allegheny" Johnson, Ewell, and Jackson could confront Banks's Federals directly. A decisive victory over Banks would enable the Confederacy to reinforce Fredericksburg or Joe Johnston with the Valley army. Lee immediately replied that no reinforcements were available, and after pondering the three scenarios for a day, he expressed a partiality for joining forces with Johnson and fighting west of Staunton first, but again explained, "I must leave the selection of the one to be adopted to your judgment." Within three days, the threat west of Staunton forced Jackson to arms.[21]

To deceive Banks, Jackson adopted a roundabout route to Staunton, joined forces with Johnson's small command, and pushed on to the town of McDowell. There, he repulsed a Union assault, but pursuit by his exhausted troops proved impossible, especially with the sloppy condition of the roads.

Meanwhile, ranking officers yanked a frazzled Ewell in three directions. As part of Banks's command hunkered down in Strasburg and a division left the Valley and headed eastward to link with Union forces under General McDowell north of Fredericksburg, Lee, Johnston, and Jackson issued Ewell conflicting orders. To folks at home the besieged Ewell griped, "I have been keeping one eye on Banks, one on Jackson, all the time jogged up from Richmond, until I am sick and worn down. Jackson wants me to watch Banks. At Richmond, they want me everywhere and call me off, when, at the same time, I am compelled to remain until that enthusiastic fanatic comes to some conclusion." All Ewell wanted to do was serve one master. Finally, Jackson resolved the multiple tug of war when he instructed an exasperated Ewell, "as you are in the Valley District you constitute part of my command." Ewell would obey Jackson's directives and alert him of any conflicting orders from headquarters.[22]

After defeating Federal troops at McDowell, Jackson hoped to turn on Banks's command and drive him from the Valley. Lee agreed. Banks appeared weaker than they had assumed, and the combination of Jackson's and Ewell's forces might enable Jackson to clear him from Virginia soil. Two days later, Lee again urged Jackson to strike Banks. A decisive Confederate victory might eliminate the Union threat in the Shenandoah Valley and draw Federal reinforcements from Fredericksburg or McClellan's army near Richmond. "Whatever movement you make against Banks," Lee advised, "do it speedily, and if successful drive him back toward the Potomac, and create the impression, as far as practicable, that you design threatening that line."[23]

One last time, conflicting orders nearly scuttled the campaign. Johnston ordered Ewell to come to his aid near Richmond or chase Shields's division, which had left the Valley to join McDowell's forces. Jackson read the disturbing news and acted quickly. He suspended Johnston's order temporarily and wired Lee for help. "I am of opinion that an attempt should be made to defeat Banks, but under instructions just received from General Johnston I do not feel at liberty to make an attack," he explained. "Please answer by telegraph immediately." Lee ran interference one more time for Jackson. He assumed responsibility for blocking Ewell's transfer if Jackson would attack.[24]

Jackson did not disappoint his protector. With cavalry acting as a screen, Jackson slipped through the gap in the Massanutton Mountains undetected, rendezvoused with Ewell's forces, and crushed a Union detachment at Front Royal on May 23. Suddenly, Banks discovered Jackson's army a scant dozen miles to his east, when he assumed his Confederate foe was closing from the south.

After some hours of indecision, Banks ordered a retreat to Winchester. The next day a huge cloud of dust blanketing the village of Middletown, some five or six miles north of Strasburg, exposed Banks's flight. With Jackson's soldiers nipping at their heels, Banks's troops discarded vast quantities of impedimenta and stores en route to Winchester. Only ravenous plundering by Rebel cavalry and infantry, much to Jackson's mortification, saved Banks's army from a horrible thrashing.

All night, with but a brief respite, Jackson drove his army to seize the prized hill southwest of Winchester. A breakdown in discipline had enabled Banks to escape once; it would not happen a second time. At daylight Jackson deployed for an attack. Simultaneous assaults from the Confederate right, center, and left caved in the Union position. But again, complete success eluded Jackson. Exhaustion, confusion in triumph, and the unwillingness of Ewell's subordinate to execute a direct order from Jackson permitted Banks to slip away. This time, however, he retreated without a fourth of his command, now prisoners of war. By midday on May 26, Banks and his mauled command gazed back toward Virginia from the north shore of the Potomac River.[25]

Banks's whipping and chaotic retreat suddenly spurred Lincoln to action. Rather than panic at the prospect of an attack on

Washington, Lincoln perceived an opportunity to trap the rampaging Jackson. The Union president ordered Fremont to the west at Moorefield to pass through a gap in Shenandoah Mountain, cross Little North Mountain, and occupy Strasburg. McDowell's Corps east at Fredericksburg, which was destined for McClellan's army, now would converge hastily on Strasburg. With a head start on Jackson and a little luck, the two Union commands could seal off Jackson's escape route from the south. Several days of good marching was all they needed. Lincoln had chomped at the bait. The plan of Lee and Jackson worked.

After his victory at Winchester, Jackson devoted the next two days to a well-deserved rest for his troops and then marched lazily toward Harpers Ferry. By May 28, he had learned of Lincoln's plot to snare his army, but the lure of Harpers Ferry and the idea of threatening a Maryland invasion proved too tempting. Not until May 30 did Jackson awake to the gravity of his situation. It was almost too late. Leaving his best unit, the Stonewall Brigade, to cover the rear, he directed one of the great forced marches of the war. McDowell's Federals, commanded by Brig. Gen. James Shields, had already seized Front Royal, and Fremont was closing in on Strasburg. This desperate predicament would have discomposed the most placid commander—but not Jackson. He summoned up that extraordinary strength of will and calmly calculated a solution. His cavalry blocked Fremont's troops and an infantry brigade checked Shields's division, while the remainder of his army slipped along the pike toward Strasburg. By noon of June 1, the elusive Jackson had slithered through Lincoln's trap.

But the race was not over. Shields's division took the road east of the Massanutton Mountains and Fremont pursued along the Valley Turnpike. Yet again, Federals were no match for Jackson's "foot cavalry." Although heavy rains slowed Jackson's march, they impeded Federal progress even more, as Jackson's horsemen destroyed the spans across the North and South Forks of the Shenandoah River.

Neither the harrowing escape nor the rout of Banks's army had quelled Jackson's ardor for battle. Most commanders would have retreated to safety; Jackson's fiery ambition refused to relent. A bold plan to strike one column, then the other before they united, began to take shape in his mind. If he burned the bridge across the South Fork near Conrad's Station, and then occupied the town of Port Republic, he would hold the vital crossroads. By controlling the bridge and the shallows there, Jackson could keep the Union commands apart and attack one, then the other.[26]

Over two days, Jackson did battle both Union columns. Unfortunately, the Yankees failed to cooperate fully in his scheme, and Jackson narrowly avoided personal capture and disaster to his army. In the end, his forces rocked Fremont and punished Shields, but the battles at Port Republic and Cross Keys cost him more than he bargained for. Neither side indicated willingness to extend the fight. His men loaded the trophies of battle into wagons and stumbled off to a gap in the Blue Ridge, euphoric from their exploits, relieved in their escape, and enervated from their arduous campaign.[27]

The achievements of Jackson and his followers were nothing short of phenomenal. Over the course of six weeks they had fought five battles and sundry skirmishes against three separate Union commands. In every instance they outmarched their opponents, and the campaign caused such mayhem that Lincoln personally devised a plan and committed troops to catch him, delaying the transfer of invaluable reinforcements to McClellan's army.

Lee heaped praise on Jackson for his leadership during the campaign. "Your march to Winchester has been of great advantage, and has been conducted with your accustomed skill and boldness," he acclaimed. Three days later, after news of the fights around Port Republic reached Richmond, Lee rejoiced in the achievements and welfare of Jackson and his army. "Your recent successes have been the cause of the liveliest joy in this army as well as the country. The admiration excited by your skill and boldness has been constantly mingled with solicitude for your situation." This Jackson executed operations to Lee's liking.[28]

The Valley Campaign launched the most effective partnership in the Confederacy. No doubt, the Lee–Jackson tandem had functioned brilliantly. Lee demonstrated a rare gift for planning on the operational level. He proposed the concept, provided invaluable advice, and prevented interference while Jackson implemented the scheme. For his part, Jackson proved himself an extraordinary operational commander. Those same qualities that elevated Jackson personally and spiritually generated his success as a military man. Most Civil War generals headed an army; Jackson truly commanded one. He imposed that towering will on his own forces and those of the enemy, disciplining his men through rigorous training methods to respond to his demands and compelling the enemy to campaign according to his own dictates. A clumsy young Thomas Jackson had learned to service a cannon through endless repetition; his army mastered the elements of warfare through rigorous instruction and drill. He compensated for any shortcomings by working his men harder than others, as he had done all his life, and forced the enemy to fight by his rules. Jackson marched his troops relentlessly, fought them aggressively, befuddled his opponents, drew vital Union manpower away from Richmond, and still won the day. It was during the Valley Campaign that Jackson matured as an operational commander.

Despite frequent contact, Lee and Jackson never established genuine intimacy. Theirs was a casual friendship, one rooted in an effective professional relationship, rather than anything truly personal. Occasionally they socialized, but there were no strong bonds between them. Neither Virginian could cast aside the cloak of propriety.

Jackson's internal focus inhibited his ability to establish deep friendships. The war, his struggle with sin, and family affairs consumed most of his day and left little time to cultivate congenial relationships. Nor were they suited to his personality. Jackson shared little about himself; he was a self-contained man. Quiet, perhaps a bit uneasy around others, he could confide his inner feelings only to his wife and a very few intimates. Before those among his inner circle, Jackson could laugh, even joke; there was a playful side to Jackson. But only a chosen handful witnessed it.

One of the few to break through Jackson's thick veneer was the dandy cavalry commander J. E. B. Stuart. Stuart and Jackson established a good relationship early in the war that soon blossomed into a true friendship. On the surface they seemed like the original odd couple—Jackson evidently introverted, rigid, and disciplined—Stuart ebullient, frolicsome, almost scandalous in behavior. Dating back to the skirmish at Falling Waters in May 1861, Jackson respected Stuart as a military man, and exposure to the cavalryman's ways convinced the pious Jackson that there was character and depth to this fellow. Jackson may have admired the way Stuart could blend this *bon vivant* personality with deep and abiding Christian belief. For his part, Stuart saw things in Jackson that others missed. Beneath the facade, the horseman perceived a gentle and pleasant side to the general whom the public called Stonewall. His presence raised Jackson's spirits as only the appearance of his wife and baby daughter (born in October 1862) did.

Like very few others, Stuart knew just how to stir up those sparks of life. The disciplined Jackson could never spoil himself with material extravagances, so friend James Ewell Brown Stuart did it for him. One day, he arrived at Jackson's headquarters with a wonderful present, an elegant new coat. Jackson could not succumb to worldly temptations by purchasing a garment of this quality for himself, but how could he decline a gift from his dear friend Stuart? Jackson donned the splendid coat with evident pride, enjoyed it immensely, but wore it sparingly thereafter. Such delight in personal possessions would only lead him down Satan's path.[29]

Unlike Stuart, most people never broke through the outer barrier. They simply viewed Jackson as a man of peculiarities. By themselves, these personality quirks and unusual habits were inoffensive enough. Taken together, they constituted bizarre behavior that warded off or discouraged others from approaching him. Certainly Jackson's introspection and open profession of God's good works struck some as odd, but many people incorporated religion richly into their everyday lives. Even though Jackson acted with excessive secrecy, a practice that frustrated subordinates to no end, many people could excuse it. After all, this was wartime, and Jackson was by nature a serene spirit. What marked Jackson as truly an eccentric, a notion that Jackson may have relished, was a host of novel customs that suited him well but struck others as weird. Among other habits, he refused to eat foods he enjoyed to rid himself of dyspepsia; he denied himself pleasures for fear of falling to Beelzebub's wiles; he sometimes raised a pointed finger in the air to improve his blood circulation; or he undertook a rigorous physical conditioning program, replete with running, rope climbing, and booming shouts to expand his lungs. All this, taken together, set him apart from his peers.

It was no wonder that high-ranking officers questioned his faculties. After some initial dealings with Jackson, Ewell doubted his sanity. When Jackson announced to Ewell that he had captured a Union wagon train through the aid of Providence, a disillusioned Ewell exploded, "What has Providence to do with Milroy's wagon train? Mark my words, if this old fool keeps this thing up, and Shields joins McDowell, we will go up at Richmond!" But in time, as he became more familiar with Jackson, Ewell learned to admire and respect him.[30]

In contrast to the painful awkwardness of Jackson in a social setting, Lee possessed all the charm and grace of the gentry. The scion of one of the finest families in Virginia, Lee felt at ease in the most exclusive social situation. He impressed men with his dignity and gentility, and enchanted women with his good looks and flirtatious banter.

Yet strangely, Lee was a man nearly everyone liked and admired but so few knew. General Joseph E. Johnston, a comrade since youth, may have been the only person in the Confederate Army who did not address Lee as "General." Nearly an entire generation separated Lee from his principal subordinates, Jackson among them, and this undoubtedly contributed to the distance between them. The same was true of close working associates such as his own staff. Not one of them glimpsed his true self. Despite hourly contact and shared accommodations, Lee perplexed them. One day he might go out of his way to perform deeds of kindness, but twenty-four hours later he could be quiet or curt with them, and on occasion he even exploded in rage. For them, life with Lee was both uncomfortable and burdensome, and their pledges of love and unerring devotion were postwar phenomena. True love Lee reserved for his family. As events unfolded, his all-consuming mistress proved to be the Army of Northern Virginia.[31]

Despite their demonstrable differences in background and personality, Lee and Jackson found common ground. Both men were devout Christians who drew upon their religious convictions in their everyday lives. Over the next year, they occasionally attended divine services together, both for personal fulfillment and to act as role models for the soldiers in their army. The Confederacy, both men believed, could not win this tyrannical struggle without God's gentle smile of approval.[32]

From a military standpoint, they shared an opinion that the overwhelming resources of the North required drastic countermeasures. The Confederate people had do all in their power to aid the war effort. They must "make every necessary sacrifice of Comfort, money & labour to bring the war to a successful issue," Lee explained to his son. Their generals needed to rely on combat multipliers such as initiative, surprise, speed, maneuverability, and concentration at the decisive point to offset Union numerical superiority. Commanders must seize the offensive and take the war into the North whenever possible.[33]

Most importantly, Lee and Jackson found comfort in the clash of arms. More than anything else in their lives, they excelled at war making. From an unusual vantage point at the Battle of Fredricksburg in December 1862, as Lee observed a counter-assault sprung on some attacking Federals, he turned to Longstreet and confessed, "It is well that war is so terrible—we should grow too fond of it." That single statement encapsulated the sentiments of both Jackson and him.[34]

Lee, the great operational commander, needed Jackson's skill as an executor. His bold plans demanded audacious implementation; Jackson could fight no other way. And Jackson, confident in combat, required Lee's keen intellect and deft interpersonal skills to elevate his performance. No one could assess enemy motives and develop courses of action like Lee. He possessed the uncanny ability to shape a campaign, to dictate its course, even when his opponent outnumbered him two to one.

As a commander, Lee's insights into human nature enabled him to elicit individual strengths among Confederate officers while camouflaging or repairing weaknesses. Jackson was a prime example. He fulfilled Lee's assignments, but in the process alienated valuable officers with his unyielding ways. A. P. Hill, Lee's best division commander, had run-in after run-in with Jackson. He contemptuously called Jackson "that crazy old Presbyterian fool," and once referred to Jackson as a "slumbering volcano," who might erupt in some irrational act without notice. Nor was Hill alone in his hatred of Jackson. Secretive, abrupt, inflexible, and a commander who held subordinates strictly accountable to the letter of his orders, Jackson left in his wake a cluster of officers who blamed their arrest or removal to Jackson's bizarre conduct. Lee could pick up the pieces. The army commander knew just how to soothe the distressed and calm the incensed. He employed the power of prestige, charm, and persuasiveness to placate victims of Jackson's arbitrariness. When Lee appealed to his subordinates to put the event or dispute behind them for the good of the cause and the army, few of them could resist.[35]

Thus theirs was a relationship of circumstance, a friendship rooted in professionalism and fashioned by war. Throughout their service, Lee and Jackson cooperated brilliantly, complementing one another's abilities and achieving remarkable successes. But there it stopped. Cordiality, consideration, and competence lay at the core of their bonds. Neither man sought nor needed intimacy from the other.

Jackson's victory over Banks, Fremont, and Shields discombobulated the Federals and boosted Southern morale, but Lee aimed at a bigger target, McClellan's army. On June 2, 1862, in the wake of Johnston's wounding, Lee assumed command of the forces around Richmond. Within days he sowed the seeds for a surprise thrust around McClellan's right flank. "Should there be nothing requiring your attention in the valley so as to prevent your leaving it for a few days, and you can make arrangements to deceive the enemy and impress him with the idea of your presence," Lee asked, "please let me know, that you may unite at the decisive moment with the army near Richmond." By June 11, Lee offered more detail. He forwarded reinforcements for Jackson's use against Federals on his front, perhaps even another diversion toward Maryland. Eventually, Lee intended for Jackson to slip out of the Valley and descend on McClellan's rear, while his command attacked in the front. Jackson's sweep would turn the Federals out of their entrenchments and enable Lee to strike them in comparatively open terrain, driving them back from the outskirts of Richmond. Secrecy, Lee intimated, was vital. "Let me know the force you can bring, and be careful to guard from friends and foe your purpose and your intention of personally leaving the valley." The plan was bold, imaginative, and brilliantly conceived on the operational level, so typical of Lee. And Jackson appeared to be the ideal individual to execute the critical flank attack.[36]

Yet neither Jackson nor his army performed up to their standards in the battles around Richmond. After sneaking out of the Valley

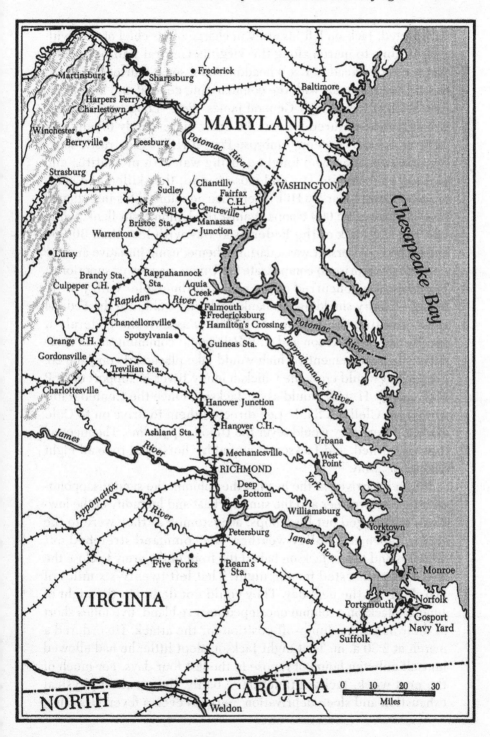

THE VIRGINIA THEATER

undetected, Jackson left his army in charge of his chief of staff with instructions to march along the Virginia Central Railroad route. Jackson rode ahead to Lee's headquarters, some fourteen hours in the saddle, to confer with the commanding general and his principals. Waiting were Major General James "Pete" Longstreet, a thickly built, good-natured fellow who grew increasingly touchy and sulky as the war went on; Ambrose Powell Hill, a thin, rustic-looking, likeable chap who fought a losing war with prostatitis; and Jackson's brother-in-law and close friend, the skilled and acid-tongued Daniel Harvey Hill. There Lee announced his intention of throwing some 56,000 troops against the Union right flank, while holding the bulk of the Federals at bay with less than 30,000 entrenched soldiers. It was a daring scheme, using initiative and the element of surprise to compensate for Union manpower superiority. The four men concurred in the plan and timetable. With J. E. B. Stuart's cavalry shielding the flank, Jackson would turn the Federal right, opening the door for A. P. Hill to assault the Federals at Mechanicsville. Jackson and A. P. Hill would communicate to coordinate their movements, which would take place early on June 26. Longstreet would cross the Chickahominy River in support of A. P. Hill, and D. H. Hill would assist Jackson. Once the Confederates turned McClellan's flank, Lee directed them to drive on to Cold Harbor, where they would sever the Union supply line. The meeting then adjourned, and Jackson mounted his horse and rode all night back to his army.[37]

When he arrived at the head of the column, the sight disappointed him. Foul weather and the summer heat and humidity of the lowlands had fagged out his troops, accustomed as they were to the cooler, more arid Valley weather. His command stretched out for miles and miles. Jackson halted the front of the army to close the line while he rested for the night. That left twenty-six miles of marching for the next day. They could not do it. On the night of June 25, Jackson's column encamped near Ashland, five miles short of their 3:00 a. m. jump-off position for the attack. He ordered a march at 2:30 a. m. That night Jackson slept little; he had allowed himself only ten hours of repose in the last four days. For much of the next week, Jackson functioned badly, the result of physical exhaustion and sleep deprivation, perhaps even a fever. His army, too, reacted sluggishly. Despite Jackson's orders, his command barely stirred to action by daylight. As he had done in the Romney Campaign, Jackson had demanded too much of his soldiers, and this time too much of himself.[38]

Waiting most of the day for word from Jackson, A. P. Hill impetuously launched an attack on a powerful Union position without him. His losses were horrible. This lack of coordination epitomized the performance of Lee's army over the next six days.

Amid the chopped-up terrain and nasty swamps, Jackson's command never seemed to locate the enemy flank. Rather than win victories by marching and outmaneuvering their foe, as they had done so splendidly in the past, Jackson's troops battered away frontally. His lack of familiarity with the region and its road network, his dependence on faulty maps, and his stupor from utter exhaustion magnified the difficulties. Much to McClellan's good fortune, this was not the same Jackson, nor was it the same army, that had accomplished such grand feats in the Valley.

Lee, too, seemed ill at ease in his first operation since the debacle in northwestern Virginia. Like Jackson, Lee suffered from poor maps, and his headquarters staff did not adapt well to operational duty. His most egregious problem was to repeat an error that surfaced in his initial campaign: Lee attempted to coordinate too many independent columns. He overburdened himself and his staff, and in the end, while his army drove the Federals back from the gates of Richmond, it squandered golden opportunities to carve up large chunks of McClellan's command. What Lee achieved in boldness of plan and combat aggressiveness he diminished through ineffective command and control.

With McClellan's army clinging to Harrison's Landing, under protection of Union gunboats, Lee terminated the campaign. A Confederate attack offered little promise of success, and McClellan indicated a greater interest in licking his wounds than in challenging the defenders of Richmond once more. The campaign had cost Lee 20,000 Confederate casualties, thousands more than the Federals, but the capital was safe, at least for the time being. Lee withdrew much of his weary army to rest, refit, and reorganize.

After barely one month in command of the Army of Northern

Virginia, as he styled it, Lee undertook a major structural rearrangement. In a summer housecleaning, he evaluated the performance of high-ranking officers and reassigned several generals, including John Magruder, Theophilus Holmes, and Benjamin Huger. Either they lacked the sort of aggressiveness that Lee sought in his commanders, or personal problems impinged on their ability to serve effectively. Longstreet and Jackson emerged from the reshuffling with supervision of multiple divisions, which Lee hoped would aid in command and control. Among Lee's division commanders, Longstreet demonstrated the most skill in handling troops, and his long service under Joe Johnston as part of the inner circle suited him well for this expansion of responsibility. Lee assigned him control of the bulk of his army.

Jackson's case was much more complex. In the Seven Days' battles, he had fallen short of Lee's expectations, and a record of nasty disputes with other officers trailed his military career. His lengthy experience as an independent commander also led Lee to wonder how he would adjust to more direct supervision and subordination. But Lee visualized strengths in Jackson that vastly outweighed weaknesses. Above all Lee's generals, Jackson had demonstrated a genuine brilliance in his previous battles and campaigns. Lee could overlook Jackson's lackluster service in the Seven Days' fight. No one in high command performed superbly in the campaign around Richmond—certainly Lee had failed to restore order and instill a responsiveness to his army during that chaotic week. Since Lee preferred to direct his officers with a gentle hand, experience as the Valley commander could only benefit Jackson. The squabbles with officers under his command and the courts-martial charges that he levied against other generals reflected Jackson's personality. Because he was somewhat awkward with his interpersonal skills, excessively secretive on campaigns, a stickler for regulations and efficiency, and exceedingly strong willed, clashes with others seemed unavoidable. Lee, though, believed he could soothe any offended officers. After all, he commanded the army and he established the tone and standards for commander–subordinate relations. It was his job as army commander to draw out the strengths of his people. Lee had confidence that the cause of the Confederacy, the critical stage of the war, and his own interpersonal and leadership skills could smooth any feathers that Jackson ruffled. For the moment, Lee charged Jackson with direction of Ewell's and his old division.

Trouble to the north spurred Lee and Jackson to action. During the Seven Days' Campaign, Lincoln united the three separate commands of Banks, Fremont, and McDowell under a single leader, Maj. Gen. John Pope. Pope, whose bombast vastly exceeded his talents, never got on track. He unwittingly insulted the troops in his army, announced that he would hold local citizens responsible for guerrilla attacks and would execute partisans without a trial, and pledged that anyone who declined to take the oath of allegiance to the United States would be forcibly removed from their homes and delivered into Confederate lines. Lee wanted Pope and his "atrocities" stopped. For some time, Jackson had been chomping at the bit to drive northward, perhaps even penetrate into Maryland. With Jackson's skill as an independent commander and his troops' reputation for lightning-quick marches and strikes, Lee considered his force ideal to "suppress Pope."[39]

As Pope's army pushed southward along the Orange & Alexandria Railroad and settled around the Rappahannock River, Jackson's command shuttled to the area near Gordonsville. Lee remained near Richmond, keeping a careful eye on McClellan's army and looking for an opportunity to detach more men to Jackson, "could I see a chance of your hitting him which did not involve its too long absence." News of Pope's advance to Culpeper Court House convinced Lee that it was time to gamble. He would double Jackson's manpower, reinforcing him with A. P. Hill's massive division, for a blow against Pope, while he occupied McClellan and discouraged that giant army from driving on Richmond.[40]

With notice to Jackson of Hill's assignment came some choice words of guidance from Lee. Take care of the wants of your men, Lee advised him, attend to their needs, and prepare your movements with great care. "I want Pope to be suppressed," he demanded. Lee then coached Jackson on how to utilize his subordinates' talents best. "A. P. Hill you will, I think, find a good officer, with whom you can consult, and by advising with your division commanders as to your movements much trouble will be saved you in arranging details, as they can act more intelligently." Effective communication with critical subordinates, Lee suggested, enhances the likelihood of success. To make such instructions more palatable, the commander explained that he delved into such subjects because "I wish to save you trouble from my increasing your command." Lee concluded by recommending that Jackson conceal his newfound strength until he was ready to attack, and after the battle prepare to return to Richmond, if necessary.[41]

In early August Jackson selected his target. He learned that a portion of Pope's force rested near Orange Court House, and he planned to launch a surprise strike on this smaller command. On August 9, at Cedar Mountain, Jackson attacked first, but Federal troops slipped around his left flank and into the rear, stampeding two brigades. Only a timely counterattack by A. P. Hill's men and the Stonewall Brigade swung the fortunes of the day in Jackson's favor. Nighttime pursuit achieved little, and as Federal reinforcements arrived on the scene Jackson fell back to Gordonsville. It was a good day's work. His army inflicted nearly twice as many casualties as it suffered, and his soldiers collected 5,300 small arms on the field of battle.[42]

Jackson had barely returned to Gordonsville when Lee ordered another advance. Reinforcements continued to augment Pope's command, and once Lee detected a large-scale movement of troops from McClellan's army to the north by water, the Confederate general realized he must strike Pope immediately. Leaving behind a part of his army, and drawing on that force as the risk around Richmond diminished, Lee ordered Longstreet and ten brigades to join Jackson. With Stuart's cavalry cutting the Federal line of retreat, Lee planned for Jackson and Longstreet to roll up Pope's left flank. But before the Confederate commander could position his troops, Pope caught a whiff of the scheme and retired north of the Rappahannock River.

Despite the size of the Union army at his front, Lee sensed an unsureness in Pope. If the Confederates could interpose a large force between Washington and Pope's command, it might rattle the haughty Union general and unnerve his troops. The movement would position the larger Union army between two Confederate wings, a perilous proposition in the face of a confident and aggressive enemy commander, but John Pope was no such person. And

Lee had the ideal man to lead this risky maneuver—Stonewall Jackson.

While Longstreet's men distracted Pope in front, Jackson and the cavalry swung along a wide arc into the rear of the Union army. It was a brilliant turning maneuver. Heavy rains foiled Jackson's crossing of the Rappahannock River for several days, but by August 25 he had slipped across the waterway and pushed on to a site near the Bull Run Mountains. The next day Jackson joined with Stuart's cavalry and seized Bristoe Station, on the Orange & Alexandria Railroad, and then occupied Manassas Junction, where Confederate soldiers feasted on Yankee bounty. Finally alerted to Jackson's true intentions, Pope began concentrating his army to attack the Rebels in his rear. Longstreet's columns, meanwhile, adopted the same wide loop around the Federal right that Jackson had chosen. The race to reach Jackson first was on, with the Federals holding the inside track.

Outnumbered three to one, Jackson drew upon his repertoire of deceptions to compensate. With Pope's army bearing down on him, Jackson divided his command and conducted a night march, sending them along different routes that eventually reunited his command in some woods at the base of Sudley Mountain. The position offered a strong defensive line nearby, with a railroad cut to protect the men, and provided easy access to the anticipated route of Longstreet. Stuart's cavalry skillfully shielded the Federals, which compounded the confusion. Again, Jackson's maneuver mystified Pope.

With the bulk of the Union army driving north beyond Manassas, a large and unsuspecting division tramped along the road a few miles to the south. Near the hamlet of Groveton, Jackson struck it with fury, catching the Federals completely by surprise. Much to Jackson's dismay, his men had attacked a plucky band of Wisconsin and Hoosier boys. Later nicknamed the Iron Brigade, these soldiers held firm and slugged it out with Jackson's troops, suffering huge losses and piling up substantial casualties in return. Only nightfall ended the vicious affair.

Over the next two days, Pope continued to make wrong decisions. Instead of continuing on to Washington, where he could have joined forces with McClellan's army, Pope ordered a concentration on Jackson the next day. But in his hasty search for Jackson's command he had denuded Thoroughfare Gap of infantry. With only Yankee cavalry to block their path, Longstreet's troops barged past the horsemen that morning and stepped quickly toward Manassas, twelve miles distant. That day, Pope battered Jackson's men in unco-ordinated assaults. Longstreet, who arrived on the scene before noon, repeatedly declined Lee's proposals to join the fray, citing a lack of good opportunities to assail the Union flank. Even though Longstreet's reluctance placed an undue burden on Jackson, it also concealed his command for the following day. Again on August 30 Pope hurled his ranks headlong into Jackson. Tenacious fighting on the part of the men in gray, aided by Longstreet's artillery that shelled the attackers in the flank, repelled advance after advance. By late afternoon, with Pope's army recoiling, Longstreet let loose his command, rolling up the Union left flank handsomely. Federals scampered in retreat toward Centreville.[43]

Lee and Jackson had not quite finished with Pope. The next morning, Jackson's veterans and Stuart's cavalry chased the Federals in another wide flanking movement. Once more, near Chantilly, Jackson hammered Pope's men. Amid torrential rains and blustery winds, which masked Confederate success and eventually brought an abrupt end to the fighting, Jackson pounded the bluecoats, inflicting 1,300 losses while sustaining 800 of his own. The remainder of Pope's ranks staggered into Washington and safety. Lee and Jackson had whipped them once more.

Pope's retreat within the protective works of Washington concluded the battles in Northern Virginia. It also culminated a series of operations that signaled the triumph of the Lee–Jackson relationship. Since Lee's reassignment to Richmond as head of all military forces, Confederate fortunes in Virginia had completely reversed. Lee had teamed with Jackson in a campaign that rid nearly the entire Shenandoah Valley of enemy soldiers and drew valuable manpower away from McClellan's primary target, Richmond. As commander of the Army of Northern Virginia, he called on Jackson to slip down to Richmond with his troops in the Valley and strike McClellan's exposed flank. In one week, they drove a massive Union army camped at the doorstep of the Confederate capital some twenty miles back, where it found sanctuary in a pocket along the James River under the shield of Yankee gunboats. Then, in August, Lee sent Jackson on a grand envelopment that bewildered the Union commander and set the stage for a Confederate rout of the Federal army in northern Virginia. Casualties on both sides had been high in the three campaigns, nearly 70,000 combined, but Lee and Jackson had accomplished the strategic objective of sweeping Federals clear from the soil of Virginia. With Lee planning and Jackson executing, the Confederacy had discovered a winning team. Together they demonstrated true mastery of the operational art of war.

In the wake of Pope's defeat, Lee had no intention of squandering the momentum that he and his army had established. He had seized the initiative in the face of overwhelming Union numbers, and to abandon it in late summer might expose Virginia to another major invasion that fall. "The war was thus transferred from the interior to the frontier, and the supplies of rich and productive districts made accessible to our army," Lee elaborated. "To prolong a state of affairs in every way desirable, and not to permit the season for active operations to pass without endeavoring to inflict further injury upon the enemy, the best course appeared to be the transfer of the army into Maryland."[44]

Lee intended the drive into Maryland as a raid, not an invasion. Permanent or prolonged occupation of portions of Maryland or Pennsylvania composed no part of his scheme. By penetrating well north of the Potomac River and maintaining a presence there for one or two months, Lee hoped to demonstrate to all Northerners the weakness of the Federal government, and perhaps to attract recruits to his army in the slave state of Maryland. He anticipated that the Union army would pursue him northward; this would allow Virginia's farmers to harvest their crops without Yankee hindrance. For more than six months, forces from both nations had lived off Virginia, draining the state of valuable provisions. If Lee could sustain his army for two months in Maryland and Pennsylvania, it would ease the burden on Virginia's agricultural producers. And in the back of Lee's mind lay the upcoming congressional elections in the North. Perhaps a presence through Election Day would influence Northern voters to cast ballots of frustration and dissatisfaction at the polls. A Congress with a strong stable of Peace Democrats and Lincoln-administration critics could hamper the Union war effort.

In early September 1862, Lee pushed across the Potomac River near Leesburg and advanced on Frederick, Maryland. He assumed that a position to the northeast of the Shenandoah Valley would compel the Federal garrisons there to evacuate and permit the Confederates to maintain a line of communication to that fertile region. When the 11,000 Union men failed to abandon their positions, Lee divided his army into two segments. After the victories in Northern Virginia, Lee believed that McClellan, back in charge again, would move cautiously, and scattering his army temporarily would risk little. Jackson, who knew the topography of the Valley as well as anyone, preyed on the garrisons there; Longstreet headed the raiding force to the north.

With the bulk of his command Jackson swung westward, slipped down across the Potomac, and marched on Martinsburg. The Yankees there and at Winchester promptly withdrew to Harpers Ferry. Jackson pursued them, bearing down on the town from the west. Two additional divisions converged on Harpers Ferry from the north, one crossing the waterway and gaining control of the high ground to the southeast while another occupied Maryland Heights north of the river. By September 13, Jackson and his division commanders had positioned their men to move on the town.

That same day, one of the most fortuitous events in the history of warfare occurred to the northeast at Frederick, Maryland. A Yankee private, rummaging in an abandoned campsite of D. H. Hill's division, discovered several cigars with a paper wrapped around them. The literate soldier scanned the document and recognized it as Lee's order to split the Rebel army, directing Jackson's men to Harpers Ferry and Longstreet's wing to the Hagerstown area. Within hours the "lost order" rested in McClellan's hands.

Emboldened by knowledge of Lee's plans, McClellan pressed Stuart's cavalry through a pass in the Catoctin Mountains and appeared headed for the gap through South Mountain. If the Federals could penetrate the pass and continue along that road a short distance, they would occupy a vital crossroad between Jackson and Longstreet. Fortunately for Lee, a heartened McClellan still advanced with some hesitancy. D. H. Hill's division raced into the opening in South Mountain called Turner's Gap, and Lee ordered Longstreet to march back from Hagerstown in support. The commanding general also alerted Maj. Gen. Lafayette McLaws, who held Maryland Heights, to beware of any Federal movement from the north through Crampton's Gap, the southerly pass through South Mountain.

By the evening of September 14, the fate of the gaps was decided. The Confederates could no longer hold out in the face of McClellan's overwhelming strength, and Lee elected to fall back west to a village called Sharpsburg, a short distance from the northern bank of the Potomac River. The combative commander notified McLaws that he, too, must move there expeditiously.

Lee chose wisely in his selection of Sharpsburg. He could concentrate all forces north of the Potomac River there, and then fall back into Virginia if necessary. From an operational standpoint, his position at Sharpsburg also defended Jackson. If McClellan attempted to break the Confederate siege at Harpers Ferry, his army must expose its flank and rear to a Lee attack. Once Harpers Ferry fell, Jackson could unite with Lee quickly and securely by marching along the south side of the Potomac River. McClellan's only move, then, was against Lee at Sharpsburg.

As Lee began positioning his troops south of Antietam Creek, a weary rider pulled up at the commanding general's quarters and delivered a note. Someone else must have accepted and opened the missive for two weeks earlier Lee had broken both his wrists in a fall. The courier brought good tidings: Harpers Ferry had capitulated to Jackson. The old artilleryman had positioned his guns skillfully, and after a little more than an hour of shelling, he convinced the Federal garrison that further resistance would not alter the inevitable. Eleven thousand Yankees, 13,000 small arms, seventy-three cannons, and assorted wagons, animals, and supplies fell into Jackson's hands. Late that afternoon, Jackson's command was off once more, this time along the Shepherdstown Road to aid Lee's army at Sharpsburg. A. P. Hill and his division remained behind to process the prisoners and take possession of the military booty. He would join them at Sharpsburg as soon as possible.

On September 16, McClellan arranged his army for an attack, then wasted the remainder of the day. Cautious to the last, he never tested the weak Confederate line. That morning Lee gambled excessively. He defended with barely 18,000 soldiers.

Hours of waiting tested every ounce of the ailing general's fiber.

Lee risked everything on Jackson, and this trusted subordinate refused to disappoint his superior officer. Shortly after noon, Jackson and his forces from Harpers Ferry began shuffling into Lee's camp. No one could move a body of men like "Old Jack." Lee directed them to the Confederate left. Still, two divisions trailed well to the rear. Not until after sunrise the next day did they trudge up from Virginia and by then the struggle had already begun. That left only A. P. Hill's fine command absent. Nevertheless, Lee's army lacked its usual strength. Straggling had taken a serious, nearly catastrophic toll on the campaign; thousands of laggard Confederate soldiers never set foot on the Antietam battlefield.

At dawn, McClellan opened a daylong series of uncoordinated assaults. Two corps pounded Lee's left. Jackson engaged them furiously. The fighting soon became so savage, and losses so severe, that the hard-pressed Jackson committed his only reserve by 7:30 a.m. It stemmed the tide—temporarily.[45]

Ninety minutes later the second Federal assault, by Edwin V. Sumner's Corps, plowed into Jackson's right, bending it back to the breaking point. At the critical moment, Lee intervened. He shifted a small division from the right, detached a brigade from the center, and parceled out his only reserve, which had arrived a few hours earlier, to Jackson. In a brilliant counterstroke, they routed the Federals, then overextended themselves in pursuit. Union troops rose up and punished them with a withering fire that chased them back. Jackson, however, had restored his line.[46]

Before 10:00 a.m., fresh Union troops struck the Confederate center, held by D. H. Hill. Hill's men occupied a sunken road, later nicknamed "Bloody Lane" as a reminder of the sanguinary action that took place there. Soon Hill's men fell back; with a bit more pressure the Yankees could split Lee's army in two. Troops from Jackson's right, exposed by Hill's retreat, entered the fray with telling effect. They struck the Yankee penetration with force, and supported by some artillery batteries, checked the advance. Then Hill scooped up a few hundred displaced soldiers and led them forward. A handful of organized regiments joined the counterattack. They were just strong enough to drive back the spent Federal assailants. Lee's center now held, barely.

By mid-afternoon, Lee and his army had endured enough harrowing moments to last a lifetime. But the crises had not ceased. On the Confederate right, where Lee had stripped manpower to save the left, a Federal corps finally geared up for a massive thrust. All morning long a pocket of Confederate resistance had repulsed attempt after attempt to seize the bridge across Antietam Creek. Early that afternoon, a mad dash finally secured the stone span for the bluecoats. Its loss was inevitable anyway, since a Federal column had forded downriver, and had pushed along the southern bank to uncover it. At 3:00 p.m., the moment of truth arrived. A massive Union corps—ponderous, powerful, and comparatively unused—rumbled into motion. To halt this onslaught, the Confederates had only a weak division. Lee rustled up some artillery support; he had nothing more. Back bent the Confederate line. Desperately, the defenders sought to halt the advance. The sheer strength of the Federal onslaught overwhelmed them.

From the rear a battery from Hill's division appeared. Help was near. But would Hill's command reach the battlefield in time? No one could see it—the hilly terrain obstructed the view. By 4:00 p.m. the Confederate line was giving way. Suddenly, a party of riders galloped up. A. P. Hill had arrived. His division was just down the road, after a grueling march of seventeen miles in seven hours. Hill had literally pushed them at point of sword.

Word of Hill's approach was electric; his attack was magical. In less than an hour's time, his brigades hammered back the Union corps.[47]

The opposing sides settled in for the night. After slugging it out for a dozen hours, all they had to show was the bloodiest day of the war. The following morning, they gazed ominously at one another. But when night fell on the battlefield, neither army had struck. While Lee then withdrew south of the Potomac River, the Federals slept. McClellan mustered only a meek pursuit. Lee's Maryland raid had ended.

As his army, worn from six months of hard marching and bitter fighting, recuperated amid the emerald slopes of the Valley, Lee assessed the recent campaign. The losses at Antietam were indeed dreadful. With Jackson's haul at Harpers Ferry included, however, the expedition across the Potomac River did achieve considerable success. It also amplified Lee's regard for Jackson's talents. "My opinion of the merits of General Jackson has been greatly enhanced during this expedition," Lee commented to the Confederate president. "He is true, honest, and brave; has a single eye to the good of the service, and spares no exertion to accomplish his object." His performance dispelled any doubts Lee had about Jackson's independent streak. Lee now viewed Jackson's ability to operate on his own as a virtue. In a reorganization of the Army of Northern Virginia, Lee requested that Davis appoint Jackson and Longstreet his two corps commanders.[48]

Late in October, Lee divided his army to block possible routes of invasion. Jackson's wing stretched along the road from Charlestown to the southwest to Berryville, where it could procure forage for animals and observe any advance in the Valley. Longstreet's wing, with Lee's headquarters, shifted east of the Blue Ridge to Culpeper Court House, in the path of another logical invasion route. Lee also strung observers all the way southeast to Fredericksburg. About the same time, the Union Army of the Potomac began its advance just east of the Blue Ridge. Jackson shadowed its movements in the Valley, ready to strike the Union flank. As Lee explained his operational intent to the secretary of war, "The enemy, apparently, is so strong that I think it preferable to baffle his designs by maneuvering, rather than resist his main force."[49]

Lincoln's replacement of McClellan with Burnside in early November 1862 shifted the direction of the Union campaign. The new Federal commander intended to trick Lee and slip across the Rappahannock River at Fredericksburg. But faulty staff work delayed the scheme and cost Burnside the valuable element of surprise. Longstreet's Corps rushed in to oppose the river crossing, and this bought Lee enough time to bring Jackson's Corps in from the Valley.

His plan a shambles, Burnside now elected to bull his way past Fredericksburg. Longstreet on the left and Jackson on the right, both occupying high ground, stood in the Union path. On December 13, Burnside unimaginatively hurled division after division into the defenders. Only in Jackson's area, where marshy ground prevented Confederate occupation, did Federals penetrate, and there Rebel reserves snuffed out the flicker of hope. Almost 13,000 Federals sacrificed themselves in the useless battle.

Throughout the winter months, cavalry raids, an aborted Union advance, and a Federal penetration in southern Virginia disrupted the monotony. Supply problems, rather than the Federals, dominated the Confederate agenda. The commanding general sent Longstreet with two divisions south of Richmond to contest the Yankee advance and gather provisions from regions untrammeled by armies. That left only Jackson's Corps, two divisions of Longstreet's Corps, and Stuart's cavalry to oppose the massive Union army to the north.

During those winter months, Lee and Jackson spent a bit more time socializing. They visited one another periodically, chatted pleasantly, and attended divine worship on a few occasions. Still, their personal relationship remained casual. That winter, Jackson was more preoccupied with his daughter, and Lee with his failing health, than they were with one another.

Without Longstreet's divisions, Lee risked much if the Federals advanced. But he had his heart set on another march into Yankeedom, and the supplies that he ordered Longstreet's men to collect were essential to his army. The new Union commander, Joseph Hooker, refused to accommodate Lee.

In late April 1863, the enormous Union Army, totaling over 130,000 men, rumbled southward. Hooker threw two corps across the Rappahannock River at Fredericksburg, while three more corps swung far to the west, waded the Rappahannock at Kelly's Ford, and descended on Lee's under-strength army, uncovering yet another shallows for two more corps to cross. Lee reacted with his usual audacity. Instead of falling back to the North Anna River, he split his small army, leaving some 10,000 men to defend Fredericksburg. He and Jackson marched against the main Union thrust. Hooker, startled by Lee's reaction, retreated from his scheme. The Union commander slowed his advance, assumed a more defensive posture, and surrendered the initiative.

And so, on the night of May 1, Lee and Jackson formulated the plan for a wide flank attack. It was their only hope of compensating for overwhelming Yankee manpower and resources. With a local guide and cavalry in the lead, Jackson began his circuitous trek at 4:00 a.m. Along roads that cut through the dense thickets and forest that locals called the Wilderness, Jackson's columns trudged. By

early evening, Rebel cavalry had located the Yankee flank and rear.
As the sun descended, Jackson meticulously arranged his attackers.
Their presence did not go unnoticed. Federals observed Jackson's
men, but the high command dismissed the notion as absurd. The
Union generals committed a fatal error in warfare—they assumed
that their opponents would act as they would. The assault roared
through encampments, stampeding bluecoats and rolling up
Hooker's flank. Union soldiers raced past so rapidly that their officers could not organize any meaningful defense.

The long march and thrill of the rout took its toll on the flankers.
Nightfall blanketed the Wilderness, as Jackson halted his men for a
quick regrouping before a final, devastating thrust. Up from reserve
came A. P. Hill's division. The two men had warred since the previous fall when Jackson arrested Hill for opening his march late one
day, and Hill was pressing Lee to bring the matter to a head. At the
moment, though, that seemed irrelevant. The minds of both men
were focused on the Yankees. Jackson wanted to close the affair that
night. As he pressed to the front for a personal inspection, sporadic
shots rang out, then a volley. Three balls struck Jackson, one in his
right hand, another in his left wrist, and a third above his left
elbow. His horse bolted, and Jackson struggled, then regained control of his mount. Within a few minutes, he collapsed. Several officers carried Jackson just off the road and attended to his wounds.
Soon stretcher bearers appeared. As they toted him rearward, one
stumbled and Jackson crashed to the ground. He winced in pain.
They then picked him up and hauled him to an ambulance wagon,
which carted the general to a hospital tent. Jackson's medical director and friend, Dr. Hunter McGuire, amputated his left arm that
night.

The next morning, Jackson awoke and dictated a message to
Lee, notifying him of the wound. Lee replied with sincere regret.
"Could I have directed events," the commanding general pledged,
"I should have chosen for the good of the country to be disabled in
your stead." Although there was much hard fighting ahead for the
Army of Northern Virginia, Lee's operational plan and Jackson's
brilliant execution had won the day, as they had done so many
times before.[50]

Five days after the wounding, pneumonia seized Jackson's lungs.

The commanding general extended words of encouragement. Tell General Jackson, Lee said, "He has lost his left arm, but I have lost my right." Within a few days, Jackson was dead. Lee "wept a good deal," as much for his fallen comrade as for the Confederate war effort. He had lost more than his right arm. In that very instant, the most effective command partnership in the Confederacy was dissolved.[51]

*Lincoln with McClellan (facing the president)
and the general's staff in 1862*
(National Archives)

3

"You have done your best to sacrifice this Army"

Lincoln, McClellan, and Union Failure in the East

On an unseasonably cold November day in 1862, Brig. Gen. Catherinus Putnam Buckingham, a War Department staff officer, boarded a private train in Washington en route to the Army of the Potomac. Buckingham bore specific instructions from the secretary of war. Snow pelted Buckingham as he clambered out of the car and wandered about the camp in search of Maj. Gen. Ambrose P. Burnside's tent. Twice before Abraham Lincoln's administration had tendered command of the army to Burnside, and twice he had declined. Buckingham came to extend the offer one more time.

After poking about camp, Buckingham discovered that Burnside had already retired for the night. His message could not wait. Awakening "Burn," Buckingham handed him an order relieving Maj. Gen. George B. McClellan, commander of the Army of the Potomac, and announcing Burnside as successor. Burnside immediately balked. A genial general whose jumbled name "sideburns" stuck ever after to his mutton-chop whiskers, Burnside declared that he lacked competence to command such an immense army, and he

51

would not replace McClellan, one of his best friends, under such circumstances.

Chilled and weary from travel, Buckingham refused to accept Burnside's demurrer. Overstepping his authority, he attempted to convince Burnside to take command. The administration, Buckingham argued, had lost confidence in McClellan and decided to remove him, whether or not Burnside succeeded to the position. If Burnside did not seize the reins, Lincoln likely would offer the vacancy to Maj. Gen. Joseph Hooker, whom Burnside detested. After mulling over these arguments Burnside reluctantly assented.

Despite the late hour, they elected to tell McClellan at once. Together they rode by horseback through the snows to a nearby town, where they caught a train to army headquarters. Buckingham and Burnside found McClellan alone, penning a late-night missive to his wife while his staff slumbered. The War Department had alerted McClellan of Buckingham's arrival, and he sensed the mission's importance. After some brief chitchat, Buckingham handed McClellan the order. He scanned it quickly and without visible emotion shifted toward his old friend and said, "Well, Burnside, I turn the command over to you." His tenure as commander of the Army of the Potomac had ended.[1]

For McClellan, it was another in a long line of failures with authority figures. In youth, he clashed with teachers, including the faculty at West Point, who unfairly deprived him of the top rank in his class, so he insisted. Throughout his military career in the 1840s and 1850s, battles with superiors plagued him. Among his sundry foe were the secretary of war and the chief engineer of the army, a brigadier general. In both instances, McClellan held the rank of only a second lieutenant, and his sheer impertinence irritated them. Even as a railroad engineer in civil life before the war, he stirred up trouble with his bosses. His struggles with the commander-in-chief, then, fit a life-long pattern.[2]

For Lincoln, the removal of McClellan culminated sixteen months of frustration. The president had taken considerable pains to assemble a massive army with staggering quantities of resources to crush the rebellion, yet McClellan had failed to advance vigorously or fight aggressively. All the while the general hurled complaints, slights, insults, brash remarks, and petulant characterizations at him.

Lincoln could endure that. But neither the commander in chief nor the nation could tolerate McClellan's hesitance to campaign actively any longer. As the president explained to a cabinet member, McClellan "has got the 'slows.'" He had worn Lincoln's cloak of patience threadbare.[3]

When the war broke out, it surprised no one, least of all McClellan, that his services were in great demand. McClellan possessed all the right qualifications and experiences for high command—graduating second in his West Point class, posting as a low-level engineer on Winfield Scott's staff in Mexico, observer at the Crimean War, several years as a successful railroad executive, and excellent political connections. The states of Ohio, Pennsylvania, and New York all vied for his services. After extensive wrangling, the industrious governor of Ohio placed the first offer on the table, and McClellan accepted. He received the rank of major general in the militia and commanded all Ohio volunteers.

Active and enterprising, McClellan promptly propelled himself into the job of organizing the Ohio enlistees. He oversaw the creation of a training camp, laid out defenses, and began the tedious process of converting civilians into soldiers. Extensive military contacts stood him in good stead when it came to accumulating weapons to arm and personnel to drill Ohio's forces. His seemingly boundless level of energy, his insistence on overseeing every detail, and his strong administrative capacity convinced soldiers, politicians, and civilians alike that he possessed a rare talent for military affairs. Within weeks he won an appointment to major general in the Regular Army.

On his fourth day in uniform, McClellan submitted without solicitation his first strategic plan of operation. Addressed to Bvt. Lt. Gen. Winfield Scott, commanding general of the U.S. Army, McClellan's proposal "intended to relieve the pressure upon Washington and tending to bring the war to a speedy close." He viewed the region between the Allegheny Mountains and the Mississippi River as one strategic theater and urged Scott to assign a single individual responsibility for it. After garrisoning critical positions along the Ohio River, he would lead an army of 80,000 men across the Ohio River and strike southeasterly up the Kanawha Valley, through the Shenandoah Valley, and on to the Confederate capital. "The movement on Richmond," he advised, "should be conducted with the utmost promptness, and could not fail to relieve Washington as well as to secure the destruction of the Southern Army, if aided by a decided advance on the eastern line." An alternative would be a drive by 80,000 troops through Kentucky into Nashville, Tennessee, and from there a march on Montgomery, Alabama. Supporting columns should fight along a Charleston, South Carolina–Augusta, Georgia axis, with the two commands ultimately targeting Pensacola, Florida; Mobile, Alabama; or New Orleans. Again, by implication he himself would command the primary army.

While McClellan certainly deserved credit for attempting to conceptualize on the strategic level, his fanciful schemes bore no relationship to the practical demands of war. His advance on Richmond ignored logistics. He could never feed and supply an army of 80,000 over such massive distances and across two mountain barriers without a complex, efficient railroad network or extensive water routes, neither of which existed. The campaign into central Tennessee overlooked Kentucky's neutrality and failed to consider the massive commitment that would be necessary from the navy. Logistically difficult but not impossible, his army would require gunboats, transports, and barges along the Cumberland and Tennessee Rivers. A movement from Nashville to Montgomery, let alone an amphibious operation against Charleston, would prove even more problematic. How he planned to accomplish any offensive with untrained three-month volunteers, McClellan never made clear.

At the time, Lincoln deferred militarily to his seasoned commander, Winfield Scott. A general officer since the War of 1812, Scott was the finest soldier in the first seventy years of the United States. He had fought splendidly against British Regulars at Chippewa in 1814, and had exhibited a mastery of command in the Mexican War. Impressive both physically and mentally in his younger days, Scott sometimes let personal vanity interfere with good judgment and clashed with his civilian leaders. Now, having lived three quarters of a century, Scott's infirm body, debilitated by gross obesity, failed him. His mind, still powerful, could no longer withstand the onslaught of corporeal decline. During meetings he contributed sage advice, but ailments and the demands of his enormous frame sapped all his energy, so that alertness deserted him after a few hours and he nodded off. Nonetheless, Lincoln regarded himself as fortunate to have a man of Scott's prodigious talents and experience available and treated Scott with kindness and respect.

Scott esteemed McClellan's ability. He had supported McClellan's promotion to major general in the Regular Army and just a few days earlier had advanced McClellan to commander of the Department of the Ohio, encompassing Ohio, Indiana, and Illinois. Rather than critique McClellan's plan, Scott drew McClellan into his confidence. The government intended to raise 85,000 men for at least three years, Scott revealed, and they would serve along with Regulars as the basis for the army of invasion. These forces would train rigorously, and in early November launch a campaign to seize the Mississippi River. Scott hoped to slice off vital portions of the rebellion, and in conjunction with a naval blockade, "envelop the insurgent States" and terminate the war with as little bloodshed as possible. "It is not improbable," Scott concluded, "you may be invited to take an important part" in the expedition downriver.[4]

Scott's sensitive response only fueled McClellan's passion to inject his own views among the high councils. Intruding on the affairs of neighboring departments, he sweetened his advice and requests to the haughty Scott with such expressions as "the general under whom I learned my first lessons in war and whom I have been and ever shall be ready to support to the bitter end" and "Next to maintaining the honor of my country, general, the first aim of my life is to justify the good opinion you have expressed concerning me, and to prove that the great soldier of our country can not only command armies himself, but teach others to do so." Meanwhile, McClellan filed protests with the secretary of war and secretary of the treasury over a lack of direction from the general in chief and a neglect to control key geographic positions. Scott rebuked him, but that did not deter McClellan. Several days later, he telegraphed the governor of Ohio, "Genl. Scott is as you are aware eminently sensitive, and does not at all times take suggestions kindly from military subordinates especially when they conflict with his own preconceived notions." By the end of May, McClellan had circumvented the entire command structure and submitted his ideas directly to the president.[5]

It did not take long for the demands of war to test McClellan, to see if he merited those laurels and positions. Confederate troops had penetrated into Unionist western Virginia, and Scott called on McClellan to "counteract the influence." From the very first, McClellan managed the campaign well, maneuvering his command masterfully in the rough terrain. He deceived his Confederate foe, and brought his vast numerical superiority to bear at the critical point. Then, in the decisive moment, he mishandled his forces. McClellan failed to press the enemy from the front to protect a flanking column. Fortunately, his Confederate opponents bungled the affair even worse, and Union troops thrashed the Rebels at Rich Mountain. McClellan proclaimed the battle a major victory, and the Northern government and public, crestfallen after the defeat at First Manassas several days later, joined him. In his own mind, McClellan twisted his performance as commander to coincide with the outcome of the engagement—if the Union had achieved a glorious victory, then surely he had directed the army skillfully.[6]

Success thrust McClellan into the spotlight. The handsome lines of Union blue that marched off to quash the rebellion at First Manassas staggered back to Washington piecemeal, more mob than army. In the face of this disaster, the Lincoln administration sought an intelligent, industrious individual to reorganize the troops and whip them into an effective fighting force. On July 22, 1861, the authorities called McClellan to Washington. Even before he arrived, the War Department had announced his appointment as commander of the Division of the Potomac. Lincoln, so he hoped, had found his man.[7]

The Lincoln–McClellan relationship dated back to the late 1850s. While McClellan was working for the Illinois Central Railroad, Lincoln had acted as one of its attorneys. Neither the man nor his politics impressed McClellan much, as the railroad executive strongly supported Lincoln's opponent, Stephen A. Douglas, during the senatorial campaign of 1858. The day after McClellan's arrival in Washington, the two men met again in the White House to discuss the new position.

The gathering at the presidential mansion was a scene of contrasts. McClellan—somewhat short, thick, mustached—appeared every bit a soldier, as if he had been born to wear the uniform. At thirty-four years of age, McClellan represented youth, power, and energy to onlookers. The tall, gaunt Lincoln looked awkward even in civilian garb. McClellan's senior by nearly two decades, the new president startled people with his unusual height, sinewy frame, and odd features. Personality accentuated the distinctions. McClellan retained a cool, aloof, proper bearing that conveyed an image of direction and businesslike habits. George Bancroft, a well-traveled Boston brahmin whom Lincoln introduced to McClellan one day, commented to his wife: "Of all silent, uncommunicative, reserved men, whom I ever met, the general stands among the first." Lincoln, by comparison, was personable, jocular, and informal, almost too casual, to some observers, for the gravity of the current crisis. As a result, most people underestimated Lincoln. No one walked away from an initial encounter with McClellan unimpressed.

Their differences transcended physical and social qualities. McClellan came from a refined Philadelphia family. Trained and educated as an officer and a gentleman, he relished his status as an aristocrat. Promotion to major general in the Regular Army, second in rank only to the septuagenarian Scott, merely fulfilled expectations for a man of his talents, breeding, training, and attainments.

Unlike the new army commander, who was groomed for a career in leadership, Lincoln had no such background or birthright. The son of Thomas Lincoln, a hardworking laborer with a knack for story telling, the new president had received scant formal schooling. Nonetheless, passionate in his quest for knowledge, young Lincoln mastered any book he could obtain. Among the volumes that shaped his mind over the years, Euclidean geometry and Blackstone's legal *Commentaries* taught him to create order from a world of complexity and chaos. As an attorney and state politico, he retained a folksy manner from his past that disguised a piercing intelligence. Quick with a joke or yarn, Lincoln reflected deeply and occasionally brooded. Always poking, always probing, hesitant to commit until the precise moment, Lincoln's ways often obscured his magnificent mind and excellent judgment from the sight of those who did not know him well.

In McClellan's opinion, the nation had chosen unwisely when it elected Lincoln president. Lincoln did not measure up to McClellan's narrow ideal of leadership. In this time of crisis, McClellan believed that the country needed a directed, forceful, and energetic leader, rather than the wishy-washy Lincoln. Lincoln neither looked nor assumed the part of a great leader. He did not project well. His level of informality rankled the cultured, aristocratic McClellan. Lincoln's casual manner—sometimes he greeted officials and dignitaries in carpet slippers—his common habits and ways, his apparently obtuse mind—posing questions, spinning seemingly irrelevant tales, and never ostensively grasping McClellan's point—all spelled disaster for the war effort. In Lincoln, McClellan sensed vacillation and weakness.

After conversing with the president and cabinet members about a wide range of military matters, McClellan visited fragments of his new army, General Scott, and important politicians. Many of them had overreacted to the defeat at First Manassas, and the mere presence of the victor of western Virginia restored equilibrium among the panicky and sense among the confused. The hero's welcome he had received went straight to his head. "I find myself in a new & strange position here—," he described to his wife, "Presdt, Cabinet, Genl Scott & all deferring to me—by some strange operation of magic I seem to have become *the* power of the land. I almost think that were I to win some small success now I could become Dictator or anything else that might please me—but nothing of that kind would please me—*therefore* I *won't* be Dictator. Admirable self denial!"[9]

These were exciting days for McClellan, as everyone fed his sense of self-importance. Crowds gathered around him and cheered. Senators, marveling at his youth, "give me my way in everything, full swing & unbounded confidence." The people looked to him, he explained to his wife, to save the nation: "All tell me that I am held responsible for the fate of the Nation & that all its resources shall be placed at my disposal." McClellan concluded that national salvation rested on his shoulders.[10]

And McClellan did take hold of the situation. After his first full day he had already determined the causes of failure, and "I am *sure* that I can remedy these & am confident that I can lead these armies of men to victory once more," he wrote his wife.[11] Delegating little responsibility, he spent long days in the saddle, inspecting troops, coercing soldiers to return to their units, reorganizing commands, and commencing drill. His tireless efforts infused a fresh confidence in the ranks, as well as in the civilian population.

McClellan built the Army of the Potomac. He organized it, he trained it, and he inspired it. His penchant for personal supervision paid great dividends with the troops. A man of rare stamina, McClellan travelled from his Washington headquarters day after day to see to the needs of his "boys." He visited commands, chatted briefly with soldiers, scrutinized their training, and observed their elaborate parades and reviews. McClellan made them feel like soldiers, and they loved him for it.

He looked every bit the commanding general. He stood a stocky 5 feet 8 inches tall, but his dark hair, barrel chest, and unusually short legs conveyed a much larger appearance on horseback. With a flair for the dramatic, McClellan knew just how to gaze upon row after row of troops or gallop down the line, staff trailing well behind, waving a hat above his head in acknowledgment of their huzzahs. His mere presence inspired confidence.

But with his organizational skills came unanticipated baggage: McClellan, ever certain of his own judgment, attempted to dictate policy. On August 2, 1861, in a lengthy strategic assessment prepared at Lincoln's request, McClellan urged a shift of the entire focus of the war from west to east, where he was now stationed. Opening with an incisive declaration of the war's ends, he noted, "We have not only to defeat their armed and organized forces in the field, but to display such an overwhelming strength as will convince all our antagonists, especially those of the governing, aristocratic class, of the utter impossibility of resistance." The heart of his plan called for a primary army for operations in Virginia of 273,000 troops, a far cry from his 80,000-man strike force across the Appalachians against Richmond. He recommended Lincoln not make this a war against property and civilians, and went so far as to suggest an alliance with Mexico to maintain its neutrality.[12]

Six days later, in a letter to Scott with a copy presented to Lincoln, he discussed the plight of the Union army in Virginia. Based on no hard evidence, McClellan insisted that the Confederate forces opposing him numbered 100,000. He anticipated an attack on Washington and announced that his army "is entirely insufficient for the emergency." In this moment of crisis, McClellan sought control of nearby departments and demanded a massive infusion of troops to his command. "I urge that nothing be left undone to bring up our force for the defense of this city to 100,000 men, before attending to any other point," he cautioned.[13]

Within two weeks, McClellan had sized up the situation to his complete satisfaction and had determined the solutions. He called for a reorientation of the war effort to his military division, escalated his needs monumentally, and through inflated estimates doubled the enemy's strength. His behavior marked a pattern that endured throughout his tenure as commander of the Army of the Potomac. He vastly overestimated the strength and threat of the enemy, exaggerated his needs, hounded his superiors for a disproportionate share of the military resources, and then placed the entire blame for failure on their shoulders. Anyone who disagreed with him was either a fool or disloyal. Since the politicians knew nothing of military affairs they accepted McClellan's opinion, at least initially, as gospel. Scott, with nearly fifty years of military experience, did not, and McClellan targeted him first.

Just days after his arrival in Washington, McClellan set his sights on his superior officer. In mid-July 1861, McClellan had declared Scott his mentor. "All that I know of war I have learned from you," he flattered the commanding general, "& in all that I have done I have endeavored to conform to your manner of conducting a campaign, as I understand the history of your achievements. It is my ambition to merit your praise & never to deserve your censure." Two weeks later, Scott was "fast becoming very slow & old," he commented to his wife. "He cannot long retain command I think—when he retires I am sure to succeed him, unless in the mean time I lose a battle—which I do not expect to do."[14]

McClellan's appraisal of war in the Virginia theater in his letter of August 8—addressed to Scott, submitted also to Lincoln, and its contents disseminated through conversations with various politicians—brazenly challenged Scott's competence to assess the military situation and intimated that Scott had neglected the defense of the nation's capital. In response, a furious Scott reassured the secretary of war that he had "not the slightest apprehension for the safety of the Government here." Yet Scott, tired and ailing, announced it was time for him to step aside for a "younger commander" and requested retirement. Lincoln declined the offer. The president trusted Scott, and he relied on his wisdom.[15]

McClellan, however, had just begun his assault on Scott for disagreeing with him. Scott stood in his pathway to full authority, and McClellan challenged the old general's intelligence, competence, and patriotism in order to pull his mentor down from power. To his wife, he exploded at Scott: "I do not know whether he is a *dotard* or a *traitor*! I can't tell which." Scott, he asserted, "is a perfect imbecile. He understands nothing, appreciates nothing & is ever in my way." A frustrated McClellan wondered how he would save the country with Scott's interference. Two days later, his diatribe against Scott continued. "Genl Scott is the great obstacle—he will not comprehend the danger & is either a traitor or an incompetent."[16] McClellan perceived Scott as the enemy. He seldom communicated to Scott, lobbied directly with cabinet members and congressmen and senators, and worked his own agenda, regardless of the wishes of the general in chief.

As days passed and Scott remained ensconced as commanding general, the scenario worsened in McClellan's mind. Magnifying the obstacles against him, the Rebel army in Virginia increased by leaps and bounds. On August 16, the Confederates opposed him with "3 to 4 times my force"; three days later, they had 150,000; by mid-September, "The enemy probably have 170,000!" Why the Confederates did not attack Washington, a mystified McClellan could not explain. The nation was fortunate indeed.[17]

Still unwilling to adopt McClellan's evaluation of the military situation, Scott continued to suffer indignities from his subordinate. And privately, McClellan held Lincoln and his cabinet in similar low regard. "The Presdt is an idiot," he informed his wife. Two months later, Lincoln was "nothing more than a well-meaning baboon," Secretary of State William H. Seward a "meddling, officious, incompetent puppy," and Secretary of the Navy Gideon Welles "weaker than the most garrulous woman you were ever annoyed by." Another time, he labeled Lincoln a coward, Seward a vile fellow, Secretary of War Simeon Cameron a rascal, Welles "an old woman," and Attorney General Edward Bates "an old fool."[18] Anyone in the administration who crossed McClellan's path and did not yield wholeheartedly to his program came in for such epithets.

Scott's days, though, were numbered. He could no longer ride. He could barely walk. He could not cope with the rigors of the job.

In short, Scott felt keenly his incapacity to command the army. McClellan then delivered the final blow when he insisted to senators impatient for action that he wanted to assume the offensive; Scott restrained him. By late October, Scott's twenty-year reign as commanding general had reached its conclusion. Without political patrons, he could no longer resist the pressure. Scott retired on October 31, 1861.

To fill Scott's shoes, Lincoln turned to McClellan. The supreme command of the army, along with direct command of the Army of the Potomac, was an immense responsibility, Lincoln warned. "I can do it all," replied McClellan.[19]

He had to do it all. McClellan trusted no one. Staff members performed few functions because McClellan failed to assign them to specific duties. "I have no one on my staff to whom I can entrust the safety of affairs," he complained to his wife. Throughout his tenure as commander of the Army of the Potomac or Commanding General of the United States Army, McClellan worked extremely long days, immersing himself in details that he should have relegated to subordinates. Deep mistrust of others precluded him from delegating responsibilities sensibly.[20]

Except for his wife, to whom he bared his soul, McClellan kept his own counsel. His wife received gossipy, opinionated letters from him that sometimes discussed military affairs. Otherwise, his plans remained secret, hidden from subordinates and superiors alike. He rationalized this tight-lipped behavior by deeming none of them qualified to scrutinize or critique his operational designs; if he revealed them to someone, they might find their way into the newspapers.

On the day Scott retired, McClellan delivered an extensive letter, prepared with the aid of prominent Democrat Edwin M. Stanton, to the secretary of war assessing the Union war effort and projecting the role of the Army of the Potomac in subduing the enemy. As he had done in early August, McClellan argued that the fate of the nation rested with his army. All Federal forces ought to work in unity, he proposed: "The entire military field should be grasped as a whole, and not in detached parts." Since he led the vital command, the other departments except Kentucky should assume the defensive and send all superfluous troops to the Army of the Potomac immediately for offensive operations. "The advance should not be postponed beyond the 25th of November, if possible to avoid."[21]

This plan of action, in conjunction with Scott's retirement and McClellan's elevation to commanding general, no doubt reassured politicians, already eager for active campaigning. But November 25 came and went. The Army of the Potomac failed to stir.

Politicians whom McClellan had cultivated now began to turn against him. For months he had lobbied for resources and Scott's removal so that he could take the war to the Rebels. Congress and the Lincoln administration had supported him earnestly, and by the late fall his precious Army of the Potomac had grown to near 100,000 men, beautifully equipped. Yet he squandered the best campaigning season of the year, the fall, with its dry roads, cool weather, and bountiful foodstuffs. Some politicians wondered out loud if he ever planned to fight his army. Others snooped around headquarters, seeking reassurance that McClellan did intend to launch an offensive. He had actively encouraged relationships with these political bigwigs; now they demanded personal audiences to pressure him into undertaking operations. McClellan had played political games; when these politicians turned against him he suffered political consequences.

In mid-October, McClellan had implored Lincoln, "Don't let them hurry me, is all I ask." Lincoln replied, "You shall have your own way in the matter, I assure you." If delays would ensure victory, Lincoln would gladly endure the public and political pressure. Then weeks and weeks rolled by, and McClellan failed to act. Whenever Lincoln sought information on McClellan's plans, his secretive commanding general rebuffed him. Time after time Lincoln called at McClellan's headquarters for news—McClellan seldom travelled to the White House to brief the commander in chief—but learned nothing more than the day's events. McClellan viewed such visits as mere annoyances; and regarded the president as a pest. On occasion he hid from "all enemies in shape of 'browsing' Presdt etc." and once blatantly snubbed his superior. Lincoln, Seward, and presidential secretary John Hay dropped by headquarters one evening, only to learn McClellan was attending a wedding reception and would return shortly. After waiting an hour, McClellan entered the house. A porter notified him of his guests; McClellan went upstairs anyway.

After waiting thirty minutes longer without an audience, the distinguished visitors dispatched a servant to remind McClellan they were downstairs. Moments later the servant returned and sheepishly informed them that the commanding general had gone to bed for the night. Lincoln discounted the insult by maintaining this was no time to make issue of trivial indignities.[22]

McClellan had the strange habit of overestimating foes and underestimating friends, especially Lincoln. He once described Lincoln as "a rare bird," an odd sort of fellow. Every time he looked at the president, he saw the anecdotal Lincoln; the nosy Lincoln; the interloper Lincoln; the uncouth Lincoln; the weak Lincoln; the apish Lincoln. He found Lincoln a pleasant peasant, a nice enough chap, but wholly unsuited for the great position that he held. It never dawned on McClellan that there was more to Lincoln than met the eye. Having sized him up early, he refused to alter his judgment.[23]

"*The original Gorilla*," as McClellan called him, manifested a depth that McClellan never noticed and could not fathom. While McClellan exhibited a powerful linear intellect, Lincoln enjoyed a splendid multidimensional mind. Like a child who explores a globe from above, below, and all around, Lincoln could examine every facet of a problem. He could comprehend difficulties and situations from the most unusual and refreshing perspectives. Then, with that uncanny, incisive logic, he could bore holes in any argument and reduce it to its fundamental weakness. His good humor and ready anecdotes camouflaged the actual workings of his genius, revealing only the core result.

But Lincoln's intelligence was not merely destructive; on the contrary, he was a builder, a man possessed of true strategic vision. He focused on the end, a reunited nation, and adapted his ways and means to fulfill it. What McClellan perceived as weakness was in fact flexibility. Lincoln fixed his eyes rigidly on the prize and adjusted policies, programs, strategies, even personnel to move the nation toward that goal. All were tools to restore the Union. Slights from McClellan, ridicule from opponents, attacks in the press, and disappointment among supporters meant little to Lincoln. He could bear it because, in the final analysis, he knew that the American public would judge him exclusively on one point: Whether or not his administration preserved the Union. Little else mattered.[24]

Before he assumed the presidency, Lincoln had only limited military background or knowledge. During the Black Hawk War of 1832, he served inauspiciously as a captain and then a private in the Illinois militia, an experience that the self-deprecating Lincoln recalled fondly and humorously. We never saw any action, Lincoln jested, but we sure had some bloody battles with mosquitoes. The only thing we assaulted were onion patches, he joked. To lead a wartime nation, Lincoln realized that he must amplify this elementary level of understanding. With that wonderful intellect, he embarked on a self-study program of military affairs, devouring sundry martial volumes in English and questioning everyone of acknowledged military acumen. Each day he learned something new and incorporated it into his corpus of knowledge, so that as the war entered its second, third, and eventually fourth years, Lincoln grasped traditional strategy and operations reasonably well.[25]

But by late fall, Lincoln still could not evaluate McClellan's war plans, not only because he lacked expertise, but also because McClellan refused to divulge them. McClellan had devised a vague scheme to advance on the Confederates around Manassas while Maj. Gen. Don Carlos Buell, in Kentucky, pushed his army into eastern Tennessee and captured Knoxville. Buell's campaign would secure East Tennessee, a high priority for Lincoln because of its strong pro-Union population, and would also sever a major railroad artery to Virginia, which would benefit McClellan's offensive. But when Buell announced that he lacked the resources to accomplish his part of the task, the entire plan collapsed.

McClellan's own personality lay at the heart of the inaction. Once again, he greatly exaggerated the strength of the enemy and undervalued his own resources. No matter how unrealistic his appraisal, or how significantly certain factors changed, McClellan formed a snap judgment of the situation and refused to alter it. Excessively cautious, he detected obstacles where none existed and readily convinced himself to abort or delay operations. Then he absolved himself of culpability. He had not sought the position of responsibility, McClellan maintained repeatedly. God must have chosen him for a purpose. He had accomplished all that was humanly possible, but the government had withheld vital resources from his army. If his command did not assume the offensive or proved unsuccessful in battle, he was not to blame.

In early December 1861, an increasingly frustrated Lincoln decided to force McClellan's hand. The president offered his own scheme to outflank the Confederates from their fortified position in northern Virginia. McClellan replied that intelligence sources indicated the Rebels could match his strength in such an expedition, but "I now have my mind actively turned toward another plan of campaign that I do not think at all anticipated by the enemy nor by many of our own people." That was it: No details, no clues, merely a cryptic reference to an unexpected approach.[26]

Actually, McClellan had conceived a rudimentary plan to transport his army by water down Chesapeake Bay and land at Urbanna, on the Rappahannock River. This would turn the Confederates from their fortified positions to the north and, if executed successfully, would leave McClellan's army closer to Richmond than the Confederates. He then would drive on to the Confederate capital and capture it or interpose his command between Richmond and the Confederate army, dig in, and force the retreating Confederates to assault his lines. McClellan had explained the idea to an engineer officer and to Secretary of the Treasury Salmon P. Chase, his patron in the cabinet. It bothered him not a whit to keep the proposal from Lincoln, nor did it strike him as improper to propound its merits to a cabinet member and not to the commander in chief.

Meanwhile, McClellan's inactivity aggravated other people besides Lincoln. Numerous congressional leaders, some of them strong McClellan supporters several months earlier, had lost all confidence in his military leadership. Flexing their own muscles, these House and Senate members created the Committee on the Conduct of the War to investigate the mobilization, planning, and execution of Union operations. Originally formed to root out the causes of failure at Bull Run and a debacle called Ball's Bluff, the committee had several Republican members who acted along strongly partisan lines; this placed Democrat McClellan in a vulnerable position.

The committee called upon McClellan, as its first witness, to flesh out his plans and explain the idleness of the Union Army. But illness struck McClellan before he could testify: He contracted typhoid fever, one of the great scourges of the war. Although his case never reached a critical stage, it had dramatic repercussions. Without his testimony, the committee formed a harshly negative opinion of

McClellan from which it never wavered, even after he presented himself for questioning several weeks later. For the remainder of his tenure as an army commander, the committee remained a thorn in his side, and McClellan, forever hypersensitive to criticism, grew more and more suspicious of Republicans in Congress and the administration. In a roundabout way, the illness also forced McClellan to be more forthcoming with his commander in chief.

With McClellan bedridden, Lincoln felt pangs of anxiety. Who would orchestrate strategic operations in McClellan's absence? Administratively, the Army of the Potomac could sustain itself, but what if McClellan never resumed command or could not return to duty for six weeks? Could the war in the East wait that long? Lincoln needed answers. Inquiries revealed that Halleck, commanding the Department of Missouri, and Buell in Kentucky lacked adequate resources to assume the offensive and had not coordinated their plans. Eight months of war and not one of his three primary commanders could deliver a powerful blow against the enemy! A disconsolate Lincoln unburdened his problems to the quartermaster general, who offered a possible solution: Confer with senior generals in the Army of the Potomac for advice.

On January 10, 1862, Lincoln brought together several cabinet members and two generals. If McClellan did not intend to use the army, Lincoln informed the group, he wanted to borrow it. He asked the generals to recommend offensives. One proposed a direct advance on the Confederates around Manassas, and the other general suggested a flanking movement by water, similar to McClellan's Urbanna plan. The next day, Lincoln held a second conference, and this time the military men agreed on the overland march against Manassas. Lincoln ordered them to develop a plan.

When McClellan caught a whiff of the meetings, he grew furious. Suspicious by nature, he perceived this as an overt attempt to usurp his authority or remove him from command. Two days later, when the group gathered for the third time, McClellan "miraculously" recovered enough to attend. To the president and McClellan's enemies, he had conveyed the impression that the bout with typhoid fever was dire. Several days prior to the meeting, though, selected individuals had secretly visited with him, and McClellan had actually conducted army business from his confinement. McClellan had used he illness as a device to reinforce his value to the nation, to make others appreciate him and feel his absence.

In a tension-packed room, Lincoln opened with a statement of why he had summoned the officers originally. When one of the generals attempted to defend his participation, McClellan silenced him icily with a curt rebuke. No one stirred for some time, and then hushed murmurs emanated from among several groups. Finally, the quartermaster general leaned over to McClellan and softly urged him to discuss his plans. McClellan announced insolently to all that Lincoln could not keep a secret—he even told his young son Tad about future campaigns. Whispering resumed, until Treasury Secretary Chase finally intervened. He called on McClellan to divulge his plan. McClellan again refused. Before the Army of the Potomac took to the field, Buell's troops in Kentucky had to undertake operations. He had already begun to arrange it. "If the President had confidence in me it was not right or necessary to entrust my designs to the judgment of others," he pronounced. "Some were incompetent to form a valuable opinion, and others incapable of keeping a secret." He would not detail his intentions unless Lincoln specifically ordered him to do so. Lincoln refused to force the matter. He asked if McClellan had settled on a date for the campaign, and the commanding general responded affirmatively. "Well," Lincoln decided, "on the assurance of the General that he will press the advance in Kentucky, I will be satisfied, and will adjourn this council."[27]

In fact, the president was not satisfied. Previously, even though he had taken an interest in military affairs, he had seldom intruded. Lincoln had ceded many of the decisions to the secretary of war and the professionally-trained soldiers. Since ultimate responsibility as commander in chief rested with him, and the war effort had accomplished little, he decided to assume a more active role in the direction of affairs. The conference marked an abrupt shift in the way Lincoln handled military matters.

Fed up with the corruption and incompetence of the secretary of war, Lincoln's first act was to ease him out of office and substitute McClellan's friend Stanton. A man of indefatigable industry and an excellent administrator, Stanton was strung a bit too tight, but Lincoln could deal with that. The president sought a tough-minded, detail-conscious individual who could galvanize the war effort and make some hard decisions, and Stanton fit the mold handsomely. McClellan was overjoyed with the appointment initially, but he soon came to despise his new superior when Stanton refused to let McClellan have his own way. Within weeks they clashed, and it was not long before McClellan branded Stanton "without exception the vilest man I ever knew or heard of."[28]

Nor did Lincoln relax pressure on McClellan. Although he did not challenge the commanding general during the conference, Lincoln denied McClellan the privilege of dictating the pace or manner of operations. In late January, the commander in chief set a timetable for action. He ordered all land and naval forces to move against the enemy on February 22. He also exercised his authority by rejecting McClellan's Urbanna operation.

Days after Stanton took office, the new secretary of war convinced McClellan to present his plan to the president. After a briefing, Lincoln concluded that the Urbanna (Virginia) proposal merely altered the site of confrontation and delayed the date of advance. In its place Lincoln specified the Confederate troops at Manassas as the target for the Army of the Potomac. Lincoln had grasped the vital need to strike the enemy armies, rather than merely occupying geographic positions.

McClellan squawked. His proposal had merits that the president apparently did not grasp, and he requested permission to submit the reasons in writing. Lincoln concurred. But before McClellan completed the task, Lincoln posed five fundamental questions about the two plans that addressed the cost in time and money, the likelihood of success, the benefits of decisive victory, and the consequences of disaster. If McClellan resolved these issues to Lincoln's satisfaction, he could undertake the Urbanna campaign.

No doubt, the Urbanna plan had genuine merit. It would turn the Confederates from a fortified position; it offered McClellan the opportunity to fight on ground of his own choosing; it might force the Confederates to attack the Federals in prepared earthworks or lose Richmond; it utilized a great Union advantage, its naval forces; and while it would require McClellan to leave a portion of his army behind to protect Washington, the logistical benefits of water and rail over land transportation compensated reasonably well. Instead of emphasizing these concepts, McClellan responded with a 3,500-word discursive essay of exoneration, excessive detail, and wishful speculation. He diluted the strengths of his plan in a morass of digressions.

Despite McClellan's rambling justification, Lincoln yielded. Still unsure of his own ability and judgment in military affairs, he preferred not to compel McClellan to adopt a campaign that as commanding general he did not embrace. At the same time, by demanding that McClellan justify his plan, Lincoln reasserted civilian control of the military establishment, a notion that his commanding general held in disdain. During the War with Mexico, McClellan had observed how the Polk administration undermined and interfered with Scott's operations. McClellan believed that politicians should determine when and where the nation engaged in war, but then turn over all details of war fighting to military professionals. By reviewing his general's strategic plans, Lincoln acknowledged that ultimately the Northern public held him accountable for the outcome of the war, and that he had a constitutional obligation to oversee all military activities. He intended to scrutinize McClellan's decisions and direct affairs whenever situations warranted presidential intervention.

Over the next six weeks, Lincoln saw little to restore his confidence in McClellan. Delays continued, and the date of February 22 passed with no large-scale operations by the Army of the Potomac. McClellan botched an attempt to clear the upper Potomac River of Confederates when his engineers brought boats that would not fit through the locks on the Chesapeake & Ohio Canal. Then the Confederate army in the Manassas area abandoned its works on March 9 and encamped much closer to Richmond. Examination of the old Rebel works in northern Virginia indicated an opposing force of approximately 50,000. The proximity of the new Confederate position to Urbanna made a landing there unfeasible, and McClellan had to substitute Fort Monroe, on the peninsula between the York and James Rivers, as the debarkation site.[29]

His plans for Fort Monroe, however, had not accounted for the rampages of the Confederate ironclad *Virginia*. Since the previous summer, naval officials had pleaded with McClellan to launch a joint army–navy operation to seize Norfolk, with its valuable navy yard.

But McClellan always found something more important to occupy his time. By early March, the Confederates at Norfolk had completed the work of converting a damaged ship to an iron-plated vessel of destruction that terrorized the U.S. Navy's wooden fleet and threatened McClellan's invasion. Eventually, the arrival of the Northern ironclad *Monitor* neutralized *Virginia*, but the Lincoln government spent several days and nights agonizing over the possible damage *Virginia* could inflict. Lincoln, who handled the crisis far better than his secretaries of war and navy, knew full well that the entire episode never would have occurred if McClellan had acted with vigor months earlier.

In response to McClellan's blunders, Lincoln now took a more active hand in overseeing the campaign and the war in general. McClellan had opted not to organize divisions into corps until after his division commanders had proved themselves in battle. Lincoln intuited this nondecision as procrastination and unwillingness to delegate authority. On advice from knowledgeable authorities, Lincoln created four corps and assigned the senior division officers to command them. Lincoln dictated March 18 as the deadline for the advance, and "the General-in-Chief shall be responsible that it moves as early as that date." Twice he specified that McClellan must leave a force sufficient enough to safeguard Washington and the area of northern Virginia.

Only days before McClellan boarded ship for Fort Monroe, Lincoln delivered a bombshell: He relieved McClellan as general-in-chief. The demands of field command, Lincoln believed, would preclude him from dealing with military affairs in other theaters. Lincoln instead delegated greater authority to Halleck and Maj. Gen. John C. Fremont, his two other military division commanders, and he and Stanton would assume responsibility for overall direction of the war.[30]

The series of events, and Lincoln's executive orders, boded ill for the upcoming campaign. Lincoln's faith in McClellan was shaken. McClellan unquestionably possessed talents, but his flaws interfered with his ability to command well under the stress of civil war. To an old friend from Illinois, Lincoln described McClellan as a man who organized well for the campaign, and as the time to move forward arrived he "became nervous and oppressed with the responsibility and hesitated to meet the crisis." With his presidential directives, Lincoln hoped to prod McClellan over the hump of indecision.[31]

Lincoln failed. Rather than driving intrepidly on to Richmond, McClellan landed his army and crept forward at a snail's pace. His bold words vanished in the face of armed opposition, as tones of pessimism and caution infiltrated his communiques from the front. Confederate commander Maj. Gen. John B. Magruder surprised McClellan by fortifying a line behind the Warwick River that stretched across the entire peninsula, and he employed all sorts of gimmicks to bamboozle McClellan into thinking that he led a large and powerful force. "Quaker guns"—wooden cannons painted black to resemble artillery from a distance—and ostentatious displays of manpower readily convinced McClellan, with his preconceptions of a Confederate army twice his size, that Magruder's 13,000 men actually represented a force equal to his own. Lapsing into his wary mode, McClellan advanced by regular siege approaches, which enabled Confederate commander Gen. Joseph E. Johnston to slip down and prepare earthworks closer to Richmond.

Worse yet, a battle fought in the Shenandoah Valley by Maj. Gen. Thomas J. "Stonewall" Jackson tipped Lincoln to another problem: McClellan's noncompliance with the stipulation that he leave a sufficient force behind to protect Washington and hold Manassas. The president feared the prospect of a Confederate advance on Washington while McClellan's army plodded its way toward Richmond from the east. That was why he had long favored the direct advance on Manassas. But McClellan, dominated by his fear of failure, had disregarded Lincoln's provision and allocated a disproportionate share of manpower to his offensive. Through some arithmetic errors and dummy forces—mostly units counted twice— McClellan calculated over 73,000 as the number of troops he had left to defend the Washington area, when an actual tabulation determined available manpower at well under 30,000. Among the ghost defenders McClellan had designated a 35,000-man command in the Shenandoah Valley. Lincoln, who had already redirected one of McClellan's divisions to another command, immediately blocked the transport of an entire corps. McClellan howled in fury.[32]

Lincoln, no doubt, overreacted. Over the next two months, Jackson and his band of gristly graycoats occupied far more Federal resources and attracted much greater concern than the threat deserved. At one moment of frustration, Lincoln intimated that McClellan "must either attack Richmond or give up the job and come to the defense of Washington." From Lincoln's standpoint, the loss of Washington might have spelled the end of the war, whereas the fall of Richmond, although disastrous to the Confederate cause, would not break the back of the rebellion. McClellan had never assuaged Lincoln's qualms on that score, and the failure to account properly for the defense of Washington exhibited gross negligence on his part. Since McClellan did not fear a Confederate advance on Washington, in his view no menace existed. It never dawned on him that the commander in chief might view matters differently.[33]

McClellan begged Lincoln to restore the First Corps. "In my deliberate judgement the success of our cause will be imperiled by so greatly reducing my force when it is actually under the fire of the enemy and active operations have commenced," he pronounced. The detainment served as a crutch for McClellan. It justified, at least in his own mind, his lapse into excessive caution. Ultimately, the president provided two of its three divisions plus many more reinforcements, all told well over 32,000, so that by the height of the campaign, the Army of the Potomac reached just a few thousand men shy of 130,000, McClellan's projected strength. According to the general's own timetable, the First Corps would not have arrived before the fall of Yorktown anyway. But that meant nothing to McClellan. He had convinced himself that a giant conspiracy was afoot, and that his enemies in Washington sought the defeat of his army.

Back and forth McClellan and Lincoln bickered. McClellan demanded the additional manpower, arguing that he needed it for the colossal battle about to take place, while Lincoln urged him to "break the enemy's line at once." When McClellan insinuated that the government had not sustained him fully, Lincoln replied that the complaints "pain me very much." In a telegram tinged with sarcasm and rife with blunt advice, the president wondered whether McClellan felt 20,000 men was force enough to resist an advance on Washington—"This is a question which the country will not allow me to evade." He admonished his subordinate to attack immediately. Time aided the Confederates, who were receiving reinforcements and continued to fortify their position; McClellan could only receive additional manpower. "And once more let me tell you it is indispensable to you that you strike a blow," Lincoln exhorted. "I am powerless to help this." Lincoln reminded McClellan that, by transporting his army to the peninsula, he was "only shifting and not surmounting a difficulty." In frank terms he explained, "The country will not fail to note, and is now noting, that the present hesitation to move upon an entrenched enemy is but the story of Manassas repeated."[34]

Such forthrightness from the president should have caused McClellan to shudder; he discounted it. McClellan knew best how to conduct a campaign, not the commander in chief. To one of Lincoln's telegrams proposing that he sever the Confederate lines, McClellan penned his wife, "I was much tempted to reply that he had better come & do it himself."[35] Methodically, McClellan positioned his artillery to blast the Rebel entrenchments. Just as the Federals arranged everything for a major push, Magruder abandoned Yorktown and its works and fell back to the main Confederate line.

Again, McClellan crept ahead timorously. This time he blamed the "horrible" roads for delays. When the president and secretary of war slipped down to Fort Monroe for a visit, though, the demands of command and his oversight of every detail precluded McClellan from seeing them. He squandered a golden opportunity to present in person his case, however weak, for more troops.

As McClellan edged up to the Confederate trenches, the size of the enemy army loomed larger, so that it outnumbered his nearly two to one. Every shred of evidence indicated that the Rebels intended to defend Richmond with "all the troops they can collect from the east, west, and south," he argued, and "I beg that you will cause this army to be re-enforced without delay by all the disposable troops of the Government." He could not bring more than 80,000 men into battle, McClellan insisted, although three weeks earlier he had informed his wife that "I have a little over 100,000 effective men." Lincoln attempted to channel the remainder of the First Corps, subsequently increased in strength to almost 40,000, to McClellan's army, so long as it continued to shield Washington. McClellan obstructed the shift. He objected to the overland route instead of water, even though the direct march was shorter and quicker. Then he protested over the restrictions on his use of the corps. Everything had to be on his terms, as he had planned it originally.[36]

By the time the War Department and McClellan ironed out the difficulties, "Stonewall" Jackson had resumed his offensive in the Shenandoah Valley with great success. Instead of reinforcing McClellan, Lincoln opted first to dispatch the First Corps to the Valley to stem the tide there, and perhaps snare Jackson. It was a matter of basic geometry: with Jackson's army in the northern part of the Valley and the First Corps and Fremont's army approaching from opposite directions to the south, a rapid march by the Federals could snare the Rebel command. Each Union force had to travel only half of the distance along the base of the triangle, while Jackson's army had to scurry down a much longer route, the entire height of the triangle. Lincoln saw the matter clearly; his mastery of Euclid had not deserted him. "It is, for you a question of legs," he instructed the First Corps commander. And that it was. Jackson's men made better use of their legs than did the Federals. The maestro of the forced march, Jackson scooted his command through Lincoln's trap.[37]

McClellan sized up the purpose of Jackson's Valley Campaign accurately: to prevent Federal reinforcements from coming to the Army of the Potomac. But his psychological spin twisted its significance. The Confederates actually employed Jackson to preoccupy the reinforcements and give the vastly overmatched secessionists at Richmond a fighting chance. McClellan viewed it as a campaign to maintain Confederate military superiority around the Rebel capital city.

In fact, even though McClellan had assumed the offensive, he had surrendered the initiative. His basic theory of command, encapsulated in a comment to the secretary of war during the *Virginia* crisis, rested in the belief that "We must take it for granted that the worst will happen." In late April, he bemoaned his plight: "It is more than probable that no General ever was placed in such a position before. Finding myself thus unexpectedly weakened & with a powerful enemy strongly entrenched in my front I was compelled to change my plans & become cautious." As his army inched its way toward Richmond, he telegraphed to Lincoln, "I wish to strengthen its force as much as I can, but in any event I shall fight it with all the skill, caution, and determination that I possess." Then, with the church spires of Richmond visible in the distance, he sounded more like a besieged commander about to capitulate than the leader of an aggressive army: "Situated as I am I feel forced to take every possible precaution against disaster & to secure my flanks against the probably superior force in front of me." The closer McClellan approached to Richmond, the more fear of failure dominated his thoughts.[38]

With the decisive operations of the campaign impending, the stress of command propelled McClellan on an emotional roller coaster. He fluctuated from buoyancy to cautious optimism to dark pessimism. When Maj. Gen. Fitz John Porter with approximately four brigades cleared out a light accumulation of Confederate forces at Hanover Court House that "seriously threatened" his right flank, a euphoric McClellan declared it a major triumph. "Porter's action of yesterday," he telegraphed the secretary of war, "was truly a glorious victory. Too much credit cannot be given to his magnificent division, and its accomplished leader. The rout of the rebels was complete—not a defeat, but a complete rout." He misleadingly claimed to have cut "all but the Fredericksburg and Richmond Railroad," and announced that the decisive battle was at hand and "If any regiments of good troops remain unemployed it will be an irreparable fault committed."

Lincoln quickly smothered the fire of McClellan's passion by congratulating the victor and downgrading the battle's depth and significance: "Still, if it was a total rout of the enemy, I am puzzled to know why the Richmond and Fredericksburg Railroad was not seized again, as you say you have all the railroads but the Richmond and Fredericksburg. I am puzzled to see how, lacking that, you can have any, except the scrap from Richmond to West Point," the Union supply, or cracker, line.[39]

Just a few days later, after McClellan had discounted the possibility of Johnston attacking him, the Confederate commander struck. Caught off guard and feeling ill, McClellan did little to influence the outcome of the battle. Disjointed Confederate assaults and Union heroics saved the day at Fair Oaks. In his first account of the fighting, McClellan embellished mildly. Johnston's army had attacked with "greatly superior numbers," and with dauntless exertion the Federals drove them back. Once fighting had ceased, McClellan's spirits lifted. On the second day of battle, his soldiers had repulsed every enemy assault and inflicted heavy losses. "Our troops charged frequently on both days," he boasted, "and uniformly broke the enemy." Ultimate victory, he predicted, was near. When the Chickahominy River dropped, he would cross the rest of his army and launch a "general attack." If he discovered the Rebels in strong works, he might call up the remaining troops at Fort Monroe, "but the *morale* of my troops is now such that I can venture much, and do not fear for odds against me. The victory is complete, and all credit is due to the gallantry of the officers and men."[40]

Then, as the days dwindled by and the moment of truth approached, McClellan's enthusiasm for the final battle cooled. Cries for additional manpower, campaigns to draw away some of the overwhelming Confederate strength, and the usual excuses bombarded the War Department over the next three weeks. Since Halleck's army had just captured Corinth, Mississippi, an important railroad junction, McClellan wanted the War Department to ship some of those troops to him, or order Halleck to occupy Chattanooga, Tennessee and Dalton, Georgia and send a large column to Atlanta. When Gen. Robert E. Lee, who had succeeded to command for the wounded Johnston, sent away some of his army to assist Jackson, Lincoln thought "it is as good as a re-enforcement to you of an equal force." McClellan interpreted the move as an illustration of Confederate "strength and confidence." To his wife he justified his hesitancy on the dearth of leadership in Washington: "when I see such insane folly behind me I feel the final salvation of the country demands the utmost prudence on my part & that I must not run the slightest risk of disaster, for if anything happened to this army our cause would be lost."[41]

On the eve of the major thrust against Richmond, intelligence information convinced McClellan that he faced 200,000 Rebel soldiers, well over double Lee's actual strength. Sources suggested that additional Rebel reinforcements from the west had arrived, and that Jackson's army had slipped down from the Valley to spearhead a flank attack. The news wholly unnerved McClellan. In an insubordinate tone, he absolved himself of culpability for the crisis, having warned the War Department repeatedly of "my greatly inferior numbers." If the impending battle resulted in disaster, he concluded, "the responsibility cannot be thrown on my shoulders; it must rest where it belongs." McClellan's horror of failure had seized control of him. Lincoln promptly scolded him, insisting, "I give you all I can, and act on the presumption that you will do the best with what you have, while you continue, ungenerously I think, to assume that I could give you more if I would. I have omitted and shall omit no opportunity to send you re-enforcements whenever I possibly can." The rebuke did no good.[42]

Deep down, McClellan believed that politicians in Washington conspired to see him fail. How else could someone explain that the Confederacy, with a white population of less than six million, could field an army of 200,000, while the Northern states, home of 22 million, could not cobble together 130,000 men for him! It was inconceivable to him that Lee, augmented by Jackson, in fact had only 85,000 troops. No! Radical Republicans, Secretary of War Stanton, and other officials withheld vital resources from his army at the critical moment of the campaign. By contrast, Lincoln was fundamentally a good person. The president wanted to aid McClellan, and in his presence promised to do so. But Lincoln was such a weak man, so easily influenced by others, that McClellan's enemies manipulated him to act in their league.

Based on the intelligence reports, McClellan took precautions to fortify his right wing against Jackson, but it was not nearly enough. No one expected Lee to risk an attack with nearly two thirds of his soldiers. On June 25, masses of graycoats stormed McClellan's right flank. Poorly coordinated, haphazardly executed, the initial assault failed to break the Federals. Lee refused to let up. Over the next six days, his troops relentlessly hammered the Army of the Potomac, driving it back from Richmond. Only sloppy Confederate staff work and lackluster leadership, along with stout Union resistance, prevented McClellan from suffering a catastrophe.

McClellan buckled under the stress. He completely abdicated control of the battlefield to subordinates and unaccountably squandered his time on rear-echelon staff duties. He slept little, ate insufficiently, and thoroughly exhausted himself. As he admitted to his wife, "You can't tell how nervous I became." Two weeks after the campaign ended, he elaborated. "I *did* have a terrible time that week—," he confided in his wife, "for I stood alone, without *anyone* to help me—I felt that on me rested everything & I felt how weak a thing a poor mortal erring man is!" The pressure and sense of isolation caused him to collapse emotionally.[43]

His messages to authorities in Washington, initially confident and composed, soon degenerated to near hysteria. After the first day, he blustered, "If I had another good Division I could laugh at Jackson." Two days later, as Confederate attacks compelled his army to abandon the field, McClellan pined, "Had I (20,000) twenty thousand fresh & good troops we would be sure of a splendid victory tomorrow." He was not responsible for the retreat, he charged the next day to the secretary of war, and if the government wanted victory, "you must send me very large reinforcements & send them at once." His concluding remark, which was so outrageous that the telegraph operator in Washington deleted it intentionally, shifted the entire burden of defeat on Lincoln and Stanton: "If I save this Army now I tell you plainly that I owe no thanks to you or any other persons in Washington—you have done your best to sacrifice this Army." By July 1, his requests had reached absurd proportions: "I need fifty thousand 50,000 more men, and with them I will retrieve our fortunes. More would be well, but that number sent at once, will, I think enable me to assume the offensive"; within three days, his needs exceeded 100,000. Confronted with failure, and so desirous to shift blame onto others, his demands had lost all semblance of reality.[44]

Throughout the fight, Lincoln endeavored to soothe his frazzled commander. When news of some disaster first reached Washington, he urged McClellan to yield ground but save the army at all costs. Once the army was secure, Lincoln dispensed some sobering remarks. He requested that McClellan "allow me to reason with you a moment. When you ask for 50,000 men to be promptly sent you, you surely labor under some gross mistake of fact." As the former commanding general, McClellan certainly knew the disposition of forces. Outside McClellan's army, the Union had barely 75,000 troops in the entire region. "The idea of sending you 50,000, or any other considerable force, promptly is simply absurd." Lincoln did not hold McClellan responsible for accomplishing more than he could do reasonably; "I only beg that in like manner you will not ask impossibilities of me."[45]

Rather than admit the near rout, within days of the end of the campaign McClellan transformed the affair into one of the great military achievements of all time. The extrication of his army from the clutches of overwhelming Confederate superiority, the stoutness of Union resistance, and the manner in which he shifted supply lines from the York River to the James in the midst of retreat manifested the brilliance of his ability to command. To his wife, McClellan crowed, "we have accomplished one of the grandest operations of Military History." He pouted after a telegram he received from Lincoln exhibited "a fatal want of appreciation of the glorious achievements of this Army" and proceeded to instruct the president, "When all the circumstances of the case are known it will be acknowledged by all competent judges that the movement just completed by this army is unparalleled in the annals of war." He had done his best, he insisted over and over to his wife. His conscience was clear. Any blame rested elsewhere.[46]

He dispatched his father-in-law and chief of staff, Randolph B. Marcy, to Washington to answer questions about events and army needs. Marcy carried a letter from McClellan, seeking "rather much over than much less than 100,000 men." In this immense crisis, "We require action on a gigantic scale—one commensurate with the views I expressed in a memorandum to the President submitted early last August," calling for an army of 273,000. By implication, Lincoln had not listened to him. He had been right all along.[47]

After Marcy's briefing, Lincoln decided to examine the condition of the army personally. He caught a speedy steamer for McClellan's army and stayed only a day. There the president held conversations with McClellan and his corps commanders and inspected the troops. All in all, the condition of the army surpassed Lincoln's expectations. When he asked the corps commanders what they should do next, continue the campaign from there or bring the army back to northern Virginia and operate along the Washington–Richmond axis, no consensus existed. Lincoln refused to tip his hand, and that bothered McClellan. "I do not know to what extent he has profited by his experience—," McClellan pondered just after Lincoln left, "not much I fear, for he really seems quite incapable of rising to the heights of the merits of the question & the magnitude of the crisis." The president's silence rankled McClellan. "I do not know what paltry trick the administration will play next—," he complained, "I did not like the Presdt's manner—it seemed that of a man about to do something of which he was much ashamed."[48]

As Lincoln boarded his vessel to return to Washington, McClellan handed him a letter which, he boasted to his wife, "will save the country" if Lincoln acted on it. A few days before the Confederate attack, McClellan had requested an opportunity to offer his views on the conduct of the war. Lincoln consented. Coolly the president scanned the document, tucked it securely in his coat pocket, and thanked McClellan for it. The policy paper called for a restrictive war, one against the Confederate army and its government. No effort should be undertaken to subjugate the secessionists or confiscate their property, including slaves. "A declaration of radical views, especially upon slavery, will rapidly disintegrate our present armies," McClellan predicted.[49]

Branded by friends of Lincoln as either outrageous or wildly presumptuous, McClellan's proposal actually smacked more of his inability to discern the changing complexion of the war and his personality flaws than anything else. McClellan, as ranking general in the army, had every right, even an obligation, to submit his opinions confidentially to the commander in chief on all military matters and policies that related to the war. The major problem was that the paper reflected his foibles. In the wake of defeat, his timing could not have been more dreadful. But in McClellan's mind, he had transformed the reality of a near disaster in which his leadership had crumbled into a mythical stellar performance against overwhelming odds. Surely, he thought, Lincoln would have to listen to his sage counsel now.

Worse, McClellan's rigid adherence to his initial assessments precluded him from comprehending the evolving nature of the conflict. He championed a continuation of the original limited-war policies, at the same time as the president was wrestling with the notion of a vastly escalated war. Their opinions gravitated toward opposite poles. Lincoln ruminated over options to expand the parameters of the war, to draw more heavily on the wide range of military, political, and economic weapons at his disposal. McClellan proposed a restrictive war, while Lincoln advocated an expansive war, one that placed more military tools in the hands of his commanders.

Lincoln did adopt a component of McClellan's program. He reinstituted the post of commanding general. Neither he nor Stanton possessed the requisite military knowledge to oversee campaign planning and day-to-day operations. The ambiguous status of McClellan's army on the Peninsula merely highlighted that inadequacy. Lincoln needed an individual of broad military knowledge who had demonstrated the capacity to supervise large-scale movements and campaigns. On the strong recommendation of now-retired general Winfield Scott, he selected Henry Wager Halleck.

A pudgy-looking fellow with bulging eyes and a thick double chin, Halleck impressed no one physically. He had gained a reputation as an army intellectual and won fame for Union successes out west, where preferred to stay. The commander-in-chief imposed on him, and the ambitious Halleck could not refuse. Immediately he undertook the task of resolving McClellan's status on the Peninsula. As the new commanding general viewed it, the Army of the Potomac could not remain inactive. McClellan's current estimates of Confederate strength surpassed 200,000—a force which, if correct, would enable the Confederates to protect Richmond and bring greatly superior numbers to bear against Union troops to the north. Forewarned by Lincoln that McClellan's manpower demands resembled a bottomless pit, Halleck went armed with a reinforcement package from Lincoln that included no more than 20,000 men. If McClellan could resume the offensive soon with that additional manpower, his army could remain on the Peninsula. Otherwise, he must transport his command back up to Washington, where it would unite with the troops under Maj. Gen. John Pope that protected northern Virginia. The two generals held conversations the first day, with McClellan insisting that he required 30,000 fresh troops to take Richmond. Halleck would not yield. The following day, McClellan unenthusiastically offered to give it a "try" with the reinforcements.[50]

The arrangement lasted just one week. McClellan continued to press Halleck for more men, and the commanding general concluded that the Army of the Potomac plus 20,000 could not advance in its present position and strength. He ordered McClellan to return to northern Virginia as rapidly as possible.

Lincoln had predicted as much. Nothing satiated McClellan's demands for additional resources, Lincoln explained to an old friend. If he provided the Army of the Potomac with 100,000 reinforcements, McClellan would be euphoric and vow to capture Richmond within days, but the next day he would receive intelligence information that suggested the Confederates had 400,000 troops, and McClellan could not proceed without more men. Before Halleck had left for the army, Lincoln had authorized him to remove the army commander if necessary. Confidentially, Lincoln had also discussed with Burnside the possibility of his succession to commander of the Army of the Potomac. A perplexed Burnside begged off, pleading a lack of competency for the post, but the conversation indicated the depths of Lincoln's disillusionment with McClellan.[51]

Halleck's decision infuriated McClellan. He perceived this as yet another blow struck against him by his conspirators to force his resignation. "The dolts in Washn are bent on my destruction," McClellan alleged to his single true confidante, his wife Nelly. "The more I hear of their wickedness the more I am surprised that such a wretched set are permitted to *live* much less occupy the positions they do." Only on the job a few days, his new superior officer, Halleck, joined the list of McClellan foe for daring to disagree with him. In barbs interchangeable with those he directed at Scott a year earlier, McClellan described Halleck to his wife as a "scallawag" and "very dull & very incompetent."[52]

He protested; he obstructed its execution; he attempted to induce Lee to attack him. Nothing had an impact. Halleck refused to rescind the order, and McClellan had no choice but to comply. Yet he failed to do so with alacrity, and Pope suffered the consequences. As Lincoln and Halleck had feared, Lee surmised the Federal movement and maneuvered first one and then the other corps to strike Pope's command before the rest of the Army of the Potomac arrived.

McClellan, meanwhile, sailed up to Aquia Creek, where Halleck assigned him the task of funneling his several corps to Pope as they arrived on transports. Again, he thwarted Halleck's directives, quibbling inexcusably and then blatantly violating orders to advance two corps as Lee's army engaged Pope's forces. In response from

Lincoln to a simple request for information on Pope's whereabouts, McClellan tipped his sentiments. He proposed two courses of action, to support the Federals in the field or "leave Pope to get out of his scrape, and at once use all our means to make the capital perfectly safe." He then mendaciously inquired "what my orders and authority are," as if he and Halleck had not communicated for the last few days. Lincoln, who regularly read message traffic to and from the War Department, knew full well that McClellan received frequent and informative telegrams from Halleck and had even consulted with him in person.[53]

At Second Manassas, Lee whipped Pope's army, while McClellan, within earshot of the battle, withheld critical reinforcements. Lincoln was furious. He honestly believed that McClellan wanted Pope to lose, and the chaos McClellan caused led the president to conclude that the general had acted "a little crazy." Stanton demanded a court-martial, and nearly the entire cabinet called for McClellan's removal. Lincoln, however, resisted the pressure. Although McClellan's conduct toward Pope was "unpardonable," Lincoln considered him "too useful just now to sacrifice." The residue of Pope's shattered command required rapid rebuilding and reviving, an area in which McClellan's talents exceeded all others. "If he can't fight himself," Lincoln told his private secretary, "he excels in making others ready to fight." Lincoln ordered McClellan to assume command of the Washington defenses, to take charge of Pope's army as it fell back into the city, and to resuscitate it.[54]

It had not been Lincoln's intention to restore McClellan to a field command. He had ordered Halleck to prepare an army from the Union forces in the Washington area for active campaigning and hoped to persuade Burnside to lead it. When "Burn" declined, Lincoln permitted the post to devolve on McClellan.

"Again I have been called upon to save the country—," the melodramatic McClellan penned his wife, "the case is desperate, but with God's help I will try unselfishly to do my best & if he wills it accomplish the salvation of the nation." Lee had followed up his victory at Second Manassas with an invasion of Maryland, and in two short weeks McClellan had re-energized the Federal army and commenced an irresolute pursuit of Lee.[55]

All that changed when the break of the war fell into McClellan's lap. A Yankee private discovered a copy of Lee's invasion plans. Within hours, McClellan knew that Lee had divided his forces—Jackson now attacking the Union garrison at Harpers Ferry and Longstreet's command pushing farther north—and he devised a scheme to defeat various components. By swift march McClellan could have split and ensnared a sizeable chunk of Lee's army. But again fear of failure seized him. He tarried. The revelation remained unexploited.

At the Battle of South Mountain, one of Lee's divisions blocked the Union advance sufficiently for the remainder of Longstreet's troops to march thirteen miles and come to its support. The stalwart defense prevented McClellan from interposing the bulk of his army between the two Confederate wings. As Lee withdrew Longstreet's command to the southwest toward Sharpsburg, along the northern bank of the Potomac River, McClellan decreed South Mountain a rout. "If I can believe one tenth of what is reported," he puffed to his wife, "God has seldom given an army a greater victory than this."[56]

Despite McClellan's assertions of a precipitous Rebel retreat and a vigorous Union pursuit, he trailed apprehensively. He still assumed that Lee outnumbered him when in fact his army nearly doubled the size of Lee's combined wings, and he would not bar the invaders from falling back into Virginia. His mindset was defensive, while Lincoln's was offensive. Lincoln wanted McClellan to "Destroy the rebel army if possible"; McClellan merely sought its withdrawal from Maryland.[57]

Lee refused to accommodate McClellan's desires. Rather than fall back across the Potomac River, the Confederate commander boldly held his ground near Sharpsburg. Throughout the late afternoon of September 15, and all day on the 16th, McClellan examined the Rebel line, hoping no doubt that Lee would slip across the Potomac River at night. But time benefited Lee, whose divisions from the recent capture of Harpers Ferry were trickling in bit by bit. McClellan had no alternative; he must drive the Confederate army from Northern soil. If Lee's forces maintained their position that night, he would attack early on the 17th.[58]

At the Battle of Antietam, the armies of McClellan and Lee suffered the bloodiest single day of the war. Unknowingly, McClellan had Lee on the ropes for much of the engagement. Until very late in the afternoon, he possessed a vast numerical superiority over the Confederates. Time and again, the Federals nearly snapped their line. Only the stoutest resistance averted a Rebel disaster. McClellan's failure to devise and impose a clear design on his subordinate commanders and his mishandling of troops all day long cost him a resounding victory.

As the sun peaked over the horizon the following day, Lee still held firm. All morning and afternoon Federals and Confederates glowered at one another. No one budged. Combined casualties of over 25,000 the previous day had deterred both commanders from striking first, and McClellan had expended every ounce of his initiative. Despite the arrival of reinforcements, the Federal general would risk nothing more.

That night, Lee did slip away across the Potomac. He had made his point. The Union army had not compelled him to abandon a field of battle. The Confederates evacuated voluntarily.

McClellan emerged from the clash with a completely distorted view of the events. In his own mind, he had commanded brilliantly and earned a great victory against overwhelming Confederate strength. "Those in whose judgment I rely tell me that I fought the battle splendidly & that it was a masterpiece of art," he jubilated to his wife. "We may safely claim a complete victory," McClellan trumpeted to Halleck. "God has in his mercy a second time made me the instrument for saving the nation," he solemnly testified to his beloved Nelly. After this grand achievement, McClellan seriously debated whether he should demand the administration dump Stanton and reappoint him general in chief over Halleck.[59]

Lincoln evaluated the magnitude of the triumph differently. The president saw nothing complete about the victory. Lee had only retreated back into Virginia, and the Confederate threat remained undiminished. Some months later, Lincoln recalled that when McClellan proclaimed he had driven the invaders from the North, saving the states of Pennsylvania and Maryland, "The hearts of 10 million people sunk within them." After all, he pithily commented, "The whole country is our soil." Rather than gaining power and influence with the Lincoln administration, McClellan's stock continued to totter.[60]

The major outcome of the "victory" at Antietam was the initiation of a policy that outraged McClellan: emancipation. Since early July, Lincoln had mulled over the notion of freeing the slaves. Despite the president's personal predilection for the abolition of slavery, the exigencies of the war dominated his decision. The Confederates had employed slaves most effectively to produce foodstuffs and a wide range of materials that aided armies in the field. Bondsmen had also labored on fortifications; road, railroad, and bridge construction; and in sundry other ways that directly benefited the secessionists in arms. A decree to free all slaves in rebellious states, supported by military resources, would strip the Confederates of their laboring force and transform them into producers for the cause of reunion. Since late July, when he had revealed his intention to the cabinet, the president had elected to await some Union success on the battlefield to issue the proclamation from a position of strength. Antietam served that purpose.

McClellan spit venom. No one in the administration had lauded him satisfactorily after his exploits, no one appreciated their significance, and now in the aftermath of his accomplishments Lincoln imposed abolitionism on the nation! "The Presdt's late Proclamation, the continuation of Stanton & Halleck in office render it almost impossible for me to retain my commission & self respect at the same time," he commented disgustedly to his wife. "I cannot make up my mind to fight for such an accursed doctrine as that of servile insurrection—it is too infamous. Stanton is as great a villain as ever & Halleck as great a fool—he has no brains whatever." McClellan prepared a vigorous protest, and before submitting it he wisely called on comrades for comments. His friends convinced him not to send it. Instead, he issued a general order that reminded his troops of the relationship between soldiers and the government. "The remedy for political errors, if any are committed, is to be found only in the action of the people at the polls," he insisted.[61]

In the days and weeks following the Battle of Antietam, McClellan demanded time to rest, refit, and reinforce his worn-out army. He had driven the invaders from Northern turf. He had accomplished enough for months to come. Lincoln, Stanton, and Halleck, however, wanted more than that. They urged McClellan to capitalize on the momentum, to follow up his victory by striking the enemy vigorously. If the Army of the Potomac had wearied in tri-

umph, Lee's forces certainly suffered worse in defeat. Lincoln visited McClellan and the army to press this case. In frank words that
persuaded McClellan of the president's friendship, Lincoln extolled
McClellan's virtues as a general officer, but pointed out his excessive
caution. The Army of the Potomac, as Lincoln had quipped to a
friend, had become "McClellan's bodyguard"; Lincoln wanted to
convert it into the vehicle that would crush the rebellion.[62]

Lincoln left the army with the impression that McClellan had
understood the administration's position and would launch a campaign promptly. McClellan, unerringly consistent in his behavior,
stalled. He fixated on a possible Confederate advance into
Pennsylvania if he shifted eastward. Without supplies, manpower,
bridges, and a railroad line from Harpers Ferry to Winchester, he
could not campaign in the Shenandoah Valley either. Halleck specifically ordered him to advance and to notify authorities in
Washington of his plans. Excuses whirled anew.

Finally, Lincoln intervened. In his inimitable fashion, the president shredded McClellan's plan with irrepressible logic and presented his own scheme, which bore the marks of an individual with
keen intellect, sound judgment, and a thorough grasp of fundamental military concepts. He scolded McClellan for "what I call your
overcautiousness" and pinpointed some underlying flaws in
McClellan's approach to planning and leadership with two questions: "Are you not overcautious when you assume that you cannot
do what the enemy is constantly doing?" and "Should you not claim
to be at least his equal in prowess, and act upon the claim?" Lincoln
prodded him on delays, insisting that McClellan's plans would waste
all autumn and "ignores the question of *time*, which can not, and
must not be ignored." While McClellan worried that Lee would
strike his line of communications into Pennsylvania, he disregarded
the fact that such an advance would expose Lee's own line with
Richmond. "You seem to act as if this applies *against* you, but can
not apply in your *favor*," the commander in chief asserted.

McClellan proposed a direct march on Lee's army in the
Shenandoah Valley, which required extensive and time-consuming
logistical preparations. Lincoln demurred. In their present positions, the Army of the Potomac rested closer to Richmond than did
Lee's forces. Lincoln wondered, "Why can not you reach there

before him, unless you admit that he is more than your equal on a march?" As the master of geometry, Lincoln noted that "His route is the arc of the circle, while yours is the chord," and, "The roads are as good on yours as his." If McClellan drove into Virginia east of the Blue Ridge, he would threaten Lee's communications. If Lee advanced north, the Federals could follow behind him, blocking his communications and coercing Lee to fight on McClellan's terms. If Lee shifted to protect his communications, McClellan could race him to Richmond, gain the "inside track," and engage Lee on ground of McClellan's choosing. All along that chord McClellan had ready access to supplies by roads, railroads, and waterways from Washington, as "spokes of a wheel extending from the hub towards the rim." With Lee's army in the Shenandoah Valley, which angled from northeast near Washington to the southwest away from Richmond, McClellan could hug the eastern face of the Blue Ridge as he marched, block the gaps or slip through them to surprise Lee, and force the Confederates to assume an even more roundabout course to reach Richmond. "It is all easy," Lincoln concluded, "if our troops march as well as the enemy; and it is unmanly to say they can not do it." The civilian had caught up, and perhaps surpassed, the professional. While McClellan's personality flaws inhibited his ability to improve as a commander and military thinker, to exploit the resources at his disposal, Lincoln's understanding of strategic thought and leadership had grown enormously over the course of eighteen months of war.[63]

As always, McClellan utterly discounted Lincoln's rebuke. He had decided on the proper course of action, and he knew better. Again, he delayed and provided a host of justifications for it. His army required elaborate bridges over the Potomac and Shenandoah Rivers for the permanent occupation of Harpers Ferry. McClellan complained of the insufficiency and inadequacy of his cavalry, which Confederate horsemen regularly bested on raids. Lincoln, his patience eroding rapidly, replied through Halleck that, "if the enemy had more occupation south of the river, his cavalry would not be so likely to make raids north of it." Since the government planned to implement a draft, McClellan inquired, could he postpone the campaign until the War Department filled his depleted ranks? A serious shortage of horses hampered his intended movements. Did the president prefer him to "march on the enemy at once, or to await the reception of the new horses, every possible step having been taken to insure their prompt arrival?" Lincoln, unyielding in his directive that McClellan undertake the campaign at once, jolted the army commander with a terse response that failure to move would serve as evidence of "such want of ability." It seemed to work. The next day McClellan informed Halleck that he would adopt Lincoln's campaign plan.[64]

The honeymoon was short-lived. By October 25, McClellan forwarded to Halleck a report from a Massachusetts cavalry regiment of ill and worn-out horses. Lincoln, his patience nearly exhausted, lashed back, "I have just read your dispatch about sore-tongued and fatigued horses. Will you pardon me for asking what the horses of your army have done since the battle of Antietam that fatigues anything?" McClellan explained his position in detail, and Lincoln apologized, but that same day more trouble erupted. McClellan asked Lincoln if drafted men could fill out old regiments "before taking them again into action." Lincoln pointedly demanded, "Is it your purpose not to go into action again until the men now being drafted in the States are incorporated into the old regiments?" McClellan unconvincingly blamed the operative phrase on a clerical error. He stood on even thinner ice with Lincoln.[65]

McClellan, too, smoldered at the perceived mistreatment. Every critical comment from authorities in Washington bristled him. For the good of the country, he would submit to insults "from men whom I know to be greatly my inferiors socially, intellectually & morally!" he griped to his wife. "There never was a truer epithet applied to a certain individual than that of the 'Gorilla.' "[66]

After weeks of prods and threats, McClellan finally threw his lead elements across the Potomac River on October 26. Seven days later, his column's tail traversed the waterway. Eschewing Lincoln's urging for a bold march, the Union army advanced at a glacial pace, tipping Lee of Federal intentions and enabling the Confederate commander to move Longstreet fleetly from the Valley to block McClellan's route. The "secesh," McClellan complained to his wife, tramped "too fast to meet my views." Union hesitancy had nullified Lincoln's plan. The president could endure no more. On November 5, 1862, the day after the congressional elections, he ordered Halleck to remove McClellan and install Burnside as army commander.

Since July 1861, Lincoln had coddled, cajoled, wheedled, nee-
dled, nudged, reasoned, and commanded McClellan to campaign,
all to no avail. Utterly exasperated by the delays, Lincoln could tolerate his "slows" no more. "Of course I was much surprised—,"
McClellan admitted to his wife, "but as I read the order in the presence of Genl Buckingham, I am sure that not a muscle quivered nor
was the slightest expression visible on my face, which he watched
closely. They shall not have that triumph," he insisted.[67]

So many Americans in McClellan's day saw the hand of God in
their lives, but few perceived themselves as specifically selected to
implement God's designs. All along, McClellan had depicted himself as a Christ-like figure. He was a chosen instrument, fulfilling
God's will. "I feel that God has placed a great work in my hands," he
explained to his wife. God "could not have placed me here for nothing," McClellan asserted. In his mind, "my previous life seems to
have been unwittingly directed to this great end." His ultimate mission was to save the nation. The long suffering that he had endured
at the hands of Republicans and the setback on the Peninsula surely
had some divine purpose, he convinced himself. Perhaps, as he
speculated in the aftermath of the Seven Days' Battles, the "fanatics
of the North might have been too powerful & reunion impossible"
had he captured Richmond. McClellan's restoration to command
after the debacle at Second Manassas and the victory at Antietam
only reinforced this sense of destiny.

During the final weeks as army commander, McClellan received
reports from friends in Washington and sensed from the tone of official letters and telegrams that his position was tenuous at best. Yet
he would do nothing different. Like Jesus Christ before him,
McClellan refused to alter or avoid that fate. His sacrifice would
cleanse the government of its rascals and cowards. His removal
would alert the public to the gross incompetence of the Lincoln
administration. From his martyred career would emerge a united
public that would cry out for fresh leadership to restore the Union.
Father Time would completely vindicate him.[68]

For George B. McClellan this was just one in a long series of
failed command relationships. A brilliant, difficult individual,
McClellan had left in his wake a history of miscarried associations
with superiors dating back to his youth. Only a handful of people—
his wife, Fitz John Porter, and a few others—maintained long-term

bonds with McClellan, and in those cases he clearly retained the dominant role.

Since childhood, McClellan had struggled with authority figures, from grade-school teachers to West Point instructors to superior officers in the Regular Army to railroad bosses. McClellan's psychological baggage impeded his ability to function as army commander and general in chief. Mistrustful by nature, he discovered deliberately threatening or demeaning remarks in innocuous comments. His excessive secrecy, need to dominate, and hypersensitivity to rank and power inhibited his capacity to labor under the supervision of Lincoln, the secretary of war, or the general in chief. McClellan formed initial or preconceived expectations and clung to them rigidly, obscuring all information that contradicted the original assessments. He grossly exaggerated the strength of obstacles, took extreme precautions, and in failure blamed everyone except himself. Severely critical of others, he reacted bitterly to criticism and justified himself at every turn. These qualities, all symptomatic of what modern psychology calls paranoid personality disorder with narcissistic tendencies, prevented McClellan from performing his duties as commanding general and general in chief satisfactorily.[69] (See Appendix.)

After reading the order removing him as army commander, McClellan agreed to assist Burnside in the transition of power by staying for a few days. Embarrassed by the awkward situation, Burnside felt "dreadfully," which convinced McClellan that his old friend had no role in the intrigue. McClellan consoled himself with the belief that "if we have failed it is not our fault."[70]

Burnside sent McClellan off well. Three days after the change of command, "Burn" called out three corps for a farewell review. A somber mood overshadowed the pageantry. The following morning, Burnside accompanied his old friend to the Warrenton train station, where McClellan boarded for Washington. Within a year, McClellan turned against Burnside, as he had against so many others.

McClellan's stay in Washington was brief. He did not see Lincoln. The War Department assigned McClellan to Trenton, New Jersey to await orders, but he requested and received permission to relocate in New York City, where some friends resided. George Brinton McClellan never commanded an army in the field again.

Throughout the course of the Lincoln–McClellan relationship, the president had supported his general wholeheartedly. He articulated military goals for his commander and provided the necessary manpower and equipment to accomplish them. But McClellan, paralyzed by his personality disorders, lacked the capacity to utilize those troops effectively.

Thus, the combination of the success of the Lee–Jackson partnership and the dismal failure of the Lincoln–McClellan association enabled the Confederacy to assume the upper hand in Virginia during the first two years of the war. Comparable Confederate achievements and Union deficiencies among command relationships out West could carry the secessionist movement to the brink of victory.

Jefferson Davis
(National Archives)

Joseph E. Johnston
(National Archives)

4

"I cannot direct both parts of my command at once"

Davis, Johnston, and Confederate Failure in the West

Jefferson Davis would have much preferred a military post to the presidency of the Confederate States of America. A graduate of West Point, he had served in the Regular Army and commanded a regiment of Mississippi volunteers with great success in the Mexican War. When the telegram from the provisional congress in Montgomery, Alabama, announcing his selection as chief executive reached him at his Briarfield plantation in Mississippi, Davis's icy reaction hinted at disappointment. Yet he dutifully acceded to the wishes of others.[1]

Certainly his military experience appealed to the delegates who cast their ballots for him, particularly if the Union opposed secession by resorting to arms, but so did other factors. Davis had held seats in Congress for many years, in both the House and the Senate. He had served on the Military Affairs Committee in each chamber and had overseen the War Department in Franklin Pierce's administration. His reputation as a level-headed secessionist drew many supporters to him. And nearly all acclaimed his unflinching integrity.

Slightly tall, with dark brown hair now invaded by patriotic grey, and a tuft of blended brown, grey, and white whiskers beneath his chin, Davis's gaunt frame evidenced his utter disinterest in food. One eye bore a murky film of blindness while the other, dark and penetrating, radiated the man's inner strength. More a man of character than a man of brilliance, Davis nonetheless possessed an intelligent, disciplined, at times nit-picking mind. Details fascinated Jefferson Davis.

On February 16, 1861, the residents of Montgomery and its distinguished visitors, many of them there to draw up a national constitution, select a president, and sit as the provisional legislature, came out in throngs to greet the president-designate. From the balcony of the Exchange Hotel, Montgomery's favorite son, William Lowndes Yancey, introduced Davis to a jubilant audience. In words that captured the enthusiasm of the moment, Yancey thundered, "The man and the hour have met."[2]

At first Davis conducted much of his business from a parlor room in the hotel, but soon the new Confederate Congress rented him space on the second floor of a modified warehouse. There he and his executive branch crowded into a dozen small rooms. Only the painted letters, "The Presdt," distinguished his office from all others. For nearly fifteen hours of every day Davis conducted the affairs of state from this room, organizing the government, greeting well-wishers, and coping with job-seekers.

Throughout his presidency, the ceaseless pace of his work schedule and the unyielding stress of the job taxed Davis, debilitating his frail constitution and shortening his temper. His sole recreation was horseback riding. Unlike Abraham Lincoln, who employed a keen wit and good humor to win over supporters and to maintain his sanity as his world appeared to crumble beneath him, Davis conveyed a stiffness and formality to almost everyone. Times were too weighty for levity.

Day after day, week after week, the procession of visitors seemed endless. A helter-skelter schedule prevented systematic thought, as the mundane affairs of government organization inundated the new president. The arrival of Joseph Eggleston Johnston broke that cycle. This fellow merited Davis's undivided attention.[3]

For more than thirty years, Davis and Johnston had known one another. Together they had attended West Point, Davis in the Class of 1828, Johnston one year behind. Although they had never been cronies, their paths had crossed numerous times since their Academy days. When Johnston resigned his commission in the U.S. Army to cast his lot with the Confederacy, he held the position of quartermaster general and carried the rank of brigadier general. Davis had chaired the Senate committee that attested to Johnston's qualifications for the post. Among Johnston's army peers, no one's reputation surpassed his.[4]

In fact, few officers in the Regular Army equaled Johnston's combat record. After graduating thirteenth in his West Point class, he had campaigned against the Sac and Fox Indians, battled the Seminoles in Florida, and fought in Mexico under Zachary Taylor and Winfield Scott. More peaceful assignments included "Bloody" Kansas, rough-and-tumble Texas, and the Mormon expedition into Utah Territory. His old mentor, Winfield Scott, once quipped that Johnston had an attraction to lead. Perhaps that was true. Several scars attested to his battlefield misfortunes.

For weeks Davis had actively sought Johnston's presence. War with the Union was imminent, and the new president needed a man of Johnston's accomplishments and talents for consultation and leadership. His passage through Davis's doorway in early May 1861 provided just the sort of relief the overburdened president required.

Over the next few days, Davis and Johnston closeted themselves away to formulate military strategy and policy, with periodic participation from the secretary of war and the adjutant general. When they emerged, Johnston would not serve as quartermaster for the Confederacy. His talents were too valuable for that. Instead, he had accepted a position in the field. Armed with a commission as brigadier general in the Confederate States Army, Johnston also carried orders appointing him commander at Harpers Ferry, which was the site of the prized arsenal, the pathway of the Baltimore & Ohio Railroad, and the gateway to the fertile Shenandoah Valley.

In this moment of crisis, Jefferson Davis anticipated great things from him. Johnston never lived up to those expectations.

Of the many perplexing personalities in the Civil War, Johnston's may have exceeded all others. On the surface he exhibited all the qualities of greatness. Johnston graduated in the top quarter of his

West Point class and impressed both faculty and students as a bright, directed, sober young man. As a warrior, Johnston ranked first among equals. His extensive combat experience and composure under fire earned him respect and admiration throughout the U.S. Army. Over his thirty years of service, Johnston had demonstrated a mastery of several critical aspects of command. He possessed a thorough grasp of tactics, and his duty as quartermaster general had exposed him to the exacting details of logistics at a high level. Perhaps most important, Joe Johnston was a leader of men.

Like his dear friend McClellan, Johnston had a presence about him that impressed onlookers. He appeared every bit a soldier, even in civilian garb. Of medium height, slightly built, and deceptively powerful, the fifty-four-year-old Johnston sported a greyish-white Van Dyke beard. His bald head, high cheekbones, and pointed jaw and beard gave his cranium a slightly domed appearance that accentuated his cerebral image. Upright, graceful, elegantly mannered and gentlemanly, he carried himself extremely well.

Johnston exuded a magnetism that drew people to him. Less flamboyant than McClellan, Johnston possessed a magical talent for establishing an intimate rapport with his troops. While McClellan won the hearts of his men by making volunteers feel like soldiers through drill and pageantry, Johnston attended to more personal considerations. He knew just how to care for his men, to fulfill their needs when others failed. Johnston looked out for their welfare, and in return soldiers loved him.

This charisma extended to the officer corps as well. Some of the finest warriors in the Confederacy professed their deep friendship and esteem for Johnston. J. E. B. Stuart, the famed cavalryman, called Johnston his best friend, and James "Pete" Longstreet, whom Lee once referred to as his "Old War Horse," longed for a return to service under Johnston. Those who treated Johnston with dignity and respect discovered in him a warmth and delightfulness that won lifelong friendships.

Yet Johnston's baggage included some less visible flaws that inhibited his success at the highest levels. In contrast to McClellan, whose psychological problems paralyzed him, Johnston was by no means dysfunctional. Rather, he lacked the capacity to grow to the level that both the war demanded and Davis had expected.

Elements of Johnston's problems surfaced in his first assignment. After two days at Harpers Ferry, Johnston announced to authorities in Richmond that he regarded the town as "untenable by us at present against a strong enemy." Because Harpers Ferry was bounded by the Potomac and Shenandoah Rivers, with heights overlooking it all around, a shrewd attacker could readily ensnare Johnston's entire command by a flanking maneuver. Perhaps an army of 15,000 could hold attackers at bay, but the defenders consisted only of a ragtag force of some 8,000, approximately 1,000 of those without weapons, and all poorly supplied and trained. "Their utter want of discipline and instruction will render it difficult to use them in the field," he asserted. He would block the river crossings and then retard any advance toward the Valley.[5]

Less than one week later, Johnston wrote to Robert E. Lee, Commanding General of Virginia Forces and Davis's primary military advisor, that an accumulation of Federal troops in Maryland threatened his position. He could not resist a Union onslaught and wondered, "Would it not be better for these troops to join one of our armies, which is too weak for its object, than be lost here?" Lee comforted his old West Point classmate and friend, insisting that every commander suffered from shortages and untrained soldiers. Johnston had deployed his forces well and Lee would funnel reinforcements whenever he could do so. "Great reliance is placed on your good judgment, the skill of your officers, and the ardor of your troops," Lee instructed him, "and should you be attacked by a force which you may be unable to resist at all points and to keep beyond your frontier, you must move out of your position and destroy all facilities for the approach and shelter of an enemy. Concentrate your troops, and contest his approach step by step into the interior." Authorities in Richmond could not direct affairs; Johnston had to rely on his own discretion.[6]

These were not the words Johnston wanted to hear, and he refused to let the matter rest. Fresh intelligence, he alerted Lee, suggested a substantial Federal army in southern Pennsylvania. Lee explained that abandoning Harpers Ferry would be "depressing to the cause of the South." Johnston replied, "Would not the loss of five or six thousand men be more so?" He again complained that authorities in Richmond had neglected to provide him with clear instructions. The burden of command fell heavily on Johnston's shoulders. The thought of becoming either the first Confederate general to retreat or the first one to lose his command seemed to consume him.[7]

A bit perplexed, Lee consulted with Davis and responded yet again. The president preferred that Johnston hold Harpers Ferry and protect the Valley. "Precise instructions cannot be given you," Lee penned, "but, being informed of the object of the campaign, you will be able to regulate its conduct to the best advantage."[8]

Already, Johnston and officials in Richmond had reached logger-heads. Davis and Lee trusted Johnston's judgment, and they refused to saddle his options with inflexible orders. After three decades of outstanding military service, Johnston had earned such considera-tion. He stood on the ground; he commanded the town and the troops; and he understood the situation better than anyone else. Davis and Lee had articulated their designs, and Johnston had to determine what he must do to carry them out. They could only express confidence in his abilities and support any decision he made.

Both Davis and Lee now grasped Johnston's underlying motive. Lee could not have been more explicit in his guidelines. And Johnston understood them clearly enough. But Johnston had been fishing for positive authority to evacuate Harpers Ferry, so as to remove the burden of retreat from his own shoulders. On the day he withdrew from the town, Johnston received a letter from Adjutant General Samuel Cooper, dated two days earlier, that cut to the heart of the matter. Military officials had attempted to grant him discre-tion, and he had balked. Cooper wrote that, since Johnston appar-ently believed that "the responsibility of your retirement should be assumed here, and as no reluctance is felt to bear any burden which the public interests require, you will consider yourself authorized, whenever the position of the enemy shall convince you that he is about to turn your position and thus deprive the country of the use of yourself and the troops under your command, to destroy every-thing at Harpers Ferry." Johnston snapped back that he had not dodged responsibility—he had, after all, ordered the retreat of his own volition—and Cooper had to soothe Johnston's wounded ego with some calming words. But the fact remained: Johnston had attempted to dodge responsibility for the retreat and avoid a blemish on his spotless record.[9]

The squabble over Harpers Ferry boded ill for the Davis–Johnston relationship. Yet at the time, Davis's confidence in Johnston appeared unshaken. In those early months, the euphoria of secession and the excitement of war imbued Davis with vast amounts of goodwill. As Cooper explained to Johnston, the heart of the president's strategy directed military forces to "resist invasion as far as may be practicable, and seek to repel the invaders whenever and however it may be done." Within that framework, Davis awarded Johnston wide latitude. Then Davis took up his pen, urging Johnston to "write whenever your convenience will permit, and give me fully both information and suggestions." Three weeks later, the Confederate president again professed his esteem for Johnston, reassuring him that "my confidence and interest in you both as an officer and as a friend cause me to turn constantly to your position with deepest solicitude." No doubt, Davis prized Johnston's judgment, and to prevent any further misunderstandings, he offered him direct access to the commander in chief.[10]

Over the next few weeks, both Davis and Johnston struggled to ascertain Union intentions in Virginia. After falling back from Harpers Ferry, Johnston played cat-and-mouse games with his Federal adversaries; they were testing each other in alternating probes. Farther east around Washington, the Federals accumulated a substantial force that threatened the Confederate Army of the Potomac, commanded by Brig. Gen. P. G. T. Beauregard, a flamboyant and intelligent Louisianian of French descent whose enthusiasm exceeded his good judgment early in the war. Davis managed to reinforce Johnston and Beauregard somewhat, but demands from every sector dispersed the limited resources. To compensate for this weakness, Johnston and Beauregard prepared to concentrate their armies in the event of a Northern advance.

The Union struck Beauregard first. On July 9, 1861, Beauregard's troops spotted Federals pouring across the Potomac River. "No time should be lost re-enforcing me here," he pleaded. Davis directed any available men to Beauregard's command near Manassas Junction, but they amounted to few. The critical manpower came from Johnston's army. At 1:00 a.m. on July 18, a telegram arrived from Cooper. It announced that Union troops had attacked Beauregard. "To strike the enemy a decisive blow," Cooper specified, "a junction of all your effective force will be needed." With all due haste, Johnston slipped away from the Federal army in his front and passed through the mountain gap toward a town called Piedmont, a station on the Manassas Gap Railroad. Embarking the men on cars, trains shuttled chunks of Johnston's army the thirty-four miles to Beauregard's rescue.[11]

By early afternoon on July 20, Johnston reached Manassas Junction. Always sensitive to status, he submitted a request to clarify his rank prior to his arrival. Davis informed him of the obvious. Johnston now held the position of full general, while Beauregard ranked only as brigadier general. "The zeal of both," Davis stated as a prediction but offered as advice, "assures me of harmonious action." And so it was on the day of the battle.[12]

Johnston, unfamiliar with the terrain and exhausted from three sleepless nights, yielded to Beauregard's plans. By early morning the next day, they were obsolete. Union forces had feigned a direct advance across Bull Run but forded upstream, beyond the Confederate flank. Johnston detected the deception first and insisted on a redeployment of troops. For some time, the decision appeared to be too late. Federals rolled back the Confederate left flank. Gathering remnants of the confused regiments, Johnston personally led a desperate attempt to check the bluecoats. With the aid of one of his subordinates, he built a patchwork line around Stonewall Jackson's brigade that halted the Union advance.

At that point in the battle, he and Beauregard wisely divided responsibilities. Johnston abdicated tactical decisions to Beauregard, who remained at the front. Johnston assumed a position about a mile to the rear, where he could direct reinforcements to the critical areas on the battlefield.

As both sides slugged each other to near exhaustion, Johnston could sense a decisive moment. Dust clouds marked an advancing column from the rear. A staff officer insisted they were foe. Johnston anxiously fixed his eyes upon them. Who was it? Who was it? Friends would win the battle; enemies would spell disaster.

It was Edmund Kirby Smith, a Confederate staff officer with four regiments from Johnston's army. "Go where the fighting is hottest,"

Johnston commanded. Instead, Smith suggested that Johnston lead these men himself. Flushed with adrenalin, the general could not resist. He pushed the troops to the left flank and directed Jubal Early's brigade to extend beyond him. The Federal line then buckled. Long, wearisome marches, stress, and all-day fighting had sapped the energy of the Union soldiers. The counterattack, led by Early but engaged along much of the Confederate left wing, shattered the Union position and hurled them pell-mell across Bull Run and back toward Washington.[13]

As the Federal line withered into dissolution, Jefferson Davis galloped up from Manassas Junction. Too eager to sit passively in Richmond, the president who preferred to be a general traveled most of the day by train, only to observe the denouement. All along the route to Johnston's headquarters, Davis coaxed stragglers to return to the fight. The sight prepared him for the worst. After a quick handshake with Johnston, he learned the truth. A protracted day of combat had resulted in a decisive Confederate victory. Davis, stirred to passion by the sight of combat, insisted on inspecting the pursuit and even crossed Bull Run to urge troops to press forward. Confusion reigned supreme. Exhausted soldiers mustered the energy to cheer the president, but their weary bones refused to respond to Davis's entreaties.

Well after nightfall, Davis rejoined Johnston for a briefing on the day's events. Davis urged a vigorous pursuit and ordered a staff officer to draw up the directive, but Johnston convinced him that prudence demanded a delay until morning. Then Davis prepared and signed a dispatch to Cooper announcing the victory. It never crossed the president's mind that Beauregard, and perhaps Johnston too, perceived this as means of stripping credit from them for the first great victory of the war.

Not long after the battle at Manassas, the relationship between Davis and Johnston showed signs of strain. Inoffensively, Lee assigned an officer to Johnston's staff, and Johnston chafed. As ranking general in the Confederate Army, he refused the officer. Davis endorsed Johnston's written reply with a single word, "Insubordinate." Barely a few days had passed when Johnston challenged another order from Lee. Since he outranked Lee, "such orders I cannot regard, because they are illegal." The directives, moreover, intruded on his authority as army commander, the sensitive Johnston claimed. Again, Davis affixed the notation, "Insubordinate," to the message.[14]

The controversy stemmed from a series of intertwining congressional laws that created the grade of general and established rank. Johnston, as the ranking officer in the United States Army who had resigned, argued that he deserved the highest rank in the Confederate Army, in accordance with the laws. Davis, quite the legalistic stickler, interpreted the maze of regulations differently. Because Johnston had vacated a staff position for duty with troops in the field, the law required Davis to base Johnston's Confederate seniority on his highest rank when serving with troops. Johnston had served in the field as a lieutenant colonel of cavalry. Two other officers, Albert Sidney Johnston and Robert E. Lee, had outranked Johnston in the cavalry. Cooper, the adjutant general in the Confederacy, held that post in the U.S. Army before the war. Because Cooper remained in the same staff position, he retaining his seniority. Davis, therefore, correctly determined the Confederate rank order of generals as Cooper, Albert Sidney Johnston, Lee, and Joseph E. Johnston.[15]

When Johnston caught a whiff that he ranked only fourth in the Confederate Army, he exploded in rage. To Davis he directed a massive epistle, close to two thousand words long, in which he declared his right to be "first general in the Armies of the Southern Confederacy." Painstakingly, Johnston established his case and concluded that the reduction of his rank "is a blow aimed at me only." He drew his sword for the Confederacy, "not for rank or fame, but to defend the sacred soil," yet he nonetheless complained that Davis's decision "seeks to tarnish my fair fame as a soldier and a man, earned by more than thirty years of laborious and perilous service." Beauregard had received promotion to general for his performance at Manassas, Johnston grumbled, but "care seems to be taken to exclude the idea that I had any part in winning our triumph." The present order of rank, Johnston insisted, was illegal.[16]

The lecture struck a raw nerve with Davis. The Confederate president had obeyed the will of Congress precisely, and Johnston's accusations of wrongdoing and injustice infuriated him. Although no doubt tempted to respond with a lengthy rebuttal, Davis resisted.

He merely acknowledged receipt of Johnston's letter and registered his opinion that "Its language is, as you say, unusual; its arguments and statements utterly one-sided, and its insinuations as unfounded as they are unbecoming."[17]

The promotion issue ended the Davis–Johnston honeymoon. For Davis, the squabble destroyed the sincere cordiality he had previously exhibited to Johnston. Kindly personal comments and references to friendship dropped from Davis's correspondence. But there the matter rested for Davis. He bore no ill feelings toward Johnston, and in no way did the fracas affect Davis's professional relationship with the general.

It was different for Joe Johnston, a driven, competitive man. During his days at West Point classmates chided him with the nickname "Colonel" for his serious, directed demeanor. Over the years, marriage and elevation in rank above his peers had damped the flames of his ambition somewhat, but in his heart the fire forever raged. Often this passion for personal success colored his perception and heightened his sensitivity to the acts and achievements of others. For Johnston, the matter of his rank festered. Now false tales that then-Senator Davis had once attempted to block Johnston's promotion to quartermaster general circulated widely in Richmond and elsewhere. Johnston, too, resurrected his battle with then-Secretary of War Davis for a promotion that both Davis and his predecessor had rejected. Eventually, Secretary of War John B. Floyd, Davis's successor and Johnston's cousin, interpreted the case in Johnston's favor and awarded him the promotion. Yet the affair continued to rankle Johnston, and his wife offered it as evidence of Davis's long-standing unkindly attitude toward her husband.

Over the next few months, Davis and Johnston maintained a polite working relationship. As ranking officer, Johnston assumed command of his and Beauregard's armies, and in October the C.S.A. War Department created the Department of Northern Virginia, officially merging the two armies. Frequently Johnston called directly on Davis for more resources—manpower, cavalry, artillery, ammunition, and provisions—and in every instance Davis attempted to fill the request or explained why he could not do so. Davis, for his part, dealt professionally with Johnston, even when Johnston's sloppy record-keeping and uninterested administration vexed the presi-

dent. Once Davis or the War Department alerted Johnston to difficulties, he too attempted to rectify or justify them promptly.

In late September 1861, Johnston, Beauregard, and Maj. Gen.
Gustavus W. Smith proposed massive reinforcements for an offensive north of the Potomac River. Johnston argued that his Army of
the Potomac occupied a position that offered little defensive value
but could serve as a springboard for an invasion of Maryland and
could possibly threaten Washington. Morale remained high as a
result of the victory at Manassas. Since no one could anticipate the
impact of a long, tough winter, Johnston speculated that this might
be the best opportunity for many months to come.

Evidently the brainchild of Beauregard, an officer noted for his
grandiose schemes, the idea intrigued Davis enough to visit army
headquarters for a conference. There he learned that the effective
force in the Army of the Potomac had dipped below 40,000, and that
for an offensive to succeed, Johnston would need 60,000 seasoned
effectives, plus substantial increases in transportation and muni-
tions. To obtain the manpower, the three generals proposed stripping the defenses from other areas of the Confederacy.

Davis dissented. As president in a democratic confederation at
war, he could not sacrifice selected portions of the nation to
strengthen Johnston's army. The political repercussions of such an
act would be severe. Davis could consent to a concentration of
resources at the expense of Confederate territory only in a crisis or if
a reasonable opportunity to win the war presented itself. Clearly
neither existed. Because of an arms shortage, Davis could not even
provide them with more than a few thousand fully equipped raw
recruits.

As an alternative, Davis suggested raids across the Potomac River.
This the generals dismissed out of hand. Federal gunboats patrolled
the Potomac, and a raiding party could become trapped north of the
river. Apparently, it never dawned on Johnston, Beauregard, or
Smith that gunboats, operating in conjunction with a sizeable land
force, could box in an army on the northern bank of the Potomac
River as well. In the end, rather than advance, Johnston's army fell
back to Centreville, a less exposed position.[18]

During these autumn months, mounting external pressures
against Davis complicated his relationship with Johnston. The six-

month presidential grace period had ended, and a chorus of opposition blasted Davis for his policies. The press criticized him for the army's inactivity; then complaints over insufficient food and inadequate medical care in Johnston's army targeted Davis and his administration as the culprits. The contents of Beauregard's report on the Battle of First Manassas, however, struck the massive blow. In his own twisted way, Beauregard presented Davis as having obstructed both the fall of Washington and a campaign that would have brought Maryland into the Confederate fold. The Louisiana general had elevated one of his absurd schemes that Davis had rejected into a grand design that would have accomplished much more than the Manassas victory. The implications fed those charges that the press and public had bandied about for weeks: that the Southern Confederacy had selected an incompetent president.

Davis exploded. Beauregard's report misled the public. Worse, it stoked the fires of Davis's opposition.

Criticism had always cut Jefferson Davis deeply. After the first meeting of Davis and his future bride, the incisive young Varina Howell sized him up shrewdly when she noted with disappointment that he took for granted that "everybody agrees with him when he expresses an opinion." Much later in life, she reflected that "he was abnormally sensitive to disapprobation. Even a child's disapproval discomposed him." Convinced of his own righteousness, Davis reacted to all reproach as an act of "injustice." The president directed his fury at Johnston's subordinate, Beauregard, who eventually altered his report. But Johnston suffered as well. For the duration of the war, the Confederate opposition to Davis assumed the political initiative and never relinquished it. Always siege-like, the atmosphere around Davis altered for the worse. Now sensitized to any criticism or disagreements, Davis lost much of his tolerance for temperamental behavior, including Johnston's. Debilitated by personal maladies, smothered by the pressures of the job, and carved up by his political enemies, Davis grew increasingly touchy and petulant. With each passing day, he became more and more like Johnston.[19]

Throughout the winter of 1861–62 Davis and Johnston clashed again and again. Disputes ranged from a squabble between Johnston and Acting Secretary of War Judah P. Benjamin, Davis's friend and arch-defender, over construction of winter quarters for soldiers to deliberate attempts by Johnston to skirt the will of the commander in chief or the secretary of war. All combined to shake Davis's confidence in Johnston and undermine Johnston's faith in his president's goodwill.

Davis first called on Johnston to reorganize his army and consolidate regiments from each of the states into state brigades. Both Davis and Congress hoped this would engender state pride, rally the folks at home, and spur enlistments. Johnston, however, viewed this as unnecessary interference into the organization of his army. Despite repeated requests to implement the policy, Johnston temporized. An anticipated Federal advance or other pressing matters always precluded brigade realignment.

A much more serious breach developed over reenlistment furloughs. In the fervor of secession and the threat of invasion, most Confederate soldiers had signed up for one-year enlistment hitches, which would expire some time in the spring. Fearful that the armies would dissolve at the height of the campaign season, Congress and the Davis administration offered an extended leave and such incentives as permission for soldiers to create new units and select their own officers to anyone who reenlisted. Johnston viewed this as a direct intrusion into his domain as army commander. Again, miscommunication between Benjamin and Johnston created the fissure; bad judgment and insistence on petty prerogatives ripped wide the gap.

Johnston learned of the furlough policy through an officer's request for information. Immediately, he sought clarification of the terms from Benjamin and insisted that granting leaves in large numbers threatened "the safety of this command." Benjamin replied that the condition of the roads would foil any attack and that he should "go to the extreme verge of prudence in tempting your twelve-months' men by liberal furloughs." This policy, Benjamin insisted, will "afford the best guarantee of your having under your orders a large force of veteran troops when active operations recommence." The Adjutant General's Office had issued Johnston a copy of the order; somehow, it got delayed.[20]

Within days, matters deteriorated. Recruiters entered Johnston's camps armed with signed furloughs or transfers as an inducement to reenlist. Johnston lashed out. Benjamin had a long history of intrusions, so much so that Johnston once cracked to a subordinate, "The Secretary of War will probably establish his headquarters within this department soon." Johnston could endure no more. He fired off a lengthy letter to Benjamin, complaining that the acting secretary of war all too frequently bypassed his headquarters and issued orders directly to officers and men in Johnston's army. This practice under-cut Johnston's authority and interfered with the internal operations of his army.[21]

When Benjamin failed to halt the practice, Johnston took his case before Davis, who some months earlier had invited Johnston to communicate freely on any issue. Davis consulted with Benjamin and responded unsympathetically to his army commander. Benjamin had not granted leaves of absence or furloughs to soldiers in the Army of the Potomac for a month now, he informed Johnston, and "those which you inform me are daily received must be spuri-ous." The president dismissed any assertions that his favored secre-tary had intruded intentionally into army affairs. Benjamin, moreover, "has complained that his orders are not executed, and I regret that he was able to present to me so many instances to justify the complaint, which were in nowise the invasion of your preroga-tive as a commander in the field."[22]

Coinciding with this tussle over furloughs, Davis and Johnston locked horns over Benjamin's interference with Stonewall Jackson's command in the Shenandoah Valley. Three months after the victory at First Manassas, Davis transferred Jackson back to the Valley to oversee Confederate defenses there. Within two weeks, the famous Stonewall Brigade rejoined its old commander, at the expense of Johnston's army around Manassas. Davis replaced them with some green troops. Although both Jackson and his men remained under Johnston's supervision, the separation of one of the army's premier brigades irked Johnston.

In January 1862, a dispute erupted between Jackson and his sub-ordinate, Brig. Gen. W. W. Loring, over the exposed position of Loring's men. Officers in Loring's division filed a grievance, which an unsympathetic Jackson forwarded to the War Department as dis-approved by him. When Davis perused the petition, he determined that Johnston should "examine for yourself into the true state of the case," report on the situation, and implement necessary changes.

Instead of handling the matter himself, Johnston foolishly sent an acting inspector general to investigate. Benjamin reacted. Based on intelligence information of a Union advance on Romney, the acting secretary of war ordered Loring to retreat to Winchester. This time, Jackson lashed out in frustration at the interference and demanded a transfer to noncombat duty or he would resign. Johnston and the governor of Virginia pleaded with Jackson to reconsider, and eventually he withdrew his resignation.

But Johnston pursued the matter further. He complained to Davis and requested that the president remove the Valley District from Johnston's overall authority, since the secretary of war and he might act at cross purposes in a crisis and cause a disaster. Again, Davis rebuked Johnston, not the secretary of war. Since he failed to investigate the controversy personally, Benjamin acted in his stead. Unity of action required a single commander, and the Valley District would remain under Johnston's authority.[23]

In barely one year, the Davis–Johnston relationship had degenerated into a running series of disputes over political policies, army administration, and command authority. Early in the war, Johnston demanded specific authorization for tactical decisions. Then the pendulum shifted to the other extreme, with the general insisting on unusual flexibility in applying policies to his army. Davis, on the other hand, perceived Johnston as a lackadaisical administrator who deliberately thwarted directives from the commander in chief or his spokesman, the secretary of war.

Embroiled in these controversies was a clash of strategic views. For political reasons, the president believed that his armed forces must protect all of the Confederacy. His strategy called for a division of the limited resources to block logical avenues of approach, and for the concentration of two or more large commands to confront a major enemy advance. To ensure cooperation, Davis created rather large departments, with all forces under a single commander.[24]

Johnston's approach to strategy, however, differed markedly. A concentration of forces, Johnston was convinced, provided the best defense for the Confederacy. "I am an enemy to much distribution of troops," he admitted to Stonewall Jackson. This concept so consumed his strategic thought that it inhibited his ability to formulate and adapt plans and operations to meet the demands of the war and prompted him to circumvent official military policies.

In Johnston's eyes, concentrated forces implied a reassuring degree of readiness. Whenever in camp, he perceived it to be his primary duty as army commander to maintain a maximum level of preparedness. But this short-term mission often conflicted with the long-term interests of his army and the Confederacy as a whole. Johnston refused to weigh his future needs against the degree of crisis at the present. He opposed the furlough program because it reduced the forces he had concentrated in northern Virginia. Like many Confederate generals, he opted for temporary readiness over the long-range benefits of an expansive leave policy. The Jackson–Loring feud cut to the heart of command prerogatives, but it also related directly to readiness and response. How could Jackson and he plan, prepare, and execute a concentration of forces or operate in synchrony "while the corresponding control is not in my hands?" Johnston argued to Davis. And if authorities in Richmond intruded on tactical decisions in his army, would they bar him from concentrating his forces if that decision opened alternative avenues to Federal invasion? Even reorganizing brigades by states would create unnecessary chaos and impair readiness, despite the possibility of future benefits from increased enlistment. Thus, Johnston's tightly-held views on strategy brought him into clash after clash with Davis.[25]

Not long after these battles with Benjamin, Johnston gained momentary revenge. At a dinner party attended by politicians, Johnston naively voiced his candid doubts that the Confederacy could win its independence with Benjamin as secretary of war. Enemies of Benjamin employed Johnston's words as evidence of Benjamin's incompetence during congressional debates on a resolution of no confidence against the acting secretary. The movement compelled Davis to withdraw Benjamin's nomination and replace him with George W. Randolph, a man more to Johnston's liking. But the joy of retaliation was fleeting. Davis appointed Benjamin as secretary of state, and he continued to act as Davis's closest cabinet advisor.

Amid this poisoned atmosphere, communications between Davis and Johnston broke down temporarily. In mid-February 1862, Davis, Johnston, and the cabinet had discussed the necessity of a retreat from the Manassas–Centreville area to the more defensible Rappahannock River. The Manassas–Centreville region offered few natural defensive positions; its great value rested in the rail connections. With McClellan's massive numbers in the Washington area, and Johnston's effective strength slipping due to illness and furloughs, he argued convincingly that the Rappahannock line would provide his army much greater security. Apparently, Davis authorized Johnston to remove heavy guns and lighten the army's impedimenta in case circumstances such as a Union advance required a move. But Davis's correspondence indicates a desire to enhance Johnston's strength and hold the current position in northern Virginia, wholly in keeping with his policy to defend Confederate territory whenever possible.

Much to Davis's shock, on the ides of March he learned that Johnston had fallen back from Manassas and its vicinity. Worse still, he conducted the retreat in a slipshod fashion. Johnston planned his withdrawal faultily and moved precipitously, abandoning or destroying fabulous quantities of prized equipment, foodstuffs, and personal baggage. Certainly the deep Virginia mud and railroad mismanagement compounded Johnston's difficulties. Yet the general unnecessarily rushed the retreat. As a consequence, he and his army discarded all sorts of valuable equipment and nourishment, along with assorted personal items that the soldiers had accumulated. "Every one is out-raged by this mismanagement," confessed one of Johnston's aides to his wife, "& Genl J is chiefly blamed. I fear he has been careless in this matter, & permitted his subalterns to neglect their duty." Johnston had opted for the short-term gains of a rapid withdrawal, rather than a more orderly and time-consuming retreat that could have preserved costly resources.[26]

To compound his woes, Johnston failed to devote proper attention to the selection of a new position. On the last day of February, Davis had instructed Johnston to undertake a "thorough examination of the country in your rear as would give you the exact knowledge of its roads and general topography, and enable you to select a line of greater natural advantages than that now occupied by your forces." While Johnston clearly had chosen a general vicinity for the army—somewhere south of the Rappahannock–Rapidan Rivers arc—on the day he notified the president of the retreat he proposed to "take such a position as you may think best in connection with those of other troops."[27]

The news stunned Davis. Not only had Johnston fallen back without notifying him, the general had failed to take adequate measures to establish a new line. In effect, Johnston had abandoned his works voluntarily and commenced a retreat without deciding precisely where he intended to halt this retrograde movement. In utter disbelief, Davis directed him to select a position "as far in advance as consistent with your safety."[28]

Whether the president mulled over Johnston's fate at this time, no one knows. He had just cause to remove the general. Perhaps Johnston's popularity in and out of the army as the hero of First Manassas discouraged Davis from acting, or Davis feared a hostile response from his flourishing opposition. Without doubt, the commander in chief exhibited uncommon tolerance for Johnston's antics.

With the spring campaign approaching, and Johnston not living up to expectations, Davis needed an outstanding military mind to coordinate operations throughout the Confederacy and to advise him and his generals in the field on important military issues. Robert E. Lee fit the bill splendidly. He ranked second only to Albert Sidney Johnston among troop commanders, and Davis trusted Lee's judgment. Strategically, the two men thought along similar lines: Neither believed in sacrificing Confederate territory except in dire circumstances.

The appointment of Lee as commanding general of all Confederate forces secured Johnston's position as head of the principal army in Virginia. Both natives of the Old Dominion, Lee and Johnston had attended West Point together and retained a friendship throughout their adult lives. Lee believed in the talents and leadership skills of Joe Johnston, and his confidence in Johnston as an army commander never flagged. Where Davis and the secretary of war stumbled in their relationship with Johnston, Lee could succeed. Lee could attend to the details that Johnston overlooked, coordinate and supervise operations better, offer alternatives, and ensure Johnston's compliance with vital government policies.

About the same time as Lee's elevation to commanding general, two Union campaigns distracted Davis from his clashes with Johnston. Burnside's command in North Carolina had captured New Bern and threatened to strike deep into the state. And possible evidence of McClellan's long-awaited spring campaign appeared with the arrival of wave after wave of troops at Fort Monroe. Davis, then, needed more than just Lee. He also required the services of an officer with Johnston's experience in this brewing crisis.

Davis and Lee reacted to Union penetrations by drawing on Johnston's command. They sent two brigades to North Carolina, and alerted Johnston to prepare twenty or thirty thousand men to march at a moment's notice for the Peninsula, where Maj. Gen. John B. Magruder, an eccentric officer who performed best in unconventional situations, was preoccupying McClellan with a phony show of strength. Union intentions remained unclear for some days. Once McClellan tipped his hand, Davis directed Johnston to bring nearly his entire command and assume control of all forces in the area.

For several weeks Davis and Lee weighed priorities and juggled their insufficient troops deftly. Throughout this period, Lee rose to the demands of his new position. He assumed greater and greater control over portions of Johnston's department beyond the Peninsula, such as Jackson's forces in the Valley, Maj. Gen. Richard Ewell's division at Gordonsville, and Brig. Gen. Charles W. Field's command around Fredericksburg. Lee also carved out Confederate strategy on the Peninsula, often in opposition to the wishes of Johnston. It was Lee who insisted, over Johnston's objections, that they attempt to block McClellan's advance along the narrow Peninsula, instead of falling back to the defenses around Richmond. Eventually the Federals compelled Johnston to retreat to the Richmond suburbs, but Lee's policy bought valuable time. Lee, moreover, successfully opposed Johnston's plan to denude the Carolinas of manpower and concentrate those troops around Richmond. Lee pointed out that Johnston's scheme might result in the fall of Charleston and Savannah. Davis again sided with his commanding general.

Throughout April, Johnston's forces held the Yorktown line as McClellan's massive army crept forward, always under protection of his field guns. Convinced that McClellan's cautious reliance on engineering and artillery spelled doom, Johnston had warned Lee that he must abandon Yorktown soon, but he never gave an exact date. His notice of an intended withdrawal on the following day caught Lee and Davis a bit off guard. A retreat would expose Norfolk with its valuable shipyard to Union conquest, and its evacuation required time. Davis implored Johnston to delay a day or two while the Confederates removed or destroyed anything of military significance.

Once Johnston undertook the retreat, confusion and delays reigned supreme. A sea of mud and faulty communications impeded the movement. Fortunately, McClellan's timidity aided Johnston's evacuation. A bold attack at Williamsburg stung the only serious pursuers, which ensured a frantic yet secure withdrawal to an area northeast of the Confederate capital city.

Johnston tensed as the weight of the campaign bore heavily on his shoulders. A man renowned for his explosions of temper, Johnston now appeared more temperamental than usual. He erupted at a wagon driver who accidentally pinned his horse up against a fence as he tried to slip by, barraging the soldier with vulgarity and demanding a pistol from a staff officer to use on the poor fellow. The teamster emerged frightened but unscathed. To Lee Johnston issued a testy memorandum, complaining that the commanding general had interfered with his orders and demanding more information from forces scattered throughout his department. In a gentle tone Lee answered Johnston's queries and responded to complaints with detail and clarity.

At the height of the crisis, as Johnston struggled to gain control of the disparate components of his army for concentration near Richmond, Davis foolishly rebuked him at length for neglecting to reorganize his regiments from the same state into state brigades. Johnston burst into fury. "I got yesterday one of the President's letters such as are written to gentlemen only by persons who cannot be held to personal accountability," he raged to his wife. "I can not understand the heart or principles of a man who can find leisure in times like these to write four pages of scolding to one whom he ought, for the public interest, to try to be on good terms with."[29]

The following day, Davis and Lee ventured out to Johnston's headquarters to discuss plans. Johnston had none. He intended to wait and hope that a McClellan error would offer an opportunity to strike a powerful blow. Several days later, to the dismay of Davis, Johnston again retreated under Federal pressure, this time near the capital. The Union army now advanced to the suburbs of Richmond, spanning the Chickahominy River.

Lee and Davis pressed Johnston for systematic designs. Days

passed with no firm plan. Johnston studied the intelligence reports, pored over maps, pondered the situation, evaluated the possibilities. Nothing brilliant leaped to mind. He lacked the ability to shape campaigns; reaction came more readily to him than action.

Fearful that McDowell's huge Federal corps pushing down from Fredericksburg would link up with McClellan, Johnston had to strike. He formulated a dire plan that would require sophisticated coordination to assault the northern portion of the Federal line. Not only were the odds of success small, but his design failed to surmount obvious pitfalls. Even skillful execution could not have promised victory. Fortuitously, Lincoln's recall of McDowell's troops to cope with Jackson's ruckus in the Valley enabled Johnston to abort the scheme. He never bothered to notify Davis that he had called off the attack.

In its place, Johnston substituted an equally complex but not nearly so desperate plan to slice off a Union corps south of the Chickahominy River. It called for a tightly coordinated convergence of three commands, all traveling by different routes, assailing Union positions from south to north with near synchrony. But confusing written orders and imprecise verbal instructions clouded the assignments and jumbled the operation. Longstreet's command marched down the wrong road and blocked one attacking column, then another. Back at headquarters, Johnston discounted reports of chaos just long enough to prevent a cancellation or delay of the fight. Unable to wait any longer, an impatient D. H. Hill ordered his men to engage the enemy, despite the absence of some of his command. Raw courage rather than skillful execution drove back the Federal line, but without Longstreet's decisive blow, and with some heroics on the Union side, Johnston gained a hollow victory.

Johnston again had neglected to inform Davis of the attack. After listening to the crack of distant gunfire for much of the afternoon, the president determined to see for himself. At army headquarters, he encountered Lee and Johnston. Like Davis, Lee knew nothing of the battle in advance and rode out to investigate the sounds of destruction. No one at headquarters seemed to know how well or badly the clash of arms had gone, and Davis, Lee, and a few others decided to reconnoiter personally. All intrepid souls, they gravitated to the front, where the whirling vortex of combat soon sucked them into the fight. Observing an assault, cheering on troops, attempting to direct a flank attack, the party attracted such heavy artillery fire that they all retired to safety.

Once a fresh brigade arrived, Davis followed it back into battle, where he viewed its tragic repulse. Then, as he rallied the survivors, Davis spotted a stretcher whose occupant bore a familiar face. It was Joseph E. Johnston. A ball had crashed into Johnston's shoulder, and shell chunks lay buried in his chest and thigh. Davis dismounted and approached Johnston as they loaded him into an ambulance. The general opened his eyes, smiled, and extended his hand to the president. Johnston confessed that he did not know the extent of his injuries but thought he had suffered spinal damage. "The poor fellow bore his suffering most heroically," Davis wrote solemnly to his wife. Johnston's wounds, although severe, were not mortal. Doctors predicted that he would require an extended convalescence, but full recovery appeared likely.[30]

Johnston's second in command, Gustavus W. Smith, assumed control of the army and held it for twenty-four hours. In Davis's eyes, Smith did not measure up to the job, and the next day the president appointed Lee as Johnston's successor. Lee immediately terminated the battle and prepared entrenchments around the city. Once he had fortified Richmond, the new army commander boldly converged the bulk of his resources on McClellan's right flank, driving the Union army twenty miles back from the city to an area near the James River. Lee, so southerners acknowledged, had saved the Confederate capital.

In spite of their consuming disputes, Davis unquestionably regretted the loss of Johnston. With the death of Albert Sidney Johnston back in April, Davis probably respected Joseph E. Johnston's military capacity more than anyone's except Lee's. To his wife Davis privately penned before Lee's attack, "Genl. J. E. Johnston is steadily and rapidly improving, I wish he was able to take the field. Despite the critics who know military affairs by instinct, he is a good Soldier, knows the troops, never brags even of what he did do and could at this time render valuable service." As a good faith gesture, Davis offered the Confederate White House as a fine place for his recuperation. Johnston and his staff respectfully declined. It was probably the worst decision they could have made.[31]

During his convalescence in Richmond, Johnston befriended a Texas senator and former brigade commander named Louis T. Wigfall. A South Carolinian by birth and a Texan by adoption, Wigfall had earned a reputation as a man who drank too much, gambled too much, and fought too much. His profligate ways had dissipated a substantial inheritance and lost him numerous friends. In Texas, where he started anew, his ardor for an independent South won him many supporters. This led to his election to the U.S. Senate and, after secession, to the Confederate Senate. Perhaps the single word that best described Wigfall was "malcontent." The man bred conflict and controversy. At first friendly to the Confederate president, Wigfall's opinion of Davis had slid some by the autumn of 1862; it took a free fall after Davis vetoed a bill that the Texan had authored. Wigfall vowed eternal hatred for Davis and became a focal point for opposition forces to the president. From a career standpoint, then, Johnston did himself no favor by sharing a house in Richmond that autumn with the Wigfalls.

Johnston, no doubt, cared deeply for Wigfall and his family, and the Wigfalls reciprocated. Wigfall provided the recuperating patient with military news and insider politics; Johnston offered extensive military knowledge and the reputation of a great military leader. Once Johnston returned to active duty, he and Wigfall maintained a vigorous correspondence, as each fed the other news, explanations, and ideas.

In the larger picture, Wigfall used Johnston as a pawn in his battle with Davis. Johnston indiscreetly complied. He allowed himself to be sucked into the controversy, to the detriment of his military career. By the time of his wounding, Johnston may have lost faith in Davis, but the president believed in Joe Johnston as a leader of troops. Unquestionably, some of Johnston's lustre as a great military man had rubbed off before Davis's eyes. But in Davis's opinion he remained a good commander and an asset to the Confederacy. From the winter of 1862 through the duration of the war, Wigfall repeatedly vilified Davis, assailing the president's views as commander in chief with ammunition from Johnston and pressing Johnston's case as a soldier of brilliance whom Davis relegated to backwater assignments and under-resourced commands. Davis, a man noted for his intolerance to criticism, despised Wigfall for it and resented Johnston's role in the disparagements.

On November 12, 1862, Johnston reported himself fit for duty. In fact, it would take nearly a year for Johnston to heal fully, and for some months to come he lacked the stamina for active campaigning. With no existing vacancies for major army commanders, Davis created a new command structure that fit well with his strategic conception and immediate needs. All along, Davis hoped that his field commanders could accumulate enough resources to assume the offensive. Most of the time, though, they would have to stand on the defensive, blocking major invasion routes with their forces. When Federals assumed the offensive, Davis sought to achieve a concentration of neighboring armies to offset the vast Union superiority in manpower and materiel. Johnston's new position empowered him with command of all Confederate troops from the Appalachian Mountains to the Mississippi River, a region of enormous size that included two major armies, the Army of Mississippi and the Army of Tennessee, several hundred miles apart. A single overall commander of Johnston's talents could not only implement this strategy of cooperation best, but he could also advise and assist the two major field army commanders out west, Braxton Bragg and John C. Pemberton. An intelligent, quarrelsome individual, Bragg had earned Davis's admiration during the Mexican War and never lost it. But his irritating nature, which alienated him from virtually every subordinate, overshadowed his military talents. By contrast, Pemberton suffered no such personality defects. A Northerner by birth, which led civilians to doubt his patriotism, and mediocre ability were his burdens. Both men had stirred up powerful critics in and out of the army.

Six months earlier, Davis had justified his veto of a bill to create the office of commanding general in part by arguing that "no general would be content to prepare troops for battle, conduct their movements, and share their privations during a whole campaign if he expected to find himself superseded at the very moment of action." On the surface, Johnston's assignment appeared strikingly similar; in reality, the new command structure was different. Technically, Johnston oversaw both armies and commanded neither of them. Davis wanted him to play the role of the troubleshooter. He would shuttle back and forth between his commands, inspecting, directing changes, coordinating operations, and preparing them for the Union onslaught. In the event of a Federal offensive, Johnston would travel to the critical area and, as the ranking officer, oversee strategy and operations, while leaving either Bragg or Pemberton to command on the tactical and lower-operational levels. This way, Davis and the two army heads would benefit from Johnston's knowledge and experience, without locking Johnston to a desk to immerse himself in the administration of these armies.[32]

Within days of Johnston's arrival in the West, a crisis developed that highlighted the principal defect of Davis's strategy—simultaneous Union campaigns. Grant had initiated an advance on Vicksburg, Mississippi, and Pemberton cried out for reinforcements. Johnston urged the president to order Lt. Gen. Theophilus Holmes, commanding in Arkansas, to send troops across the Mississippi River to assist Pemberton. Bragg's army, already outnumbered, required every one of its troops to bar the way in the event of a Union push toward Chattanooga, and the transportation time alone from the position of Bragg's army to Vicksburg would consume a month. Davis dismissed the proposal. Holmes commanded far fewer troops than Johnston knew, and occupation demands had compelled Holmes to scatter them throughout the state. It would take him thirty days before he could aid Pemberton.

There the matter rested until Davis dropped in on Johnston and Bragg one week later. Reports of difficulties in his beloved Mississippi had convinced the president to examine the situation personally. En route, Davis stopped at Chattanooga to inspect Bragg's troops and consult with Johnston. The condition of Bragg's army and the confidence Bragg expressed in checking any Federal drive toward Chattanooga led Davis to order Johnston to send a division from Tennessee to aid Pemberton in Mississippi. As insurance, he called for cavalry raids against the Union supply lines between Louisville and Nashvile and between Memphis and Grant's army. Then Davis and Johnston embarked for Mississippi. The division from Bragg's army arrived just in time to participate in the tail end of a Union repulse at Haynes' Bluff.[33]

Unfortunately, Bragg could have used the division even more. In late December, the Federal army launched a campaign against Bragg's command. At Stone's River, near Murfreesboro, Tennessee, the opposing armies battered one another for two days, inflicting mammoth losses in a stalemated engagement. Davis's strategy for the region, then, lacked the means to cope with simultaneous advances.

In the aftermath of the two campaigns, Johnston found fault with his new position on two levels. Again he objected to Davis's strategy and called for a concentration of forces. Johnston wanted to strip areas east and west of the Mississippi River of troops, occupy Port Hudson, Louisiana, and Vicksburg with a defensive detachment, and create an army of 40,000 for field duty in Mississippi. Bragg would manage affairs with his current strength.

It was the same argument they had debated in Virginia the previous spring and Davis, as usual, objected. Concentration of forces did not bother the president. After all, he had consented to Lee's plan that brought together commands from the Shenandoah Valley and the Carolinas to drive McClellan from the outskirts of Richmond. What disturbed Davis was that Johnston's proposal would unnecessarily expose vast areas of the Confederacy to Union troops. Lee concentrated forces for a battle; Johnston intended to concentrate men, then look for a battle. In Davis's mind, the distinction was monumental.[34]

Perhaps more critical, Johnston opposed the new command structure. Davis had intentionally configured the position with enormous latitude for a man of Johnston's experience and accomplishments. But Johnston was not the general to fill the power vacuum, to expand his authority to its outer limits. Dominated by a rigid sense of command prerogatives and authority, he conceived this new assignment narrowly, to protect the rights of his army commanders. Thus, Johnston's limited vision restricted his own power and undercut the position's usefulness.

He wanted no part of this new assignment. "The impossibility of my knowing [the] condition of things in Tennessee shows that I cannot direct both parts of my command at once," he alerted Davis. To Wigfall, he elaborated on the problem. "The president's idea that I am to take command of these armies successively, at my pleasure would be a very mischievous one in practice," Johnston grumbled. "It is virtually having two generals for one army." He complained that he would almost certainly design a system and formulate a course of operations that differed from those of the two army commanders. Once he left those armies, each commander "would naturally go back to his own system." Therefore, it made little sense for him to develop such a plan of operations. "For more than three months," he pined, "I have been doing next to nothing."[35]

Johnston misconceived Davis's entire concept. The president believed Johnston's knowledge and talents as a military leader vastly surpassed those of Bragg and Pemberton. Davis intended for Johnston to impose on them his own "dispositions & a plan of operations" which, Davis presumed, would be superior to their own. Johnston would assume command of an army in times of crisis, but if he could not, Pemberton or Bragg would implement the plan as he had formulated and explained it to them. Davis wanted Johnston to prepare for various contingencies; the general could not envision them.[36]

Rather than head a department, Johnston sought command of his own army once more. And an opportunity arose that offered just such a prospect. He possessed the authority to investigate the conduct of the Army of Tennessee at Stones River, assess Bragg's performance, and ultimately recommend his removal. Several distinguished officers exhorted him to adopt just that course. But Johnston resisted. Bragg had commanded the army well, Johnston insisted. Anyway, to render a decision that would lead to Bragg's replacement, when Johnston himself likely would succeed him, smacked of impropriety.

Johnston coveted his old command. Davis, he wrote to Wigfall, should return him "where Yankee missiles found me." Enviously, Johnston directed barbed missiles of his own at Lee, who had usurped his position not only as its permanent commander but also as first soldier of the Confederacy. "What luck some people have," Johnston jealously mused after Burnside assaulted Lee at Fredericksburg. "Nobody will ever come to attack me in such a place." He had heard that the president and secretary of war described Johnston's assignment as "the highest in the Confederacy." Johnston wondered, "If they so regard it ought not our highest military officer to occupy it?" That would enable Lee and him to swap jobs. Since he deemed the command structure unworkable, "Under all the circumstances, if the government cannot be convinced of the correctness of my views, it seems to me that the assignment of Lee to this command, & to me my old army, would be a good & pleasant solution to the problem." It never happened.[37]

While Johnston lamented his plight as departmental commander, U.S. Grant finally cracked the topographical conundrum of

Vicksburg. By tramping down the opposite side of the Mississippi River, then slipping across below Vicksburg, Grant caught Pemberton, Johnston, and Davis by surprise. Johnston, in his sickbed from a flare-up of his old wounds, responded to Pemberton's request for additional manpower by seeking reinforcements from outside his department. "They cannot be sent without giving up Tennessee," he exaggerated. As he had done throughout his tenure in command, Johnston sought a concentration on his own ground at the expense of other areas of the Confederacy. This time, though, Johnston's hand included a trump card. The Union and Confederacy now battled for Davis's home turf. The president drew forces from as far away as coastal South Carolina to augment troop strength in Mississippi.[38]

Then everything seemed to unravel for the Confederates. Grant maneuvered his troops brilliantly, marching swiftly, cutting loose from his supply base, and pounding Confederate commands at every opportunity. Davis, who took a proprietary interest in the campaign, communicated directly to Pemberton, admonishing him that "To hold both Vicksburg and Port Hudson is necessary to a connection with Trans-Mississippi."[39]

Meanwhile, the Confederates squandered critical response time. Hampered by his injuries, Johnston had remained in Chattanooga until May 9, 1863, when the secretary of war ordered him to Mississippi to "take chief command of the forces." Late on May 13, Johnston reached Jackson, Mississippi, with token reinforcements, declaring to the secretary of war, "I am too late." Grant had interposed his army between Pemberton's and Johnston's forces. Only if Pemberton battled his way through the Federals to the east could the two commands concentrate. That, however, required Pemberton to abandon his sole charge, Vicksburg. Instead, he elected to strike Grant's line of communication to the south, then changed his mind after Johnston rebuked him for disobeying orders. Now it was really too late. Federals shoved Johnston's command out of Jackson to the north and then bore down on Pemberton's army. At Champion's Hill Grant's bluecoats delivered a pasting, and Pemberton's command, scarcely intact, stumbled back to Big Black River, just ten miles from Vicksburg. Pemberton had one last chance to escape. He opted instead to risk the army and hold Vicksburg. Pemberton lost both.[40]

Johnston reoccupied Jackson and began the laborious process of accumulating a large enough army to break Grant's grip on Vicksburg. Not only did he have to draw in manpower, but most of the reinforcements lacked ammunition, wagons, and horses, all of which Johnston had to supply. The job was daunting, and time played into the hands of the Union. With each passing day, the Federal position grew stronger. Fresh Union troops poured into Mississippi, and Grant employed his soldiers at the construction of field works in opposite directions—one to the west toward Vicksburg and one to the east in the event of a Johnston attack. To break the Union line and link up with Vicksburg's defenders, then, Pemberton and Johnston would have to assault both fortified lines simultaneously.[41]

As the Confederacy confronted the fall of Vicksburg and the loss of the entire Mississippi River, tensions between Johnston and authorities in Richmond heightened. Since late May, Johnston had collected 24,000 effectives. But by mid-June, he still had not acted. He insisted on more reinforcements. Davis wondered why he had not drawn more men from Bragg's army. When Johnston claimed to lack authority, the relationship cracked.

In his defense, Johnston disingenuously asserted that the order directing him to assume command of the forces in Mississippi had removed him from departmental responsibilities. Actually, he again objected to the broad discretionary powers that his position entailed. Barely three months earlier, he insisted to Wigfall, "I have never complained of want of official authority, but have been trying ever since I ascertained the fact practically to convince the government that such authority can not be exercised beneficially to the service." Johnston's limited view of command restricted his ability to wield the power. "It is for the Government to determine what department, if any, can furnish the re-enforcements required," he averred hollowly to the secretary of war. "I cannot know here General Bragg's wants compared with mine. The Government can make such comparisons." Two days later, he elaborated: "To take from Bragg a force which would make this army fit to oppose Grant, would involve yielding Tennessee. It is for the Government to decide between this State and Tennessee."[42]

Distraught over the prospects of Mississippi's fall to Union hands,

Davis projected his anger for the sorry state of military affairs on Johnston. He pored over every piece of correspondence from Johnston, seeking evidence to support the general's contention that he had been removed from his own departmental command. None existed. Petty debates ensued, which aggravated Davis all the more. Both stubborn men, neither tolerant of criticism, and both insistent on the final word, they refused to drop the issue.

On June 15, Johnston telegraphed authorities in Richmond that "I consider saving Vicksburg hopeless." The secretary of war responded forcefully: "Vicksburg must not be lost without a desperate struggle." Even if Johnston could obtain no more resources, "you must hazard attack." Johnston waited too long. On July 3, he issued instructions to Pemberton for a cooperative assault on Sherman's portion of the Union line. One week later, Pemberton received the communication. It was too late to change anything; he had surrendered on the Fourth of July. Pemberton's decision to save Vicksburg and not his army had caused the crisis, but Johnston's inability to utilize the resources at hand assured defeat.[43]

The fall of Vicksburg freed up Davis to gather more evidence against Johnston. In a massive three-thousand-word letter, reminiscent of the legendary tomes he had once written as secretary of war to Commanding General Winfield Scott, the president rebuked Johnston for his unjustified interpretation of the order assigning him to command in Mississippi. Beneath the surface, Davis seethed because Vicksburg had been lost without a bold relief attempt. Johnston replied with two thousand words of defense. From there, the dispute spilled over into the press and politics, with partisans on each side defending their favorite. This only fanned the flames of bitterness between them.[44]

At the root of the dispute lay the command structure. "No general can command separate armies," Johnston contended during the Vicksburg Campaign. Davis had devised a position of command to utilize Johnston's talents and experience, and Johnston lacked the capacity to fill it. On July 22, Davis acquiesced to Johnston's wishes. He carved out the Department of Tennessee, which included Bragg's army, from Johnston's domain. And he never forgave Johnston for the loss of his beloved Vicksburg.[45]

Johnston's banishment from important command did not last

long. After Federal forces routed the Army of Tennessee at
Missionary Ridge in November 1863, Bragg submitted his resignation. Too many subordinates despised Bragg for Davis to retain him.
But then the question arose: Whom to replace him with? Corps
commander William J. Hardee accepted the post temporarily but
declined permanently. He suggested Joe Johnston. An old and dear
friend of Davis's, Leonidas Polk, recommended him, too. Even the
unobtrusive Lee endorsed Johnston. The president had few options.
Among field commanders, the choice narrowed to Johnston or
Beauregard. In Davis's mind, Johnston was the lesser of the two
evils. During mid-December, Joe Johnston received his Christmas
wish—command of a single army.[46]

Johnston provided just the sort of therapy the Army of Tennessee
required. His charismatic, soldier-oriented approach buoyed morale
in the ranks and ensured a staff that responded to the needs of the
men. Johnston's reputation, still towering within military circles,
quelled unrest among officers and pieced the fragments into a whole
once more. In short, Joe Johnston soothed what ailed the Army of
Tennessee.

Unfortunately, misleading information convinced Davis that
Johnston could accomplish even greater things. On December 17,
1863, Hardee submitted a report to the adjutant general in which he
requested reinforcements for an offensive while his Union opponents were scattering their strength in Tennessee and Mississippi.
Obtaining supplies for horses and men, according to Hardee, "pre-
sents a source of infinite trouble." He anticipated that Tennessee
and Kentucky would fill those wants. One week later, in a letter to
authorities in Richmond, he claimed that since taking over as acting
commanding general, he had increased troop strength, replaced
artillery and horses, granted furloughs, and resolved supply difficulties. Hardee took great pride in turning over to Johnston an army in
"fine condition." A visit to the army by Davis's aide-de-camp cor-
roborated Hardee's evaluation.[47]

Statements from Hardee and from Davis's emissary directly contradicted previous reports on the Army of Tennessee. And Davis all
too willingly accepted them as the actual state of affairs, when in fact
the army lacked the capability to assume the offensive. Just six days
earlier, Confederate Secretary of War James A. Seddon had issued

Johnston instructions that addressed the force's disastrous condition. Seddon referred to "disheartened" troops and the lack of ordnance and materiel. Johnston, he hoped, would "restore and supply its deficiencies in ordnance, numbers, and transportation" and "use all means in your power" to rectify the food and forage problem. Then, two days before Christmas, Davis altered the agenda. Because the condition of the army "is encouraging," Davis called for "prompt and vigorous action" to "reoccupy the country" that the Army of Tennessee had lost during the year. Johnston should formulate his own designs. Davis merely requested that the general "communicate fully and freely with me concerning your proposed plan of action." But the Rebel president was thinking wishfully, not realistically.[48]

Johnston resisted on both counts. He discussed neither strategy nor plans with the authorities in Richmond, and he correctly dismissed the idea of an offensive as impractical. Perhaps in May or June 1864, when the three-year Federal enlistments would expire, army strength would equalize and he could assume the offensive. Much more worrisome was the possibility that the immense Union army in the Chattanooga area would "drive us back whenever it pleases." Throughout the winter and into the spring, the effective strength of the Army of Tennessee hovered around 42,000, despite vigorous efforts to increase manpower. Days prior to the opening of the spring campaign, he complained to Wigfall that the administration had dashed his hopes for large-scale reinforcements. "Those coming," Johnston notified his friend, "are too small to be considered in deciding upon a course of action."[49]

Just as he did in the face of McClellan's masses, Johnston intended to fight on the defensive, seeking an error that would provide an opening for a counterattack. Thus, he abdicated the initiative and permitted Sherman to dictate the contours of the campaign. More important, Johnston neglected to think through his course of action. With his army in a strong defensive position at Dalton, Johnston anticipated that Sherman would hurl his blue waves at the Confederate fortifications. His army would then exploit any weaknesses that the vanquished Federals exposed. But his plans failed to account for the likelihood of a Rebel retreat. Rather than taking precautions to scout the terrain rearward, to lay out alternate defensive positions, and to design traps to spring on Sherman's army in case he needed them, Johnston devoted scant attention to the country-side between Dalton and Atlanta. As a consequence, whenever Sherman's forces compelled the Army of Tennessee to withdraw during the campaign, Johnston and his staff had to scramble to select and prepare a new line of defense. They could implement the adjustments on the tactical level effectively; from an operational standpoint, they struggled.

Several times Johnston planned to deliver a blow against Sherman's columns, only to see the opportunity slip away. Either maladroit execution or Sherman's talent for command disrupted the attempts. Sherman always seemed to be one step ahead of Johnston. And each time Johnston retreated, Davis grumbled. Yet the com-mander in chief continued to aid and support Johnston. He had no replacement. By mid-June, reinforcements had elevated the effec-tive strength of the Army of Tennessee to over 60,000, an increase of more than 14,000 since the campaign began. Near the end of the month Sherman committed his worst blunder of the campaign, a frontal assault on Kennesaw Mountain. But its failure provided Johnston with no chance for a counterattack.[50]

As Sherman's army shoved the Confederates back near Atlanta, his lengthening supply line, the railroad to Chattanooga, offered an inviting target. Repeatedly Johnston called for cavalry from the neighboring Department of Alabama, Mississippi, and East Louisiana to break the railroad. Davis and his new military advisor, Braxton Bragg, wondered why Johnston did not employ his own horsemen. According to field returns, Johnston's army reported over 11,000 effective cavalrymen. The Department of Alabama, Mississippi, and East Louisiana had already contributed 14,000 troops to the Army of Tennessee, and now it could barely neutralize the Federal forces within its own boundaries. Johnston responded by insisting that "our own cavalry is so weak compared with that of the Federal army."[51]

In reality, Sherman's advantage in manpower was not quite so overwhelming as Johnston asserted. While Sherman tabulated his effective strength on June 30 at 106,000, those numbers did not directly confront Johnston's army. Union and Confederate forces determined effective strength differently, which inflated Federal totals by some 7 percent. Then, for each mile Sherman's army advanced into Georgia it had to peel off more than 230 men to guard its rail supply line. By the time it had reached the outskirts of Atlanta, over 20,000 men, one fifth of his effective strength, had been left behind to protect the railroad. By contrast, Johnston, who drew supplies through friendly country, devoted only small numbers to guarding his logistical pipeline, and as he fell back he incorporated these troops into his front-line command. He also benefited from nearly 10,000 militiamen in Atlanta. The Rebel commander again demonstrated his incapacity to use the resources at hand effectively.[52]

Davis grew increasingly impatient with Johnston's retreats. Behind the scenes, Lt. Gen. John Bell Hood, an ambitious, aggressive corps commander in Johnston's army whose war wounds cost him a leg and the use of an arm, had fed Davis tales that Johnston had recoiled from assuming the offensive. Davis never questioned the information's veracity. It merely reinforced what Davis had suspected all along: Johnston had spurned the offensive. When Johnston notified Richmond authorities that he had withdrawn to the Chattahoochee River, some ten miles from the heart of Atlanta, Davis intervened. The message "renders me more apprehensive for the future," the president expressed to Johnston. With the army's back to the river, heavy rains could make it unfordable, thereby trapping the Confederate command. And if Johnston withdrew to the south bank, he would open Alabama to raids. Davis could offer no means of "averting calamity." The administration had stripped other areas of manpower to reinforce him, and no more would be forthcoming, other than some Georgia militia whom the governor could muster.[53]

To investigate the situation, Davis sent Braxton Bragg. The president chose badly. As the former army commander and a man beholden to Davis for his current position, Bragg could not act objectively. Nor did Bragg's abrasive personality work well toward bridging the Davis–Johnston gap. Upon arrival, he reported a retreat from the Chattahoochee River and a decline in the condition of the army. After holding conversations with senior officers, he paid two visits to the army commander. Bragg learned nothing. "He has not sought my advice, and it was not volunteered," Bragg informed Davis. "I cannot learn that he has any more plan for the future than he has had in the past." Bragg's only positive statement was that he suspected Johnston "is now more inclined to fight." Bragg's sole job was to learn about the military situation and the commander's intentions; inconceivably, he did not ask.[54]

Davis had to act. Possession of Atlanta, a major industrial center and a critical railroad junction, was essential to the Confederate war effort, and the president needed assurances that Johnston would hold it. "I wish to hear from you as to present situation, and your plans of operation so specifically as will enable me to anticipate events," Davis telegraphed. In reply, Johnston again explained how "we must be on the defensive" with only half of the Federal numbers. "My plan of operations must, therefore, depend upon that of the enemy. It is mainly to watch for an opportunity to fight to advantage." He then expressed a hope that the Georgia militia could hold Atlanta for a day or two to provide his army with flexibility to maneuver and fight.[55]

That was it. Johnston had no specific plan, and he had not pledged to hold Atlanta. Davis had given him one last opportunity. Johnston bungled it. The next evening, a message arrived from the adjutant general. Since "you have failed to arrest the advance of the enemy to the vicinity of Atlanta" and "express no confidence that you can defeat or repel him, you are hereby relieved from the command of the Army and Department of Tennessee." Johnston surrendered command to Hood and communicated his intentions: to strike Union forces as they straddled Peachtree Creek, similar to his attack at Seven Pines, and, more vaguely, to swing around and attack Sherman's flank. Before he left, however, Johnston fired a brief parting salvo at authorities in Richmond. He had outperformed the great Lee in retarding Union penetrations, Johnston insisted. Then, he conluded with a flourish of sarcasm: "Confident language by a military commander is not usually regarded as evidence of competency."[56]

Like Lincoln and McClellan, Davis and Johnston lacked effective communication. In the Union situation, McClellan's psychological drawbacks impaired his ability to function properly. Johnston's failure with Davis lay in the general's inability to conceptualize on the level that Davis demanded and that Johnston's rank and responsibility required. Johnston's limited strategic and operational vision and restrictive view of command prerogatives prevented him from employing the resources at hand most efficiently. This, in turn, resulted in clash after clash with the chief executive. Once a schism occurred, neither Davis nor Johnston possessed the interpersonal skills to bridge it. Both personalized the dispute, Johnston more so than Davis. Over time, the two men drifted farther and farther apart.

For five months Johnston stewed at home, standing on the sidelines as the Confederate war effort collapsed. On February 22, 1865, he returned to command of the Army of Tennessee. Johnston's old classmate, Robert E. Lee, who had recently received the appointment of general in chief, ordered Johnston to assume command of all forces he could pull together and "drive back Sherman" as his old nemesis stormed through South Carolina. Lee still believed in Joe Johnston. Despite misgivings that this might be a Davis scheme to sully his reputation by reinstating him to the command of an army at the eleventh hour, he accepted. The reply was vintage Johnston: "It is too late to expect me to concentrate troops capable of driving back Sherman. The remnant of the Army of Tennessee is much divided. So are other troops. I will get information from General Beauregard as soon as practicable. Is any discretion allowed me? I have no staff."[57]

Johnston did assemble an army, one top-heavy with generals and bottom-weary with privates. They fought for him well at Bentonville, North Carolina, under a plan devised by the skillful cavalry leader Lt. Gen. Wade Hampton and approved by Johnston. But the brute strength of Sherman's army proved too much. Despite effecting an initial rout, Johnston's army lacked the power to exploit it and then nearly suffered a disaster during a Federal counterattack a couple of days later.

Over the next few weeks, Johnston's sole hope rested with Lee. Somehow, the two armies had to link up and deal first with Sherman, then with Grant. The unification never happened. At the end of March, Grant finally broke Lee's lines. Richmond fell into Union hands, as Lee dashed for Lynchburg and the railroad to the south. All along the way, Grant severed portions of Lee's command, and at Appomattox Court House he boxed in the remnants. Lee surrendered.

Davis, meanwhile, had evacuated the capital and fled south. At Greensboro, North Carolina, he halted to convene a meeting with cabinet officials and senior officers on the future of the Confederacy. Combative to the end, Davis advocated a continuation of the war, even after learning of Lee's surrender. A pall of silence descended on the room. Nearly all knew Davis was wrong but they shied away from challenging the headstrong president. Only one man refused to accede. It was Joe Johnston. In no uncertain terms, he proclaimed to Davis that the Confederacy had lost.[58]

No one disappointed Jefferson Davis more than Joe Johnston. Based on Johnston's reputation and record in the prewar army, Davis had anticipated great things from him. Johnston never lived up to expectations. Instead of resounding battlefield triumphs, petty jealousies and simmering feuds characterized the general throughout the war. Johnston defined and circumscribed the world around him and responded heatedly to any intrusion or interference, regardless of the source. A tender ego eclipsed his better judgment. He reacted to the slightest provocation, and his competitive nature demanded the final word.

While most ambitious individuals seek greater responsibilities and more difficult assignments, Johnston dodged them. He eschewed departmental leadership with separate armies, opting for one of his own. There, as an army commander, Johnston could share in its fate, influence its destiny, and win kudos for its accomplishments. He, the soldiers, and the public would identify him with that command. The army's victory would be his victory. In Johnston's mind, army leadership was the surest path to success.

Johnston refused to fill the power vacuum that the Confederate command structure and the demands of war created. He despised departmental command with separate field forces because he could not imagine how one officer could control distinct armies dozens, sometimes hundreds of miles apart. Trained in the peacetime world of a lean army, he locked into a narrow perception of command. Despite the exigencies of warfare on a massive scale, he proved incapable of breaking free from the past, of elevating his talents to another level. With a good eye for terrain, he could form sound tactical decisions on the spot. But Johnston never made the transition from the tactical to the operational and strategic levels. He needed to stand on the ground and observe personally to direct forces. The more abstract thought required for operational and strategic movements eluded him. In short, Johnston lacked effective operational and strategic vision.

Even as an army commander, he could never dictate the conduct of a campaign. Lee and Jackson, the truly great Confederate commanders in the war, imposed their will on the enemy. By seizing and maintaining the initiative, these leaders determined how and where their armies fought campaigns and battles. They explored possibilities, considered eventualities, and executed plans. As Johnston rose in rank and stature, the boldness of command that he had exhibited on the small-unit level vanished. He merely reacted to his adversary. In response to enemy movements, he wishfully sought an opening that would enable him to strike a blow. Johnston never grasped the art of compelling an opponent to act according to his own designs, and his plans frequently exhibited both an inattention to vital details and systemic confusion. His strategic and operational decisions displayed a surprising inability to grasp or predict their repercussions.[59]

Thus, Joseph E. Johnston possessed a hodgepodge of strengths and weaknesses. A charismatic leader, one well grounded in tactics and logistics, Johnston captured the hearts and minds of most of the officers and men who served under him. Yet a temperamental nature and limited vision inhibited him from elevating his talents to satisfy the demands of large-scale warfare. Lacking the attributes of an effective military leader, Joe Johnston proved incapable of exploiting the manpower and resources at his disposal. As a result, the Confederacy failed to established a strong command relationship for the war in the West.

Ulysses S. Grant at Cold Harbor in 1864
(National Archives)

William Tecumseh Sherman
(National Archives)

5

"If I got in a tight place you would come—if alive"

Grant, Sherman, and Union Success in the West

In a postwar interview on his relationship with Grant, the glib Sherman once wisecracked, "He stood by me when I was crazy and I stood by him when he was drunk; and now, sir, we stand by each other always." Typical of Sherman, the statement blended sarcasm with fundamental truth. In contrast to the professional relationship of Lee and Jackson, theirs was a partnership founded on amity, intimacy, and collaboration. Though they were mere acquaintances before 1861, the war thrust these men together; there they formed a most unusual and symbiotic partnership.[1]

Grant was the eldest son of a successful tanner. Born and raised in Ohio, young Grant had little interest in military matters; a passion for horses consumed him. But on a Christmas vacation in Grant's sixteenth year, his father announced that he would receive an appointment to West Point. Ulysses protested, but his father insisted he would attend, and "I thought so too, if he did."[2]

At the Academy, Grant attained inconspicuousness. His only outstanding achievement there came on the back of a horse, when he set a school high-jump record. Otherwise, he melted into the mass of students. Grant graduated 21st of 39 in the class of 1843, and in the Army's infinite wisdom, it assigned this great horseman to the infantry.

During the Mexican War, Grant fought in the campaigns under Generals Zachary Taylor in northern Mexico and Winfield Scott in central Mexico. His excellent performance earned respect from his peers and three citations for bravery and meritorious conduct from the army. Wartime letters to his fiancee and others provide a glimpse into the "Civil War" Grant. His descriptions of battles, places, and peoples were so thorough and insightful, yet so cool and detached, that it appeared as if Grant stood above the fray, rather than acting as a participant. He possessed a genuine feel for warfare; strangely enough, he found comfort in its element.

After the war, Grant married Julia Dent, the sister of a West Point classmate and a woman of character who had a steadying influence on her husband. But prolonged absence from Julia and the tedium of army life in peacetime led him to disillusionment, depression, and drunkenness. Resignation saved him from the disgrace of a court-martial. Until the outbreak of the Civil War, Grant kicked around at various occupations in several locations, never succeeding at any of them.

Sherman, too, hailed from Ohio. The third son in a family of eleven, his father died when young "Cump" was nine. Although his father had been a successful lawyer, his mother lacked the means to rear all the children alone, and she parceled him out to a prominent attorney named Thomas Ewing, who "ever after treated me as his own son." Ewing eventually served as United States Senator and as a cabinet official, and he had no difficulty procuring an appointment to West Point for Sherman. Much more the intellectual than his Civil War companion Grant, Sherman posted excellent grades at the Academy. Only an abundance of demerits for pranks and a disregard for rules deprived Sherman of the fourth spot in the class of 1840. He then entered the artillery.[3]

While classmates, juniors, and seniors earned kudos in Mexico, Sherman commanded occupation troops in California. Military assignments eventually brought him east, but a promising banking venture lured him away from the army and back to California in 1853. In the civilian world, Sherman struggled, too. The banking enterprise in California failed, due to no fault of Sherman's. He then tried the legal profession, real estate speculation, and finally settled as superintendent of the Louisiana Military Seminary, the forerunner of Louisiana State University.

Two men could hardly have been more different. Grant was short, of modest build, with brown hair and a well-trimmed beard. Sherman, gangling and slightly built, had reddish hair, a patchy beard, and a weather-worn face, "the quintessence of Yankeedom," so noted a staff officer. Grant seldom talked. Sherman spoke incessantly. While Grant's temperament seemed unflappable, Sherman was a bundle of emotions. Sherman was as intense as Grant was placid. Grant could sit quietly and contemplate for hours. Few could penetrate that impassive demeanor, and perhaps only his wife Julia and his adjutant John A. Rawlins ever truly understood him. Sherman could not sit still for more than a few moments. He was in perpetual motion, jerking in one direction, then the next, contorting his wrinkles as he blurted out wise counsel on a host of topics. For better or worse, people always knew how Sherman felt or thought.[4]

Not only were they mismatched physically and emotionally, their mental processes functioned on completely different levels. Grant comprehended problems in all their simplicity; Sherman grasped them in all their complexity. Sherman viewed life as chaos and confusion. Such bedlam and disarray grated on his nerves, and throughout his years Sherman strove to restore some order to the world around him. For Sherman, who perceived all possibilities, a world of chaos merely complicated matters or distracted him from the essentials. While he had the capacity to make difficult decisions, Sherman often agonized over them. Life's obfuscations compounded the anguish of decision making for him. Grant, on the other hand, paid no attention to confusion; it neither bothered nor distracted him. Unlike his less secure friend, Grant did not need to recognize or understand all the possibilities, because only a few were truly relevant or important. He possessed an uncanny knack of zeroing in on the critical factors. As a result, responsibility for decision making was rarely a burden to Grant.

In a revealing and insightful conversation with James Harrison Wilson late in the war, Sherman compared Grant with himself:

Wilson, I am a damned sight smarter than Grant; I know a great deal more about war, military history, strategy, and grand tactics than he does; I know more about organization, supply, and administration and about everything else than he does; but I'll tell you where he beats me and where he beats the world. He don't care a damn for what the enemy does out of his sight, but it scares hell out of me.

Sherman then added:

I am more nervous than he is. I am more likely to change my orders or countermarch my command than he is. He uses such information as he has according to his best judgment; he issues his orders and does his level best to carry them out without much reference to what is going on about him and, so far, experience seems to have fully justified him.[5]

With overlapping West Point and Regular Army careers, Grant and Sherman certainly knew one another for years before the war. As a first classman at the Academy, Sherman had scanned a list of incoming cadets, among them a chap with the peculiar name of U. S. Grant. Undoubtedly, Sherman sought out the fellow Ohioan and knew him a bit, but their class differences and army assignments limited contact between them.[6]

Their true relationship dated from February 1862. At the time Brigadier General Grant had orders to transport his command of 15,000, accompanied by naval gunboats, up the Tennessee River and to secure Fort Henry, which blocked waterway traffic and military penetration into central Tennessee. After disembarking his troops just north of the fort, he directed an overland advance. Yet Grant's columns arrived too late. Winter rains and ensuing floods had swamped Fort Henry, making it indefensible. Instead, Confederate forces concentrated on firmer ground at Fort Donelson, a dozen miles east on the banks of the Cumberland River, leaving behind only a paltry garrison of artillerists. Those remnants at Fort Henry quickly succumbed to Federal navy shelling.

Grant immediately shifted his focus to the Confederates at Fort Donelson. Unlike so many Union officers, Grant grasped the value of initiative in warfare. Those commanders who dictated how, when, and where to engage the enemy had tremendous advantages. He intended to "keep the ball moving as lively as possible," perceiving his mission as the defeat of Confederate armies, rather than just the occupation of territory. Without specific authorization from his more cautious superior, Maj. Gen. Henry W. Halleck, Grant directed two divisions to slog their way through the mud to the outskirts of the Confederate positions. The succeeding day, a third division arrived by transport along the Cumberland River, and with the aid of Federal gunboats, Grant invested the Rebel forces.[7]

This, Grant's first great campaign, exhibited all the qualities that became his trademark. Along with initiative, Grant demonstrated a tenacity of purpose and a spirit of aggressiveness that few, if any, surpassed in the war. Through plunging temperatures and a blizzard, Grant's grip on the enemy remained firm. Federal troops who had discarded their overcoats during the Indian-summer days now shivered, stamped their feet, and cursed the biting cold, but kept to their posts. When a desperate Rebel attack popped through the Union line, Grant restored his dominance of the campaign by launching a counterattack that not only sealed the breakthrough but occupied some vital positions in the original Confederate line as well. Unable to withstand another Federal assault, the Confederate commander requested terms for capitulation. Grant's terse reply, wholly in character with his approach to warfare, captured the imagination of the Northern public: "No terms except an unconditional and immediate surrender can be accepted. I propose to move upon your works immediately."[8] The Rebel commander, an old friend of Grant's, angrily relented, and Grant had gained the first important Union victory of the war.

In the background of the Henry and Donelson Campaign loomed William Tecumseh Sherman. As commander of the District of Cairo, Illinois, Sherman had received the task of forwarding soldiers and supplies to Grant's force. The senior brigadier general of the two, Sherman nonetheless subordinated himself to Grant in an effort to ensure success. He performed his mission with alacrity and skill, funneling all that Grant required up the Cumberland River. With shipments came notes of support and encouragement. "I should like to hear from you," Sherman penned, "and will do everything in my power to hurry forward to you reinforcements and supplies, and if I could be of service myself would gladly come, without making any question of Rank with you or General Smith." On another occasion, Sherman vowed his "faith" in Grant and urged, "Command me in any way." Few high-ranking officers would have volunteered to waive rank and lead a subordinate command in another's army, or would have pledged such unrestricted support as Sherman had done.[9]

All this greatly impressed Grant. At a time when individuals seemed only too willing to compromise national interest for personal pettiness and gain, Sherman stood above all that. His selfless commitment to the pronounced goal of the Northern government, the restoration of the Union, and his efficient performance of duty convinced Grant that this was a dependable officer.

Grant, too, advocated this creed. Both he and Sherman had military ambitions, but neither man would permit personal glory to supersede national welfare. They fought to accomplish the nation's objectives, not to enhance their postwar political careers as so many others did. "I care nothing for promotion," Grant commented to Sherman after the fall of Fort Donelson, "so long as our armies are successful and no political appointments are made."[10]

One month after the close of the Henry and Donelson Campaign, the relationship between Grant and Sherman took a major step forward when Sherman arrived at Pittsburg Landing with a division of new troops to join Grant's command. Within three weeks, they fought the desperate battle of Shiloh. A vicious Confederate assault had caught Grant and Sherman unprepared and their troops without field fortifications, yet the bulk of the Federals resisted stoutly. Twice balls nicked Sherman, and a third round passed through his hat. Confederates shot three horses from under him. Unfazed, Sherman was everywhere, urging on his command, handling his brigades and regiments skillfully, and instilling confidence among his green troops by his coolness under fire. Sherman, Grant crowed to his wife, had commanded superbly. "There has been nothing like it on this continent, nor in history," he hyperbolized.[11]

That evening, Grant approached Sherman with his assignment for the next morning. During the day Grant had barely staved off disaster. The Confederates had driven the Federals through their camp and pressed them rearward near the banks of the Tennessee River. Grant, combative to the core, ordered Sherman to assume the offensive. In the struggle for Fort Donelson he had learned an important lesson: At the height of the engagement, both sides had exhausted themselves and appeared defeated, but the one that seized the initiative and attacked had won the day. Reinforced by fresh troops, Grant struck back early in the morning and by afternoon swept the field. Sherman then attempted to organize an effective pursuit, but it was too late. The Federals were as confused in victory as the Rebels were in defeat.

Without doubt Grant reaped the benefits of commanding such an outstanding subordinate as Sherman. And Sherman, too, began to thrive under Grant's leadership. After directing a brigade at the battle of First Manassas, Sherman was transferred to Kentucky, where he soon assumed the position of Commanding General, Department of the Cumberland. Limited resources and unrealistic government policies exacerbated the pressures of command and led to what most likely was a nervous breakdown. The media then blasted Sherman as crazy. Mortified by the public accusations of insanity, Sherman confessed to his brother, "I do think I should have committed suicide were it not for my children."[12] His family rushed to his aid, and Halleck, an old friend, arranged for a transfer to a position of light duty until Sherman had recovered satisfactorily enough to resume strenuous labor. It was Grant who resurrected Sherman. "Until you had won Donelson," Sherman explained to Grant, "I confess I was almost cowed by the terrible array of anarchical elements that presented themselves at every point; but that victory admitted the ray of light which I have followed ever since."[13] For Sherman, Grant had transformed chaos into order.

Neither Grant nor Sherman basked in the glory for long. What Grant won on the battlefield he lost in the eyes of the Northern public. The unprepared state of the army and the massive casualties at Shiloh, over 13,000 on the Union side alone, appalled Northerners, and calls for Grant's removal resounded from all around the country. Halleck stepped in to lead Federal forces at Shiloh in a campaign for Corinth, Mississippi, stilling the public clamor against Grant but also displacing him. While Grant stewed in his nominal post of second in command, Halleck cautiously maneuvered his ponderous army of over 100,000 and eventually occupied Corinth.

At the end of the campaign, a distraught Grant requested and received an extended leave of absence. "It is generally understood through this army," he complained to Halleck, "that my position differs but little from that of one in arrest." Grant's severely limited duties entailed no responsibility, and he found his assignment awkward and embarrassing. Halleck simply had no need for his services.[14]

When Sherman discovered Grant's intention to vacate the army, he paid the disillusioned general a visit. Since the outgoing Sherman's arrival at Pittsburg Landing, he and the introverted Grant had founded a burgeoning friendship. Sherman described Grant to his wife as "not a brilliant man" but a "good and brave soldier, tried for years; is sober, very industrious and as kind as a child." Just a few weeks earlier, Grant had sung Sherman's praises to his wife, averring, "In Gen. Sherman the country has an able and gallant defender and your husband a true friend." As an obligation of that friendship, Sherman felt compelled to offer his perspective on Grant's unfortunate position. He explained that he understood Grant's frustration since he had faced a similar dilemma himself. During service in Kentucky earlier in the war, overwork and stress had so debilitated him that reporters branded him as crazy. Months passed before Sherman could shake the charges. A division command in Grant's army was Sherman's salvation. At Shiloh he had fought well, and now he was "in high feather." He urged Grant to stay. If Grant returned to the North, he could do no good and would never regain favor. But if Grant remained in the field, some opportunity might develop that would enable him to retrieve his fortunes, just as Sherman had regained his own fortunes through fighting alongside Grant.[15]

Struck by the logic and the kindness of Sherman's argument, Grant concluded to remain in the department. Six weeks later, authorities ordered Halleck to Washington and appointed him general in chief, and Grant resumed charge of his old army. Patience had won Grant a reprieve.

For several months afterward, Grant and Sherman did little but battle raiding parties and guerrilla bands. After the fall of Corinth, Halleck had scattered his mammoth army, and Grant lacked sufficient forces to launch another offensive. Runaway slaves, cotton trading, guerrillas, Confederate raids, and offended civilians absorbed the time and energy of both generals. Campaigning, it seemed, had taken a back seat to policing secessionist territory.

As both men grappled with the complexities of guerrilla fighting and the headaches of occupation duty, Grant sought a confidant with whom he could sort through the issues. With Grant headquartered at Corinth and Sherman stationed at Memphis, Grant called on Sherman to "write more freely and fully on all matters of public interest." Sherman, with his fertile, active mind, could provide Grant with a host of alternatives and fresh perspectives, from which the decisive Grant could choose. It was an offer of collaboration that the cerebral Sherman could not resist.[16]

Among the two, Sherman was the bona fide intellectual. He had a voracious appetite for information and uncanny recall. Decades after his travels through Georgia and the Carolinas as a young lieutenant, Sherman could recollect with astonishing accuracy terrain features and other regional characteristics. His knowledge of military affairs was the product of years of reading, reflection, and personal experience. Sherman had a remarkable ability to assimilate vast quantities of information and convert them into workable form. His orders were models of clarity and thoughtfulness, and they covered almost every imaginable subject. Sherman, moreover, devoted the requisite time for contemplation. He slept little and, as Grant once mentioned, he liked to "bone" his campaigns, or "study them hard from morning till night."[17]

Grant's intelligence in military matters was much more instinctive. He openly admitted that he had not read widely on martial affairs, and he was not a great thinker like Sherman. Other than his gift for writing clear, concise orders and letters, which was primarily a product of his extensive reading of literature, Grant had no real intellectual training that prepared him for command. What separated Grant from others was his capacity to formulate effective decisions under the enormous stress of battle and command. "My only points of doubt were as to your knowledge of grand strategy, and of books of science and history," Sherman wrote him in early 1864, "but I confess your common-sense seems to have supplied all this." Sherman thought that Grant's greatest quality was "the simple faith in success you have always manifested, which I can liken to nothing else than the faith a Christian has in his Savior." He marveled at the way Grant "completed your best preparations" and entered battle "without hesitation, . . . no doubts, no reserve." Such quiet conviction instilled confidence in those around him.[18]

During the next few months, the Grant–Sherman correspondence delved into such topics as journalists, trade with Southerners, partisan activities, occupation policies, military campaigns, and, most important, efforts to quell the rebellion. Together they ascertained how highly Southerners valued property—"They are about as sensitive about their property as Yankees," Sherman quipped—how the confiscation of slaves aided the Union and damaged the Confederate war effort, and how dispersing forces into small garrisons failed to subdue or stifle the guerrillas. Laboring their way through these problems, Grant and Sherman teased out the rudiments of a raiding strategy that would coerce Southern whites to return to the Union. First proposed by Sherman, its premiss rested on the belief that "all the South is in arms and deep in enmity," and that "We cannot change the hearts of those people of the South, but we can make war so terrible that they will realize the fact that, however brave and gallant and devoted to their country, still they are mortal and should exhaust all peaceful means before they fly to war." Sherman argued that Federals "hold the river absolutely and leave the interior alone. Detachments inland can always be overcome or are at great hazard, and they do not convert the people. They cannot be made to love us, but may be made to fear us, and dread the passage of troops through their country." By controlling the Mississippi River, they could land troops and launch powerful raids into the heartland, to destroy railroads and to "make ourselves so busy that our descent would be dreaded the whole length of the river, and by the loss of negroes and other property [they] would in time discover that war is not the remedy for the political evils of which they complained." Over the next two years, Grant and Sherman refined this basic concept, incorporating new ideas and lessons learned from other campaigns, and converting it into a workable strategy for the defeat of the Confederacy.[19]

Before Grant and Sherman could sharpen their ideas, though, circumstances in the theater began to change. In late October 1862 Grant assumed command of the Department of Tennessee, and within a week additional reinforcements arrived. More importantly, a politician turned general, John A. McClernand, had received authority from President Abraham Lincoln to raise a command to capture Vicksburg, a Confederate bastion on the banks of the Mississippi River that impeded travel and transport. Grant knew McClernand well. They had served together at Forts Henry and Donelson and later at Shiloh. Grant had serious doubts about McClernand's ability and temperament to lead such an expedition, judging him "unmanageable and incompetent," and at the urging of Halleck he decided to preempt McClernand's Vicksburg Campaign by attempting it himself.[20]

Grant's plan called for two forces, widely separated, to advance simultaneously and without communication, a risky proposition at best. While Grant personally led an army south along the Mississippi Central Railroad toward Jackson, hoping to draw Confederate forces out for a fight, Sherman would slip down the Mississippi River on transport vessels and land near Chickasaw Bluffs, just north of Vicksburg. Sherman's troops then would brush aside the light Confederate opposition and seize the city.

Unfortunately, execution proved more difficult. Two Rebel cavalry raids severed Grant's supply line, and he fell back under the misapprehension that his feint had succeeded and Sherman had captured Vicksburg. The Confederates at Vicksburg, however, did not budge from their works, and when Sherman tried to storm the bluffs in late December, Confederate shells and balls cut bluecoats down by the hundreds. Then, much to Sherman's chagrin, the press targeted him as scapegoat for the repulse.

The new year brought a blend of headaches and hope for Grant and Sherman. On January 2, 1863, McClernand arrived by transport north of Vicksburg with his newly created army in tow. Armed with a commission as major general of volunteers in his pocket that ranked him above Sherman, McClernand took command of all forces there. They had no prospects of capturing Vicksburg from below Chickasaw Bluffs. Sherman, therefore, proposed a joint army–navy operation against Fort Hindman, often called Arkansas Post, on the Arkansas River, from which Confederates had launched nettlesome raids against Federal transit along the Mississippi River. McClernand endorsed the concept so warmly that he eventually declared it his own, while Admiral David Dixon Porter needed coax-

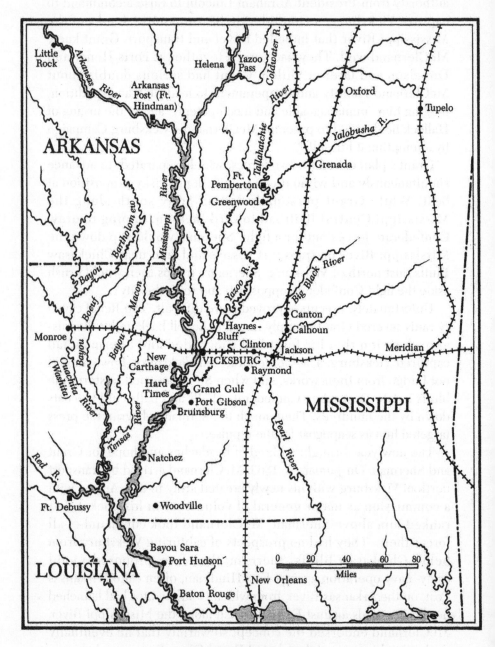

THE VICKSBURG AREA

ing from Sherman. Porter had all the confidence in the world in Sherman and none in McClernand, and as a result he extracted a promise from McClernand that Sherman would run the operation. On January 9, the Federal expedition reached the vicinity of Arkansas Post, and within two days, Porter's bombardment compelled the defenders to raise up the white flag. Nearly 5,000 prisoners fell into Union hands.

Grant, meanwhile, had resolved some important questions in his own mind about the upcoming Vicksburg Campaign. Since McClernand lacked fitness to command, Grant would assume the burden and supervise operations himself. McClernand, Sherman, and a Grant protegé named James B. McPherson, a personable engineer officer who had graduated first in the West Point class of 1853, would each command a corps. Grant also decided that the approach overland from the north offered little possibility for success. Due to the bluffs that shielded Vicksburg to the north and west, an army had to advance on the city from the east. The logical approach, south along the Mississippi Central Railroad to Jackson and then west following the Vicksburg & Jackson Railroad into the city, had failed once before. By hugging the railroad, too, Grant would have to peel off critical manpower to protect his lengthening supply line, and the Confederates still might break it as they had done in December.

To get at Vicksburg, Grant undertook a variety of schemes, from digging a canal that would bypass Vicksburg to cutting a levee and flooding bayous for navy transport that would land troops on the high ground northeast of Vicksburg. None proved successful, but all served a purpose. The public, the army, and the Lincoln administration could not endure idleness. All demanded action. At least these creative projects occupied public attention while the floods subsided and the roads dried a bit.

When the last effort to turn Vicksburg on the right failed, a "perplexed" Grant had come to the forlorn conclusion that only an assault at Haynes' Bluff, near where Sherman had failed last December, offered any chance of success. "Heretofore I have had nothing to do but fight the enemy," a dejected Grant commented to his wife. "This time I have to overcome obstacles to reach him."[21] He, Sherman, and Porter had even reconnoitered the area to select the best places to land troops and storm the works. Despite projections of massive losses, Grant viewed it as his sole option to conquer Vicksburg.[22]

Almost in a flash, several separate strands came together in Grant's mind that provided him with a fresh option. Throughout the entire campaign, he had only considered approaches that would turn the Confederate right flank. But perhaps he could swing around the *left* of the Vicksburg works! For months authorities in Washington had urged unity of action between Grant and Maj. Gen. Nathaniel P. Banks, Federal commander in Louisiana, who was attempting to capture Port Hudson, also on the Mississippi River. Yielding to War Department wishes, Grant had offered to send down a corps to assist Banks. Then Banks's entire command could sweep up from the south and turn the Confederates out of their strong works on high ground near Vicksburg. To transfer the corps, Grant's men had toiled strenuously to clear a water route west of the Mississippi River that would link them with Banks's forces. It suddenly dawned on Grant: rather than supporting Banks, could he not send troops southward along the west side of the river, cross over the Mississippi, and then march them northward?

Back in February, a substantial Confederate artillery force at Warrenton, along the river less than ten miles below Vicksburg, had begun harassing Federal navy vessels. After some investigation, Sherman determined that with only a little work his troops could construct a road that would enable the Federals to shift and deploy an artillery battery with some troops on the west bank of the Mississippi River across from Warrenton. Since then the water level had fallen, which would make road construction on the west bank even more feasible. As Confederates reinforced Warrenton in the intervening weeks, Grant had toyed with the idea of cooperating with the navy to ferry two regiments to seize those fortifications. A plan to turn the Rebel bastion's left flank gelled.[23]

Grant's solution required boldness and speed. He would pass his army below Vicksburg, ferry it across the Mississippi River, and then strike rapidly: directly north to Vicksburg, or up toward Jackson and swing across to Vicksburg, or cooperate with Banks to the south. The major obstacle was maneuvering troops below Vicksburg. Passage on transports was too risky. The scheme required Grant to march them along the west side of the river. Then Porter's transports could run past the Vicksburg batteries and cross troops from the west to the east bank of the Mississippi.

Even though Grant kept his own counsel when he formulated this new operational plan, throughout much of the Vicksburg Campaign he had consulted with Sherman. Now more than ever he needed Sherman's services. Lacking the dynamic or effective personality to win others to him, Grant impressed few people and won converts slowly. Until he achieved great success, his only apostles were Sherman and McPherson, and he relied on them heavily. Sherman complemented Grant well. He brought to the relationship a fabulous mind that could provide Grant with all sorts of alternatives. Together they could discuss military matters confidentially and candidly, without fear of hostility or alienation. Grant also had in Sherman an individual of unwavering loyalty who adopted Grant's plans as if they were his own and executed them skillfully. While Grant focused on the main elements, he needed Sherman to handle the more peripheral yet vital aspects of assignments. Sherman rarely disappointed Grant.

During those months of failure and frustration, the bonds between them strengthened to the point where Grant, who found little comfort in the presence of others, exhibited signs of genuine pleasure in company with the gregarious Sherman. As their relationship warmed, Grant exposed more and more of his inner world to Sherman, so that by early 1863 he and Sherman were fast friends and confidants. For Grant, this friendship was somewhat of a breakthrough. Inherently retiring, he found little comfort in the presence of others. But for the extroverted Sherman, whose intellectual appetite seemed to suck in everything around him, these were merely tantalizing glimpses of Grant's character. "To me he is a mystery," Sherman once exclaimed, "and I believe he is a mystery to himself."[24]

Grant's reticence never deterred Sherman from offering advice. When Grant took command from McClernand, Sherman suggested that the army return to Memphis, reorganize, and embark on a fresh campaign. Although Sherman's proposal made sense from a military standpoint, Grant realized that the Northern public would interpret any retrograde movement as a defeat; he therefore declined to act on it. In early April, after Grant had revealed his designs, Sherman objected in a confidential discussion and later in a letter to Grant's Assistant Adjutant General Rawlins. Sherman thought that fighting a campaign with their backs to the river placed the Union forces in unnecessary jeopardy. He also feared that if Grant's efforts failed, McClernand would claim that no one had listened to his ideas. Sherman suggested that all corps commanders submit their opinions in writing, then proceeded to volunteer his plans first. He focused on operations north and east of Vicksburg, recommending that they establish a base on the Yalabusha River, advance along the Mississippi Central Railroad, and then shift over to the Vicksburg & Jackson line. Sherman asked Grant to give his plan "as much or as little weight as it deserves" and reminded him through Rawlins, "Whatever plan of action he may adopt will receive from me the same zealous cooperation and energetic support as though conceived by myself."[25]

Grant took Sherman at his word. McClernand's Corps prepared the road that enabled the army to march along the west side of the Mississippi River to an area below Vicksburg, and McPherson's followed it. Porter then ran gunboats, transports, and barges past the Vicksburg batteries to support the landing on the eastern bank. To disguise Grant's real intention, he requested that Sherman feign an attack on Haynes' Bluff. In the wake of Sherman's defeat there in late December, Grant knew that Sherman's troops and the Northern public might interpret the movement as another failure, so he hesitated to order it. But he also mentioned that "the effect of a heavy demonstration in that direction would be good so far as the enemy are concerned." Sherman promised to act immediately. His soldiers "will all understand the purpose, and will not be hurt by the repulse," and as to the Northern public, the crusty Sherman noted, "it is none of their business." In Sherman's eyes, the matter was quite simple: "You are engaged in a hazardous enterprise, and, for good reasons, wish to divert attention; that is sufficient to me, and it shall be done."[26]

Sherman's bluff worked. His demonstration, coupled with a cavalry raid to the interior, so confused the Confederates that Grant's troops slipped across the Mississippi River unhampered. Again Sherman alerted Grant to foreseeable problems, this time in the area of logistics. Grant, Sherman predicted, would create a logistical snarl by attempting to supply his three corps over a single road unless he halted and took pains to organize his wagons.

Once again, Grant surprised Sherman. His plan required swift movements against a substantial enemy army. For the campaign to succeed, Grant needed an agile force that maximized its firepower. Rather than fritter away precious troops and time in creating and maintaining a supply and communication line, Grant decided to march light, cut loose from his base, and forage on the Mississippi countryside. As a young quartermaster in the Mexican War, he had observed Maj. Gen. Winfield Scott supply his invading army from the peasantry. After the Confederate cavalry cut its supply line in December, Grant's command had lived for two weeks by confiscating food and fodder from the locals. He had little doubt that the plantations and farms in such a rich agricultural region could feed his soldiers and their animals.[27]

In a campaign of initiative, audacity, and power, Grant's army fought five distinct battles. Every time the Federals concentrated larger numbers at the point of attack, and every time Grant's troops won. His army first pushed the Confederate forces north toward Vicksburg, then drove a second Rebel army back through Jackson. Finally, he turned on the Confederate defenders in Vicksburg and pounded them back into their fortifications, narrowly failing to cut off a large segment of them. Instead of saving his army and abandoning Vicksburg the Rebel commander, Lt. Gen. John C. Pemberton, elected to defend the bastion. After two attempts to storm the works failed, Grant tightened his noose around the city, and on the Fourth of July its garrison of nearly 30,000 men capitulated. Pemberton had proved himself Grant's "best friend."[28]

As the two generals occupied the high ground that Union soldiers had attempted to seize back in December, Sherman confessed that until that moment he had been unsure of success. To a coterie of officers and men just minutes later, he plainly admitted, "Grant is entitled to every bit of the credit for the campaign; I opposed it." But from Grant's perspective, Sherman's contributions to success were greater than if he had designed the campaign himself. Grant's trusty subordinate had lived up to his words. Sherman had executed all assignments brilliantly and selflessly, with the same zeal he had vowed six weeks earlier. "His untiring energy and great efficiency during the campaign entitled him to a full share of all credit due for its success," Grant recorded in his memoirs. "He could not have done more if the plan had been his own."[29]

Sherman's wholehearted cooperation and skillful execution had cemented the bonds between them. From that point Grant's confidence in Sherman never wavered. Less than three weeks after the fall of Vicksburg Grant urged Lincoln to promote Sherman to brigadier general in the Regular Army. He praised Sherman's ability, performance, high character, and unyielding commitment to Federal victory. After listing Sherman's long and outstanding service with him, Grant averred that his accomplishments at Vicksburg "entitle General Sherman to more credit than it usually falls to the lot of one man to earn."[30]

Throughout the remainder of the war, as Grant succeeded to new positions of rank and responsibility, he placed Sherman in his old post. Sherman had emerged as Grant's most valued and reliable subordinate. After the Union debacle at Chickamauga, where Confederate forces routed the Federal Army of the Cumberland, the War Department promoted Grant to head the Military Division of the Mississippi. Sherman filled his shoes as commander of the Department and Army of the Tennessee. When authorities in Washington directed Grant to send reinforcements to help break the Confederate siege at Chattanooga, he called on Sherman and troops from the Army of the Tennessee. After the rout of Confederates at Missionary Ridge, Grant again dispatched Sherman to relieve the besieged Federals under Maj. Gen. Ambrose E. Burnside at Knoxville. And when Lincoln elevated Grant to lieutenant general and commander of the Union Army, Sherman assumed Grant's old position as Commanding General, Military Division of the Mississippi.

Perhaps more than anything else, trust cemented the Grant–Sherman relationship. Above all others in the war, Grant could count on Sherman for frank advice and skillful execution. Likewise, the more nervous Sherman fought with the reassurance that he could act boldly because he always had Grant to support him. "I knew wherever I was that you thought of me," he explained to Grant, "and if I got in a tight place you would come—if alive."[31] Thus Grant fortified the high-strung Sherman.

Sherman was probably the only officer to whom Grant truly warmed, apart from his personal staff. At Chattanooga, Maj. Gen. Oliver Otis Howard described Sherman's entry into a wall tent that he shared with Grant. As Sherman came "bounding in after his usual bouyant manner," Grant's face lit up with pleasure.

"How are you, Sherman?"

"Thank you, as well as can be expected," came the reply.

Grant then proffered a cigar, which Sherman instantly accepted and lit, "without stopping his ready flow of hearty words." To break Sherman's monologue, Grant had to "arrest his attention by some apt remark," and then offered Sherman the premier seat in the tent, a high-backed rocker.

"The chair of honor? Oh, no! that belongs to you, general," Sherman replied.

Grant, unabashed by the compliment, proved unrelenting: "I don't forget, Sherman, to give proper respect to age."

"Well, then, if you put it on that ground, I must accept." Howard noticed that Grant's bearing with Sherman was "free, affectionate, and good-humored," in striking contrast to his demeanor around other officers.[32]

Despite their great differences in personality and thought processes, the Grant–Sherman collaboration had produced a united approach to warfare. Instead of squandering valuable manpower and materiel on the occupation of Confederate territory, they advocated a concentration of forces for an aggressive, raid-oriented strategy that fixed on the enemy soldiers, war resources, and Confederate population as its primary objectives. An effective blow struck at one of those targets damaged the others, initiating a cycle of defeat. Raids devastated logistical networks and undercut support among civilians, which in turn reduced war resources and weakened soldiers' morale. Confederate armies, now battling with dwindling supplies and faltering spirits among their troops, suffered a decline in combat effectiveness, which impaired their ability to protect citizens from destructive raids. And once the Union armies had locked up their foes in combat, the Confederates could no longer peel off portions of their armies to reinforce other commands or to protect the countryside from Federal raids.

Unlike other Union strategists who sought merely to put down the rebellion, Grant and Sherman aimed to crush it. They understood that this was a revolution, and that the Union forces had to convince the Confederates and their supporters that "war and individual ruin," so Sherman argued, "are synonymous terms." They were fighting not only hostile armies but hostile people.[33]

During the winter of 1863–64, Grant and Sherman proposed a revised version of the raiding strategy they had collaborated on back in the fall of 1862. Confident now that an army could march very light and subsist well on the goods of Southern farmers, Grant and Sherman foresaw the possibility of extensive raids of destruction which would sever large segments of the Confederacy from the war effort. In early December, Grant recommended an advance from New Orleans to Mobile, one of the last Rebel ports still open, and then a continued drive deep into Alabama and perhaps Georgia. Three weeks later, Sherman suggested and Grant endorsed a plan to abandon control of the interior near the Mississippi River and to hold four river ports for staging raids against guerrillas and the Confederate logistical network. Occupation of the interior, so Sherman argued, "requires a vast force, which is rendered harmless to the enemy by its scattered parts."[34] Specifically, Sherman offered to lead raids up the Red River and through northern Mississippi. Competing priorities undermined the Mobile and Red River campaigns, but Sherman did launch a strike through Mississippi to Meridian in January 1864, with the object of clearing Rebel troops from the region and destroying the railroads, thus "preventing the enemy from drawing supplies from Mississippi." A prototype of Sherman's massive raids of late 1864 and 1865, his army consumed Rebel food, wrecked anything of military value that it encountered, and subverted civilian morale.[35]

When Grant learned that Lincoln had submitted his name to fill the newly created rank of lieutenant general, he reported the news to Sherman and thanked him and McPherson, who "above all others, I feel indebted for whatever I have had of success." Sherman replied with warmth, modesty, and his usual friendly advice. After crediting Grant with his own achievements and assessing Grant's greatest attributes as a soldier and a man, Sherman pleaded with him not to settle down at the nation's capital, where political intrigue would sap his strength: "For God's sake and for your country's sake, come out of Washington!"[36]

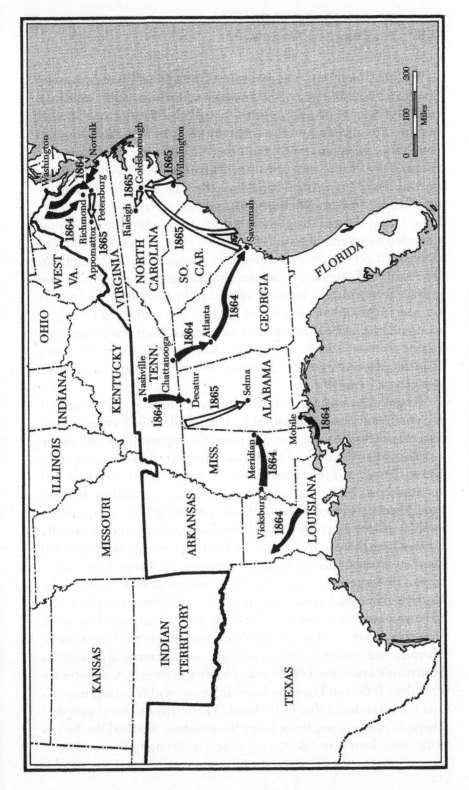

MAJOR UNION CAMPAIGNS, 1864–65

By mid-March 1864, Grant returned to Nashville and summoned Sherman from Memphis. The demands of the war, Grant explained, required him to occupy a position near Washington, and he had decided to accompany the Army of the Potomac, the principal Federal command in the East, in the field. Sherman would succeed Grant in the West. Since pressing affairs required Grant's presence in Washington, to save time they rode the train to Cincinnati together, plotting strategy and discussing personnel changes. Two weeks later, Grant issued his plan in writing. Characteristically, Grant intended to assume the initiative that spring, "to work all parts of the army together, somewhat toward a common centre," something the North had intended to accomplish but failed to execute for two years. "You I propose to move against Johnston's army, to break it up, and to get into the interior of the enemy's country as far as you can, inflicting all the damage you can against their war resources." Grant refused to dictate a campaign plan; Sherman had earned such latitude. He merely requested that Sherman submit a copy of his operational designs.[37]

Neither the campaign against Johnston's army nor the one against the Confederates under Robert E. Lee fulfilled their expectations. Sherman's wide flanking movement nearly trapped Johnston's entire command at Resaca, but McPherson hesitated to attack, fearing heavy losses, and Johnston's army escaped. Grant, too, met stiff resistance in the Wilderness and suffered high casualties. Both he and Sherman pressed their foe, Grant pounding Lee's army repeatedly in major engagements and Sherman striking and eventually outflanking Johnston from strong defensive positions. Both operated in close contact with their foe, to prevent one Confederate army from reinforcing the other. Only at Kennesaw Mountain, where he hurled his troops against a superb Confederate position, did Sherman blunder seriously. By early July, Grant and Lee were locked in trench warfare around Petersburg, while the troops under Sherman and Johnston sparred with one another north of Atlanta. As Sherman's army worked its way closer to the city, Confederate President Jefferson Davis replaced Johnston with a young, impetuous commander, John Bell Hood. Three times Hood assailed Sherman's forces, and three times the Federals repulsed the Rebels with heavy losses. In late August Sherman swung to the southwest, severed the final railroad line into Atlanta, and compelled Hood's columns to evacuate.[38]

Although Sherman had failed to neutralize the Confederate army, he had inflicted heavy damage to the Rebel ranks and seized a critical railroad and industrial hub. Lincoln extended "national thanks" to Sherman and the army, and Grant fired every artillery gun along his front "in honor of your great victory." The fall of Atlanta assured Lincoln's re-election bid, which guaranteed war for four more years, if necessary.[39]

Hood's army limped off to the west of the city. There it rested and refitted, as Sherman's forces did in Atlanta. Soon, however, the Confederates launched a new campaign, publicly trumpeted by President Jefferson Davis, to force Sherman to yield all the ground he had gained in the spring campaign. Hood directed the Rebel offensive against Sherman's extended supply line, a railroad from Chattanooga to Atlanta. Sherman responded to the bait: he left a portion of his army to hold Atlanta and marched rearward after the Confederates. But Hood's army, much smaller and more mobile than Sherman's command, fell back into northern Alabama. Sherman could not catch the elusive Hood.

The attack on his supply line vindicated Sherman's previous assertions that occupying Atlanta and maintaining such a vulnerable railroad were bootless. Months earlier, he and Grant had discussed the possibility of a campaign toward the Atlantic coast, taking some supplies with the army but gathering much of it from the inhabitants of Georgia. Such a march would expose the futility of Confederate armed resistance. Southerners had joined the Rebel army to protect their hearths and defend their rights to own and utilize property—specifically slaves—as they saw fit. Sherman's idea would demonstrate that the Southern military forces had failed on both counts, as his army marched through the heart of the South and confiscated slaves for the Union cause. Before the Atlanta Campaign commenced, Sherman had collected census tables and tax records for Georgia from 1860. He calculated the amount and value of crops and livestock throughout the state, so he knew the types and quantities of food and fodder that his army would find en route to the ocean. Hood's advance to the north opened the door for Sherman's massive raid.[40]

On October 1, 1864, Sherman suggested a plan of operations: He would transport a portion of his army north to cope with Hood and take the remainder on a raid to Savannah or Charleston. "We cannot remain on the defensive," he urged in justification of his scheme.[41] Eight days later, Sherman proposed a more specific campaign, to Savannah via Milledgeville, the state capital. "By attempting to hold the roads we will lose 1,000 men monthly, and will gain no result," he telegraphed. "I can make the march, and make Georgia howl."[42] Despite Sherman's repeated emphasis on the value of initiative and the attrited effects of territorial occupation, Grant preferred that Sherman deliver a single knockout blow to Hood's army, but agreed reluctantly to "trust your judgment." Sherman's response assuaged Grant's uneasiness. "Instead of being on the defensive," he explained, "I would be on the offensive; instead of guessing at what he means to do, he would have to guess at my plans. The difference in war is full 25 per cent."[43]

The underlying concepts struck a responsive chord with Grant. An advance across Georgia would, as Sherman predicted, demonstrate the vulnerability of the Confederacy and undercut the influence of President Davis, who had announced in public that Atlanta would be to Sherman what Moscow was to Napoleon—a disastrous overextension of power. From that point on, Grant fended off challenges to Sherman's raid from Lincoln and others, even though he possessed his own doubts. Only once more did Grant recommend the alternative of Sherman chasing Hood, and he quickly reversed himself. His belief in Sherman superseded his confidence in the plan.

In mid-November 1864, Sherman began his legendary March through Georgia. Swinging south toward Macon and then northeastward through Milledgeville and near Augusta, his army of over 60,000 destroyed railroads, confiscated slaves and animals, and foraged liberally on the inhabitants. As Sherman had forecast, the raid did demonstrate to the people of the South how defenseless they really were. In mid-December, Federals contacted the blockading fleet near Savannah, and several days before Christmas, they occupied the city.

With his new celebrity status, Sherman had opportunities to criticize Grant for the slow progress of his war in Virginia. Others would have relented to the temptation, but not Sherman. He defended his friend and publicly lauded the lieutenant general's direction of the war effort. Grant was pleased. "Sherman's letter shows how noble a man he is," he commented to wife Julia. "How few there are who when rising to popular favor as he now is would stop to say a word in defence of the only one between himself and the highest in command." Then Grant patted himself on the back for finding such a talent and friend as Sherman. "I am glad to say that I appreciated Sherman from the first feeling him to be what he has proven to the world he is."[44]

Prior to the fall of Savannah, Grant proposed that Sherman fortify a base along the coast and transport the bulk of his infantry to Petersburg to break the stalemate with Lee. Soon afterward, Grant learned that it would take two months to accumulate the necessary vessels to ship Sherman's men to Virginia. Sherman, however, offered an appealing alternative. Rather than waste months in idleness, he recommended an overland jaunt through Columbia, South Carolina and north toward Raleigh, North Carolina, again living off the land and destroying railroads and anything of military value along the way. Grant approved it enthusiastically, and in late January 1865, Sherman inaugurated his march through the Carolinas.[45]

Sherman and his army next surfaced in Goldsboro, North Carolina, in late March. After having covered almost 450 miles in seven weeks, wrecking rail lines, burning towns, destroying an arsenal, and intimidating Southerners, his soldiers sensed that the Confederacy was on its last legs. "It is the talk with the Boys now that our next move will be in the direction of Richmond," commented an Iowa veteran from Sherman's army, "but they say it is hard to tell which way Crazy Bill (Sherman) will go for he goes where he wants to and the rebs cant help themselves."[46]

On April 10, Sherman's command, reinforced by two corps under Maj. Gen. John M. Schofield, began its final drive against the Confederates opposing them. Two days later, news arrived from Grant that Lee had surrendered on April 9. From November through March, Grant had held Lee's army fast, so that Sherman's troops could devastate the war resources of the Confederacy. All the while, Grant had lengthened his line, and casualties, sickness, and desertion had attenuated Lee's strength. Finally in late March the Federals turned the Confederate position at Petersburg, and Lee fled with his army westward in desperate hope of linking with the Rebels in Sherman's front. When Grant's forces blocked Lee's path at Appomattox, the Confederate general surrendered.

With the capture of Lee's army Sherman's old nemesis, Gen. Joseph E. Johnston, requested a cessation of hostilities to negotiate a surrender of his forces. Misinformed about the sorts of surrender terms Lincoln had requested, Sherman negotiated a deal far too lenient for authorities in Washington to accept. He permitted Confederate soldiers to take their arms with them and to deposit them at their home state arsenals; he recognized state governments; he restored the franchise in the Rebel states; and he failed to discuss emancipation. Had Lincoln still been president, the matter would have been disposed of expeditiously and quietly. But in the aftermath of Lincoln's assassination on April 14, near hysteria gripped many officials in Washington. Secretary of War Edwin Stanton intimated in a letter published in the *New York Times* that Sherman was a traitor. The new president, Andrew Johnson, and the entire cabinet plus Grant rejected the surrender terms.[47]

In a final gesture of devoted friendship, Grant now volunteered to visit Sherman personally and straighten out the affair. By directive from the new president through Stanton, Grant was to supersede Sherman. He would have no part in that. Instead, Grant quietly slipped into Sherman's camp and notified him that Sherman must offer Johnston the same terms as he, Grant, had given Lee. After a bit of wrangling, Johnston accepted Sherman's offer, and the surrender was consummated.

On May 24, Sherman's army participated in the Grand Review through the streets of Washington. The previous day, the spit-and-polish Army of the Potomac had proceeded along those same thoroughfares in brilliant fashion—handsomely uniformed, well accoutred, and exquisitely drilled. Sherman dreaded the event. After a year of active campaigning, his men had ragged uniforms, dirty and scraped-up weapons, scuffed or torn shoes, and a gait more suited to prolonged marches than to dress parades. He feared that their shabby appearance would detract from the great reputation they had earned over the course of three or four years of fighting. That morning, the sun shone, the temperature was delightful, and dense crowds lined the streets to view this near-legendary army that had marched through Georgia and the Carolinas. At 9 a.m., Sherman rode forward slowly, followed by his command, to the cheers of thousands. As he turned onto Pennsylvania Avenue near the Treasury Building, he peered back. Much to his amazement, "The column was compact, and the glittering muskets looked like a solid mass of steel, moving with the regularity of a pendulum." He passed the reviewing stand, saluted, and pushed on to the presidential grounds, where he turned over his horse to an orderly. Sherman then returned to take his place with the president and other dignitaries to view his army. Grant was there, too. It was only appropriate that he and Sherman now should stand by one another once again.[48]

Although Grant and Sherman could scarcely differ more in personality and thought patterns, the two individuals shared values and formulated common conclusions about war. Both men professed a wholehearted commitment to the reunion of the United States and voiced the conviction that men of military training, rather than politicians, ought to command armies. So, too, did many other West Point graduates. What distinguished the Grant–Sherman relationship from all others was its deep friendship, founded on trust and nurtured in an atmosphere that fostered the free, frank interchange of ideas. Other Union generals maintained relationships; Grant and Sherman established a partnership. Together they forged an unyielding bond through selfless collaboration, devising and implementing a fresh concept of warfare that utilized manpower and resources with maximum effectiveness and culminated in Union victory.

David Dixon Porter
(National Archives)

6

"I am ready to cooperate with anybody and everybody"

Grant, Sherman, Porter, and Successful Army–Navy Collaborations

*I*n early December 1862, during a dinner party on an army quartermaster's river boat at Cairo, Illinois, Acting Rear Admiral David Dixon Porter was feasting on roast duck and champagne when a stir on deck disrupted the festivities. The host politely exited, and moments later returned with a surprise guest: a slightly built, shabby-looking fellow in a brown civilian coat and gray trousers bearing a fresh coat of dust. The quartermaster introduced the unimpressive visitor: "Admiral Porter, meet General Grant."[1]

As the admiral and the general shifted to a table by themselves, Porter, attired in his military finery, felt a twinge of self-consciousness. A navy man who had continually bucked the system for over three decades, Porter would have preferred a different atmosphere for his initial encounter with Grant. He feared that if the army general fell victim to first impressions, he might conclude that Porter was just another naval officer, full of himself and his pomp and ceremony, one who had forgotten along the way that a military man was here to fight. Grant's expressions failed to provide a clue about his inner sentiments. All Porter could detect in that "calm, imperturbable face" was an overpowering sense of "determination." No one could ever read the inscrutable Grant.[2]

Porter's predisposition led him to look unfavorably on Grant. Before this gathering, he had studied the attack on Forts Henry and Donelson and admired Grant's "bulldog courage." He also had to admit that Grant demonstrated a capacity to cooperate with the navy during that campaign. But from animosity between the services he inferred that Grant's attitudes toward the navy were no different from those of any other army officer. "I don't trust the Army," he commented to the assistant secretary of the navy just three weeks earlier. "It is very evident that Grant is going to try and take Vicksburg without us, but he can't do it."

The admiral had mistakenly prejudged the general. In person, all he saw clashed with that view. The two men spoke in earnest, assessing difficulties honestly and calculating how to overcome them most effectively. There was no hint of superiority, no evidence that Grant perceived the navy as a weaker sister service. Instead, his "bull-dog tenacity" convinced Porter that this chap Grant could accomplish great things.[3]

For twenty minutes the two men discussed a plan of campaign against Vicksburg, the critical Confederate stronghold on the Mississippi River. Grant had advanced south toward Grenada along the railroads in northern Mississippi, but a long supply line and repairs to a railroad bridge currently delayed his march. Along the Mississippi River, the Federals had begun to accumulate manpower for a blow at Vicksburg. The problem was that Grant held its proposed commander, Maj. Gen. John McClernand, in low regard and wanted his trusted subordinate, William T. Sherman, to direct the movement. Since McClernand was dawdling in Illinois, Grant elected to seize the opportunity and implement his own plan. He would march along the Mississippi Central Railroad, holding the Confederates in his front, while Sherman slipped downriver and stormed the bluffs overlooking the Yazoo River outside Vicksburg. From the high ground Sherman could sweep into Vicksburg or drive south to the railroad from Jackson and then march on the city. Grant needed Porter's gunboats to provide fire support for Sherman's landing and assault and to assist in the reduction of Vicksburg. Porter approved the concept, and the meeting adjourned as abruptly as it had begun.[4]

Grant and Sherman could not possibly have done better than David Dixon Porter. Born the son of a famous naval officer, Porter lived only for the sea. He sailed on his first voyage at thirteen. Over the next three years, he joined the Mexican Navy, fought in a battle against a Spanish warship, and suffered through six months in a Cuban jail as a prisoner of war. At sixteen, young Porter joined the U.S. Navy. The bulk of his duty for the next thirty years consisted of coastal and harbor surveys, which paid great dividends along the shifting channels of the Mississippi River in the Civil War. During the conflict with Mexico, Porter exhibited courage and dash, side-stepping the orders of his superior and achieving considerable results. But his audacious performance did little for his career. In the postwar years, the navy lapsed into stagnation. Only a political-ly-charged assignment in New York Harbor, where Porter success-fully marked courses through the treacherous Hell Gate and Buttermilk Channel, earned him public acclaim. As the 1860 elec-tion took place, Porter was weighing a lucrative offer to leave mili-tary service and sail vessels for a commercial firm.

When the war broke out, Porter bypassed the Navy Department and went directly to Lincoln with a plan to save Fort Pickens near Pensacola, Florida. It worked. Later, he masterminded a scheme to capture New Orleans, even overseeing the construction of some novel mortar boats for the campaign. Porter's contraptions lobbed huge shells into the forts below the Crescent City, damaged them heavily, and enabled his foster brother, Commodore David Farragut, to sail up the Mississippi River and compel the authorities to sur-render the largest city in the Confederacy. After falling out of grace for indiscreetly criticizing McClellan and his Army of the Potomac—he had advocated an attack on Norfolk to seize the navy yard back in 1861—Porter returned to duty as commander of the Mississippi Squadron in late October 1862 with a rank of acting rear admiral. He had entered the war sixteen months earlier as a lieu-tenant of twenty years.

At only five feet six inches tall, a height that near starvation in prison during his teens may have stunted, Porter projected a much stronger image. His black slicked-down hair, darting brown eyes, long sharp nose, and dark curly beard hardened his appearance. A high-pitched voice seemed to detract from his presence until it gamely joined in repartee or spouted witticisms. Blessed with a photographic memory and keen analytical powers, Porter thought and reacted quickly, sometimes too quickly. His penchant for speaking his mind, at times rashly, provided immediate gratification but caused him subsequent grief. Numerous times during his career Porter occupied the seat of honor in the naval doghouse for blunt talk, and this doubtless retarded his progress on the promotion track. A tendency to lapse into exaggeration, and occasionally sarcasm, augmented this problem with superiors. Porter's unconventionality and peculiar assortment of qualities led many to undervalue him. Lincoln called Porter "a busy schemer" and underestimated his ability throughout much of the war. Stanton considered him "a gasbag, who makes a great fuss and claims credit that belongs to others," which some may have thought a more apt autobiographical assessment.[5]

The most influential event in Porter's life occurred in his youth, when his father resigned from the navy. Commodore David Porter emerged from the War of 1812 as a national hero, one of a cluster of brilliant naval officers. Like his gifted son, though, Commodore Porter never walked away from a squabble. In a dispute with several congressmen, selected naval officers turned against him and in a court-martial suspended him without pay for six months. His father served out the sentence and promptly left the service. The impressionable lad never forgot or forgave. Throughout his career, David Dixon Porter challenged authority. He despised the stodgy navy leadership, with its fixation on mindless tradition and lack of progressive reform. In fact, his favorite hobby was to poke fun at ranking officers who resisted change, either through indiscreet quips—he openly described them as "fogies"—or burlesque sketches. Porter's stance unquestionably earned him the wrath of certain "superiors." The slow advancement of an individual of his talent, sometimes behind his peers, represented their punishment. But David Dixon Porter refused to succumb to the dictates of the Old Guard. He battled the stagnation that so appalled him, and he endured the consequences. Young naval officers adored him for it.

Several days after the Cairo meeting, Grant notified Sherman of his new designs and asked him to visit that evening. Together, they hammered out the details of the operation. While Grant organized his forces for an overland advance, Sherman would head back to

Memphis to gather troops for the Vicksburg landing. That night, Sherman telegraphed Porter to meet him in Memphis. "Time now is the great object," and Sherman, a thorough planner, wanted everything arranged in advance.[6]

For over a month, Sherman and Porter had exchanged numerous informative letters that pledged harmony of action and established a superb tone for joint army–navy operations. In mid-November, Porter advised Sherman that Grant ought to use his gunboats in any attack on Vicksburg. "I wish to cooperate with the army in every way where I can be of service, and if you can get any message to or from General Grant on the subject, and give me an idea of what is going on, I shall be much obliged to you." Sherman responded with maps and other information and a call for unity of command. "My opinion is that a perfect concert of action should exist between all the forces of the United States operating down the valley; and I apprehend some difficulty may arise from the fact that you control on the river, Curtis on the west bank, and Grant on the east bank," Sherman explained. "Were either one of you in absolute command, all, of course, would act in concert." Porter agreed. "I am ready to cooperate with anybody and everybody," penned the admiral, "and all I ask on the part of the military commanders is their full confidence and a pull together." Thus, when Porter visited Sherman, he expected a warm reception.[7]

As Porter entered Sherman's Memphis headquarters, what he saw reassured him. It reminded him a bit of McClellan's command post—officers waiting, clerks scribbling rapidly, orderlies racing about on horseback, and sentries pacing back and forth—but there was a striking contrast. No one wore lace and feathers, there were no velvet carpets; it was a working headquarters, not a showroom. "Everything was rough and ready," Porter noted with satisfaction.[8]

Then some confusion crushed the admiral's upbeat spirit. Staff greeted Porter and seated him in a waiting room, and there, for an hour, Porter stewed. Finally Sherman entered, and after introductions he apologized to the admiral—no one had told him of Porter's arrival. When Sherman broke off the discussion to complete business with a subordinate, Porter nearly erupted in rage. For some reason, though, he hesitated, and after conversations resumed for a few moments, Sherman had more than regained Porter's faith and confidence. "He turned towards me in the most pleasant way," Porter recalled, "poked the fire and talked as if he had known me all his life." Rarely had Porter met anyone so direct. Sherman chatted openly about preparations he had completed and what steps he intended to take next, interrupting his monologue periodically to dictate some terse message to a subordinate. Porter marveled at this loquacious general whose mind danced from subject to subject with such facility. Like his headquarters, this was a working general— attired casually, informal in manner, and immersed in his labors. Within minutes, the two men bonded as if they had known one another for years.[9]

By December 19, 1862, Sherman's troops had climbed aboard transports for the strike against Vicksburg. En route, they picked up another division at Helena, Arkansas. Porter's fleet had gained control of the Yazoo River, just north of Vicksburg, and Sherman hoped to land, drive on to the Vicksburg & Jackson Railroad, and force his way into the city. Porter's gunboats would provide an invaluable shield and soften defensive positions around Vicksburg. If Grant could just detain the Confederates to the northeast near Grenada, Sherman would encounter only token opposition.

But in no time the intricate scheme began to unravel. Rebel cavalry raids severed Grant's supply line and compelled his retreat. Rather than block Grant's movement the Confederates held tight in Vicksburg. And Sherman, wholly unaware of Grant's fate, attacked directly into the lion's mouth. Bayous so cut up the area that Sherman found two routes to reach the base of the bluffs, only one offering any promise of success. With Federal gunboats and mortars shelling adjacent woods to isolate the target area, he ordered his troops to storm the heights on December 29. The Federals charged with a will, surmounting obstacles and groping up the slick slopes toward the Confederate line. But the defenders and their fortified position proved too strong. Heavy losses dissipated the attackers' power, and they never gained a foothold in the earth works. That night, torrential rains drenched the troops and so slopped the assault route that operations there promised nothing but failure.

During the next day, Sherman and Porter gathered to assess their options. From this conference emerged a new plan. Sherman would maintain his current position and feign an attack, while Porter would lead his gunboats and 10,000 soldiers farther upriver. With close fire support from the vessels, these troops would storm the heights there. That night, however, a dense fog blanketed the region and precluded any movement by water. Porter canceled the operation. The attempt to carry Chickasaw Bluffs ended in utter defeat.[10]

From the misery of the Yazoo, where over 1,200 Federals sacrificed their lives or sustained wounds and another 550 fell into Rebel hands, a burgeoning friendship formed between the two military men, Sherman and Porter. Their respect for one another's professional conduct cemented the personal rapport they had established in Memphis. Porter not only directed his naval forces skillfully, he cooperated wholeheartedly. The admiral provided sound advice and proved to be a resourceful leader. For his part, Sherman impressed Porter with his mastery of all aspects of the operation and the way in which he drew Porter into his confidence. Sherman accepted Porter as a full partner, a refreshing change of pace for a naval officer. To the secretary of the navy on the last day of 1862, Porter expressed his complete confidence in the army commander. "General Sherman is quite equal to the emergency," he insisted, "and nothing daunted by his want of success."[11]

Several days after the assault on Chickasaw Bluffs, Maj. Gen. John A. McClernand arrived at the mouth of the Yazoo River to supersede Sherman as army commander. A longtime political friend of Lincoln's, McClernand had served with Sherman as a division commander at Shiloh. He impressed neither Grant nor Sherman with his military talents. Porter, who had met McClernand in Washington a few months earlier, held him in even lower regard, calling him a "hybrid general" and interpreting his appointment as an insult to Grant.[12]

Sherman immediately recommended that McClernand withdraw the army to Milliken's Bend, which the new commander did. He then suggested that McClernand employ the army in conjunction with the navy in a campaign against Arkansas Post, a Confederate bastion on the Arkansas River. During the fight along Chickasaw Bluffs, a Rebel vessel from Arkansas Post descended the river and captured a steamer towing coal and ammunition barges. Unless the Federals silenced the fortress, it would annoy traffic on the river and hinder any Union attempts to capture Vicksburg. At the time

McClernand had no specific plans and only a general one to seek the fall of Vicksburg, yet he hesitated to adopt Sherman's recommendation. Sherman then alerted Porter to the problem. Apparently, the two had discussed this as a possible course of action a few days earlier, and Sherman felt sure that "General McClernand will do anything you ask." When they arrived at Porter's flagship, McClernand presented the operation as his own conception. The admiral was outraged. Porter had disliked McClernand beforehand, and now, because he had expropriated Sherman's plan, he resented the political general even more. Only a private conversation with Sherman convinced him to participate in the venture. But Porter insisted on a price: Sherman would command the assault force. McClernand concurred.[13]

A massive convoy of Federal transports and gunboats ascended the Arkansas River. By January 11, the troops had debarked and assumed positions for an assault. Porter's gunboats opened an impressive barrage, and field artillery and infantry joined the fray. In short order they silenced the Rebel artillery, and before Sherman could order an assault, defenders raised the white flag. Nearly 5,000 Confederates surrendered. McClernand assumed much of the credit, but according to Sherman it was Porter's gunboats that won the engagement. Porter merely chalked up the lack of magnanimity to army egoism. "I find that army officers are not willing to give the Navy credit (even in very small matters) they are entitled to," he commented with disgust.[14]

When Grant linked up with the victorious joint command near the mouth of the Arkansas River, Sherman and Porter confirmed what he had already anticipated. McClernand lacked the capacity to lead an important expedition. Sherman, of course, would obey McClernand's orders as his superior officer, but the army needed Porter's aid to reduce Vicksburg, and the admiral looked upon him with "distrust." Whereas Porter viewed Sherman as "every inch a soldier, and has the confidence of his men," he believed "McClernand is no soldier, and has the confidence of no one, unless it may be two or three of his staff." Since McClernand's arrival, "I have twice the work to do now that I had before," he grumbled. "Sherman used to help me to think, but now I have to think for McClernand and myself." Both Sherman and Porter urged Grant to assume command. Their pleas were too late. Grant had already decided to direct the operations against Vicksburg.[15]

Over the next two months, Grant employed his forces in a host of projects that would enable him to strike Vicksburg without assaulting the bluffs. Each enterprise, regardless of the likelihood of success, received Porter's complete support. Grant attempted to dig a canal that would bypass Vicksburg. But the Confederates realized that by repositioning some guns they could shell the entire course of the man-made waterway, thus eliminating it as a worthwhile Federal venture. West of the Mississippi River, Grant ordered his forces to clear a passage from Lake Providence through a series of narrow bayous and waterways into the Red River. Yet slow progress and the length of this circuitous route, approximately 500 miles, limited its utility.

East of the Mississippi River, Grant undertook two difficult schemes to reach the upper Yazoo River and avoid the powerful positions near Vicksburg. By breaking the levee along the Mississippi River across from Helena, Arkansas, Grant hoped to restore an old channel to Moon Lake. From there, soldiers and sailors would wriggle their way through a series of waterways that form the Yazoo River. Confederates felled trees and prepared other obstructions to discourage the Union advance. After much labor, the army–navy contingent worked its way to the intersection of the Tallahatchie and Yallabusha Rivers, where the Confederates had constructed a fort. With no means of attacking from land, the job of eliminating the position lapsed to the navy. Twice gunboats shelled it, and twice the Rebel gunners kept them at bay. An effort to flood the defenders from the fort also failed, and Grant had to seek a means of entering the Yazoo River west of this tiny bastion.

The other proposal called for soldiers and sailors to enter Steele's Bayou from the Mississippi River not far from Milliken's Bend, travel south into Black Bayou, east to Deer Creek, north to Rolling Fork, east to Big Sunflower River, and finally south into the Yazoo River, some ten miles above Haynes's Bluff. Porter personally supervised this operation, forcing his gunboats along waterways at times barely several dozen yards wide. Limbs stretching over the water chewed up his smokestacks and tree stumps below the surface scraped his hulls. Aggressively, Porter pushed on, plowing all obstacles from his path. Sherman, in command of ground forces, pursued slowly by land. As the gunboats worked their way along Deer Creek, approaching Rolling Fork and more open travel, the Confederates started cutting down timber to obstruct their passage. Several vessels stuck fast in submerged willow branches. In the distant rear, Porter and his sailors could hear locals chopping down trees behind them. Then Confederate snipers began taking potshots at his men. The admiral's mortars blindly tossed shells into the woods, to no avail. His situation had suddenly become critical; the Confederates had them trapped. On tissue paper he scrawled out a plea for help and entrusted a freedman with its delivery to Sherman.

As darkness crept over his crafts, Porter loaded all guns, secured the portholes, and huddled his sailors below deck. Minute after minute ticked away; Porter agonized over the condition of his ships and crew. In the hours before dawn, he even prepared detailed plans for the destruction of his vessels rather than letting them fall into the hands of the Confederates. Sunrise brought small comfort. His situation was unchanged. The mighty gunboats sat helpless with enemy all around.

Shortly after noon, Porter's men could hear the distant crack of rifles. Straining to detect any clues, the sailors finally deciphered the noise. It was Sherman's advanced party, skirmishing with the Confederates. Ninety minutes later, Sherman himself, covered with mud, rode up on an old horse to the huzzahs of the seamen. Once he received word of Porter's plight, he had immediately pushed forward the few troops he had on hand. That evening three boatloads of soldiers arrived at Black Bayou. By candlelight, Sherman led them through the dense thickets on a night march covering over twenty miles. Six weeks ago, when the press harangued Sherman for his assault on Chickasaw Bluffs, Porter had come to his salvation, releasing letters had written to the secretary of the navy during the campaign that absolved Sherman of blame and even lauded his talents as a general officer. Now, Sherman came to Porter's rescue.[16]

"Halloo Porter," the general cried, "what did you get into such an ugly scrape for? So much for you navy fellows getting out of your element; better send for the soldiers always."

Porter took the ribbing good-naturedly. "I never knew what helpless things ironclads could become when they got in a ditch and had no soldiers about," he confessed. The sight of Sherman and the men of the Army of the Tennessee, whom he aptly described as "half horse, half alligator, with a touch of snapping turtle," utterly delighted him.[17]

The failure of the Deer Creek expedition turned Grant back reluctantly to an assault on Haynes' Bluff, to the north of where Sherman had lost 1,500 men the previous December. He had run out of options.[18]

Then two separate strands meshed in Grant's mind. Rear Admiral David Farragut had cruised up the Mississippi River and communicated with Grant, requesting a party to assist him in knocking out the batteries at Warrenton, about ten miles below Vicksburg. At the same time, Grant was searching for a means of shipping up to 20,000 men along a route west of the Mississippi River, crossing them over to the east side, and reinforcing Maj. Gen. Nathaniel P. Banks's command around Port Hudson. After its fall, Banks could march north on Vicksburg, hugging the river and receiving protection and supplies from the Union gunboats. It suddenly dawned on Grant that his best option might be to move troops, supplies, and transports along the western side of the Mississippi River, shuttle them to the eastern bank below Vicksburg, and attack from the south, rather than the north. As the winter floods receded and the rains subsided, roadbeds that could carry Grant's men and wagons dried. The only remaining problems were accumulating enough barges and transports and running a few gunboats past the Vicksburg gauntlet. From despondency bloomed promise.[19]

For Grant's new plan to work, he needed the navy's support. In communications with Porter, Grant revealed his intentions and requested gunboats. "Will you be good enough, admiral, to give this your early consideration and let me know your determination?" Only a week after his near disaster, Porter did not hesitate. "I am ready to co-operate with you in the matter of landing troops on the other side," the admiral committed, "but you must recollect that, when these gunboats once go below, we give up all hopes of ever getting them up again." If he sent vessels below, he preferred to employ his best craft, "and there will be nothing left to attack Haynes' Bluff, in case it should be deemed necessary to try it." Two days later, Grant, Sherman, and Porter reconnoitered the prospective attack site at Haynes' Bluff. The following day, Grant announced his decision. An attack there "would be attended with an immense sacrifice of life, if not with defeat. This, then closes out the last hope of turning the enemy by the right."[20]

Porter was lukewarm to the new plan. Yet he not only pledged resources, he consented to supervise the preparation and movement of all vessels that passed the batteries. He agreed simply because Grant had urged them. "So confident was I of the ability of General Grant to carry out his plans when he explained them to me," Porter told the secretary of the navy, "that I never hesitated to change my position from above to below Vicksburg." While Grant accumulated the boats and barges, Porter had them packed with grain sacks, heavy logs, and wet hay for protection and to conceal the fires under the boilers. He also assigned sailors to man several army boats on the hazardous journey.[21]

But before Grant could bring down all the necessary transports and barges, Porter received a blistering rebuke from the secretary of the navy. Dismissing the worthwhileness of Porter's support for Grant's various schemes around Vicksburg, the secretary announced the president's view that patrolling along the river between Vicksburg and Port Hudson "is of far greater importance than the flanking expeditions which thus far have prevented the consummation of this most desirable object." Porter, who never dodged a fight, responded with clarity and force. "I am sorry the Department is not satisfied with the operations here, but you will please remember, sir, that I was ordered to cooperate with the army, and sagacious officers deem these flanking movements of great importance." Control of the river above and below Vicksburg, he reminded the secretary, would not necessarily lead to the fall of the city. "While it is my desire to carry out the wishes of the Department in relation to all matters connected with operations here, still I must act in accordance with my judgment and a more full knowledge of affairs than the Department could possibly have." Nevertheless, Porter immediately notified Grant that a Navy Department directive "will compel me to go below the batteries with the fleet sooner than I anticipated," with whatever vessels the army had on hand.[22]

On the night of April 16, seven gunboats and several transports, with an assortment of steamers and coal barges lashed to the side, drifted quietly downriver. Detailed instructions that Porter had issued nearly a week earlier carefully outlined the order, fire direction and range, and spacing between boats. He even included contingency plans in the event a vessel sustained a serious hit. Porter personally led the convoy. At 11:16 p.m., the Confederates opened fire on his ironclad, *Benton*, and within minutes the Rebels ignited huge bonfires on both banks to illuminate the river. For two and a half hours the Vicksburg garrison poured shells into his squadron. Almost miraculously, only one craft, an army transport, sank, although every one sustained some hits.[23]

Just as Porter's gunboat passed out of range, he heard a cry from a small boat, *"Benton* ahoy!" It was Sherman. He pulled up alongside to check on the condition of Porter and his crew. After receiving the status report, Sherman could not resist a bit of needling.

"You are more at home here than you were in the ditches grounding on willow-trees," he teased. "Stick to this, old fellow; it suits Jack better." Then off the tireless Sherman went, to examine each vessel as it emerged from the fire.[24]

Throughout the staging process for the movement across the river, Porter regretted Sherman's absence. Everything was chaos; he needed an experienced officer who could supervise the loading process. "I wish twenty times a day that Sherman was here, or yourself," he complained to Grant, "but I suppose we cannot have all we wish." Within the army, Porter confided to a friend, Sherman "has more brains than all put together."[25]

Grant had other duties in mind for Sherman. While the bulk of the army embarked for the east bank of the river below Vicksburg, Sherman led a feint at Haynes' Bluff to draw away the attention of the city's defenders.

Problems continued to develop, and Grant had to adapt to overcome them. A drop in the water level prevented the army from drawing supplies through the swamps so more vessels, loaded with supplies, had to run the Vicksburg gauntlet to feed the troops. The original landing zone along the east bank of the Mississippi River, Grand Gulf, proved unsuitable as well. Porter's gunboats could not silence the Confederate batteries there, and the secure defensive position on the bluffs precluded a frontal assault. The Federal troops had to trudge farther south, and on April 30, 1863, Porter's ships began shuttling Grant's army across the Mississippi River. After fifteen weeks of toil, Grant finally had positioned his forces to operate against Vicksburg.[26]

While Grant conducted a brilliant campaign against separate Confederate forces, Porter slipped down to the mouth of the Red River to relieve Farragut of some of his duties. He returned, however, in time to assist in the fall of the city of Vicksburg. On May 18, Porter could hear the pop of musketry from the area around Chickasaw Bluffs. It was Sherman's Corps. Several hours later, he received wonderful reports of a lightning operation that continually kept the Rebel armies off balance.

Throughout the siege, the admiral secured the cracker line and provided fire support for the army. On May 19 and again three days later, he employed his gunboats and mortars to cover the assaults and disrupt the defenses.

On May 27, Sherman requested a gunboat to attack the water battery that anchored the Rebel left flank. The vessel, *Cincinnati*, closed on the target and fought aggressively. In the process it sustained numerous hits and in minutes plunged to the bottom of the river, with the loss of forty crewmen. Sherman, who witnessed the entire affair from the bluffs, felt horrible. Porter chalked it up as one of war's misfortunes. He would agree to lose all his boats, Porter told Sherman, if they would secure Vicksburg. Porter meant it. Back in December, one of his gunboat commanders struck a mine in the Yazoo River while maneuvering closer in order to fire on the Rebel positions. His vessel sank. When the commander, one of Porter's best, asked about the date of a court of inquiry, the admiral erupted: "Court! I have no time to order courts! I can't blame an officer who seeks to put his ship close to the enemy." Porter then ordered the fleet captain to find the officer another gunboat and chugged away.[27]

When Vicksburg fell on the Fourth of July, 1863, Grant and Porter gathered briefly for some warm congratulations. Two days later, in his after action report, Grant's acclaim for Porter's aid had not abated. He expressed "thankfulness for my good fortune in being placed in co-operation with an officer of the Navy" such as Porter. The admiral and his subordinates "have ever shown the greatest readiness in their co-operation, no matter what was to be done or what risk to be taken, either by their men or their vessels." Grant then concluded that

"Without this prompt and cordial support, my movements would have been much embarrassed, if not wholly defeated."[28]

Sherman, too, heaped praise on the admiral. From his position on the Black River, he regretted that he could not meet Porter on a wharf in Vicksburg to celebrate. "In so magnificent a result," Sherman expounded, "I stop not to count who did it. It is done, and the day of our nation's birth is consecrated and baptized anew in a victory won by the united Navy and Army of our country. God grant that the harmony and mutual respect that exist between our respective commanders, and shared by all true men of the joint service, may continue forever, and serve to elevate our national character, threatened with shipwreck." From a more personal standpoint, Sherman admitted that, "Whether success attend my efforts or not, I know that Admiral Porter will ever accord to me the exhibition of a pure and unselfish zeal in the service of our country." On July 18, in the governor's mansion in Jackson, Mississippi, Sherman and a party of generals joined in a hearty chorus of "Army and Navy forever." The next day, after describing the scene the night before, Sherman pledged eternal support for his navy friend: "To me it will ever be a source of pride that real harmony has always characterized our intercourse, and let what may arise, I will ever call upon Admiral Porter with the same confidence as I have in the past."[29]

For Porter, exposure to officers of Grant and Sherman's caliber transformed his opinion of professionally-trained army officers. Earlier in the war he confessed to the assistant secretary of the navy, an old friend, "I don't believe in our generals any more than I do in our old fogies of the Navy." Interservice mistrust and rivalry and early war experiences had soured Porter's assessment of high-ranking army personnel. Grant and Sherman won over Porter through their professional conduct, sensitivity to Porter's rank and position, and the refreshing atmosphere of cooperation that they fostered. "Grant and Sherman are on board almost every day," the admiral noted with pleasure in early March. "Dine and tea with me often; we agree in everything, and they are disposed to do everything for us they can." More than anything, Porter feared "for the sake of the Union that nothing may occur to make a change here."[30]

Porter accorded full credit for the Vicksburg Campaign to Grant. In his report to the secretary of the navy, the admiral asserted that "the late investment and capture of Vicksburg will be characterized as one of the greatest military achievements ever known. The conception of the idea," he continued, "originated solely with General Grant, who adopted a course in which great labor was performed, great battles were fought, and great risks were run; a single mistake would have involved us in difficulty, but so well were all the plans matured, so well were all the movements timed, and so rapid were the evolutions performed that not a mistake has occurred from the passage of the fleet by Vicksburg and the passage of the army across the river up to the present time."[31]

To be sure, Porter liked this pleasant-looking man with an unobtrusive disposition, but his fondness for Grant derived predominantly from his enormous respect for the general's military talents. Grant's quiet confidence, aggressive approach to warfare, and doggedness earned Porter's deepest admiration. No one Porter ever met could focus on a problem, such as the conquest of Vicksburg, and labor at it so relentlessly as Grant. He attempted scheme after scheme just to gain a position from which to launch an attack on Vicksburg. Behind that unaltering countenance of Grant's worked an adaptable, resourceful, creative mind that impressed Porter.

Grant, like Porter, refused to bind himself to conventional methods and thought. He experimented with varying approaches to reach the high ground near Vicksburg. Once he had slipped below the city, Grant cut loose from his supply base—a bold decision that Sherman opposed—to speed his march and enhance his maneuverability. He drew skillfully upon the resources at hand, particularly the navy. Unlike most army generals, Grant grasped the possibilities of joint operations. Selflessly committed to victory, and convinced that an army–navy team offered the only hope of success, he had no qualms about dealing with Porter as a peer, something few army officers would do. And Porter proved himself more than worthy of coequal status.

By contrast, Sherman and Porter established a much more personal relationship. Both quick-tongued, energetic, extremely intelligent, and wholly devoted to their profession of arms, these two men bonded during their first encounter, and within a week they were fast friends. Whether they were telling jokes, teasing one another, or damning the world of politics, Sherman and Porter were at ease with one another. A rich chemistry existed between them; Sherman and Porter were soul mates.

Like Grant, Sherman appreciated the navy. But while Grant's interest was utilitarian, the maritime had a special charm for Sherman. Since his travels to California in the 1840s, sailors and the sea had intrigued Sherman. With his unquenchable curiosity, Sherman enjoyed poking around Porter's gunboats and talking naval matters. He entered the admiral's world with enthusiasm, setting himself apart from most army officers and winning new friends, especially Porter, within the sister service.

Sherman's relentless pursuit of mastery of the art of war appealed to Porter. A naval officer who had spent years charting channels, he appreciated Sherman's passion for maps and geographic features. Porter possessed a photographic memory for the written word; Sherman, it seemed, nearly had a photographic memory for the ground. "The General himself," Porter wrote with but slight exaggeration, "had one peculiarity and that was a very correct knowledge of the topography of all places he had operated in or was about to operate in. He never forgot a house, a road or a bayou—in fact he seemed to possess all the crafts of a backwoodsman and never even forgot a 'blazed' tree." During active operations or in preparation for them, the general was almost a man possessed. "Sherman's whole mind was so absorbed in whatever work he had before him," Porter observed, "that he never thought of eating, sleeping or his dress." Instead, noted the admiral, "The General's great delight was to pore over maps and he seemed to take in all the roads, fields and rivers, as if they were good to eat and drink, or he would spend the night in writing out general orders, which were always very full and explicit." Sherman, Porter informed a friend, was "the moving spirit" of the army.[32]

Throughout the Vicksburg Campaign, Porter noticed that he and Sherman agreed with each other time after time. They conceived problems similarly and generated comparable solutions. That same consensus existed in their fundamental approach to war. As they communicated more and more, it occurred to both men that their thoughts on how the Union should conduct the war effort converged. After eighteen months of observation, contemplation, and analysis, Sherman had concluded that occupation of Confederate territory squandered resources and did little to subdue the rebellion. The Union needed to gain control of the Mississippi River and use it as a springboard for raids directed at the interior of the Confederacy. Federal troops would eat the food, steal the slaves, destroy the railroads, and make life so miserable for the inhabitants that they would realize secession and war were not proper solutions to their political complaints. "The possession of the river, with an army capable of disembarking and striking inland, would have a mighty influence," he insisted to Porter. War's devastations had already sapped many Confederates of their passion for secession, and his new troops, the men of 1862, "came with ideas of making vigorous war, which means universal destruction, and it requires hard handling to repress excesses." Porter not only vowed that "Whatever control I have on the river shall be exerted to help the army," he endorsed Sherman's approach to the war. "I am of the opinion that there is but one way to make war, and that is to harass your enemy all you can. I have tried to be as unpleasant to the rebels on the river as possible, and hope that the new armies now going into the field will give them (the rebels) a taste of devastation that may bring them to their senses." The army general and navy admiral thought as one.[33]

In comparing Grant with Sherman, Porter marveled at their marked differences. "I don't suppose there ever was a greater contrast between any two men," he averred, "than between Grant and Sherman." He described Grant as unimposing physically. Still, he was a congenial-looking fellow with agreeable features, simple in taste and calm in demeanor. Sherman, however, was "a hard weather beaten soldier, with naturally a corrugated face, a nervous, restless, active man." Grant resembled any private; Sherman looked "every much a general." Porter once doubted that he ever held more than a twenty-minute conversation with Grant. Sherman gabbed almost incessantly. Grant chose good people and could delegate work, while Sherman "attended to all the details himself." In fact, Porter thought that "They were unlike in everything except in their skill as soldiers, yet they agreed perfectly." What made the tandem so successful, Porter concluded, was that "Grant and Sherman together combine qualities possessed by no one general that ever lived; what one wants the other possesses."[34]

Porter shared characteristics with both men. Temperamentally more akin to Sherman, he could act decisively, a quality that most observers regarded as one of Grant's strongest features. Intellectually, Porter fit more comfortably with Sherman, and he certainly found Sherman's company more enjoyable and intimate. But there was something reassuring about Grant, his quiet confidence and serenity soothing the more mercurial admiral. Like Grant and Sherman, Porter possessed a resourceful nature, and results, not methods, dominated his approach to military service in wartime. Once, after responding to a series of hypothetical questions from a young officer, Porter snarled back with his biting sarcasm: "All I have to say is that when the time comes to use your judgment you must use it; and if you do it right, you will hear from me damned quick; and if you do it wrong, you will hear from me a damned sight quicker!"[35]

The Vicksburg juggernaut brought Grant, Sherman, and Porter together as only such an operation could. From their difficult experiences, they learned to depend on one another, and they developed mutual respect as individuals and as warriors. With each man possessing different talents and skills, they fed off one another, exchanging ideas, each increasing his knowledge of the other service, and evolving and maturing as joint commanders. The Vicksburg Campaign tossed the three together, and from it they emerged with powerful professional and personal bonds. In the years to come, rich and lasting friendships blossomed among them, but the heart of the relationship stemmed from the demanding service along the Mississippi River.

Days after the surrender of Vicksburg, Port Hudson fell to Union control, and now the Mississippi River ran "unvexed to the sea." All three men received promotions for their invaluable services. Porter earned a commission with the permanent rank of rear admiral, and the War Department elevated Grant to major general and awarded Sherman a brigadier generalship, both in the Regular Army.

Although Sherman and Porter continued to communicate and cooperate, they never again joined forces for a large-scale operation. As Sherman commented in mid-October, "You have almost finished your job and can and will, doubtless with infinite pleasure, help us who must live whilst we penetrate the very bowels of this land." The intimacy between them never waned. When personal tragedy struck Sherman, he poured out his heart to the tough-minded admiral. "I lost, recently, my little boy by sickness incurred during his visit to my camp on Big Black," a heartbroken Sherman revealed. "He was my pride and hope of life, and his loss takes from me the great incentive to excel, and now I must work on purely and exclusively for love of country and professional pride." Sherman concluded by saying, "To you I can always unfold my thoughts as one worthy and capable of appreciating the feelings of a soldier and gentleman."[36]

In Sherman's absence, Porter prepared chatty, informative letters of considerable length, which the admiral wittily justified by admitting that "sailors will spin long yarns—it is part of their nature." Porter continued the practice with periodic reports throughout the remainder of the war. The two friends could accomplish more through direct, personal communication, resolving problems and kicking around ideas as they had done at Vicksburg, than by working through official military channels.[37]

With Grant's assignment in central Tennessee, communication between Porter and him slowed to a trickle. Only terse, businesslike dispatches passed over telegraph lines from one to the other. Though they were warm and caring friends, their personal relationship did not have the same intimacy as Grant and Sherman's or Porter and Sherman's, and Grant's primary focus had now shifted to this new area of concern. When trouble erupted back in the Mississippi River Valley, though, Porter did not hesitate to bring the matter to Grant's attention, using a belated congratulatory message to write his friend a lengthy letter. "If I have not sooner congratulated you on your splendid victory at Chattanooga," explained the admiral, "it was not because I did not share in the joy of your triumph, for you have no greater well-wisher than myself. I congratulate you now with all my heart, and now that you have finished that business so well, I must tell you that the guerrillas are kicking up the mischief on the river." Grant replied that Sherman was returning there to quash the partisans and launch his raiding strategy along the river. Porter was delighted. "I was glad to receive yours of the 20th instant, and to hear that I was soon to see my old friend Sherman, whom I esteem as you do. Indeed," joked the whiskered admiral, "we have been so much together and in so many hard places that we look upon him as the property of the navy."[38]

Time permitted Sherman to organize a march on Meridian, Mississippi, living off the land and demolishing the railroad as he travelled. But other pressing matters precluded his intended raid up the Red River. The president had elevated Grant to lieutenant general, and Sherman would direct one of the two major Union thrusts that spring, with his target the Confederate army in northern Georgia. The campaign up the Red River lapsed to Porter and, by default, to Nathaniel P. Banks.

Porter was worried. He feared the consequences of a volunteer commander directing a joint operation. Sherman allayed the admiral's uneasiness by assigning 10,000 of his own troops under a trusted subordinate, Maj. Gen. A. J. Smith, to assist in the endeavor. As it turned out, the Porter–Smith combination could not secure victory, only stave off a disastrous defeat. Three converging columns— one under Banks, another under Maj. Gen. Frederick Steele that never materialized, and the third under Porter and Smith—were to link at Alexandria, Louisiana, and then advance as far upriver as Shreveport, breaking up Confederate opposition and gathering valuable supplies of cotton. Alexandria fell to Porter and Smith; despite promises, Banks started late and arrived after the fight. At that point, low water nearly terminated the campaign. Sherman had authorized Porter to cancel operations if the gunboats could not pass up the rapids. They barely did. Banks then led the column on, and at Sabine Cross Roads a Confederate command routed his forces. Smith's two divisions along with some other Union troops abruptly halted the Rebel pursuit at Pleasant Hill. But Banks had enough. The next day, his troops continued their precipitous retreat. Rebel batteries and dropping water levels made the withdrawal a living hell for Porter. Only the imaginitive labors of a Wisconsin officer, who erected a dam to raise the water level and float Porter's fleet over the rapids, saved the admiral from an utter catastrophe.

Porter laid full blame on Banks's doorstep. "You know my opinion of political generals," the admiral fumed to Sherman after the two battles. "It is a crying sin to put the lives of thousands in the hands of such men, and the time has come when there should be a stop put to it." Two days later, he approached the failure more philosophically, but his attitude toward Banks and officers of his ilk had not budged:

You know I have always said that Providence was fighting this great battle its own way, and brings these reverses to teach us, a proud, stiff-necked, and unthankful people, how to be contented under a good Government if peaceful times come again. I hope it will teach us not to place the destinies of a great nation in the hands of political generals and volunteer admirals.[39]

Porter survived the Red River Expedition with his reputation largely intact, perhaps not with the public but certainly with the Navy Department. And as Grant locked up with Lee around Petersburg, and Sherman battled his way to the outskirts of Atlanta and eventually captured the city, Porter returned east. The secretary of the navy wanted Porter to head a flying squadron in the Atlantic that would chase blockade runners. Porter respectfully begged off. Such mundane duties offered no appeal; he best served the nation as a combat commander. Some days later, the secretary proposed a joint army–navy operation to North Carolina to seize Fort Fisher, which controlled the blockade runners' last haven, Wilmington. Porter leaped at the opportunity.

Immediately, Porter paid his old friend Grant a visit at his head-quarters in City Point, Virginia. After lengthy discussions, Grant endorsed the concept and assigned Maj. Gen. Godfrey Weitzel, a brainy engineer officer, to command the army. Soon, however, problems developed. Fort Fisher was part of Maj. Gen. Benjamin Butler's department, and he proposed an idea that intrigued authorities in Washington. Butler suggested that they load an old vessel full of gunpowder and explode it near the fort, either demolishing the bastion or so stunning the garrison that an assault would carry the works swiftly. Porter, whose nature attracted him to fresh methods and bold ideas, thought it was worth a try. Grant considered the project ridiculous, but he refused to expend capital to block it. Then Butler, another political general who had tussled with Porter during the campaign for New Orleans in 1862, decided to head the army contingent personally.

Not until mid-December 1864 did the expedition get underway. Incompetence ruled the army operation. Poor preparations, inexcusable delays, and a lack of aggressiveness hounded Butler's command, and gale-force winds worsened its woes. The gunpowder ship explosion proved a pyrotechnic spectacle, but it did no damage to the fort, and Porter had to rely solely on his naval gunfire to soften the enemy positions and support the landing. Again, Butler's men were thirty hours late, and only 2,500 soldiers went ashore. Weitzel reconnoitered and found the defenses too strong. Much to Porter's mortification, he and Butler cancelled the attack. By imputation and later accusation, the naval bombardment had failed to dislodge enough cannons in Fort Fisher for an assault to succeed.

Porter was livid. To the secretary of the navy, he bemoaned the incompetence of the army officers who headed the expedition and beseeched the secretary not to withdraw his fleet until they had conquered the fort. All the army needed, Porter insisted, was a skilled commander. That day, he dispatched his top subordinate, Capt. K. Randolph Breese, with a letter for Sherman to come up and take control of the affair. "This," Porter enticed his comrade, "is merely on your way to Richmond. Take this place and you take the 'crème de la crème' of the rebellion." Sherman's masterful handling of the operation would "let our people see the folly of employing such generals as Butler and Banks. I have tried them both, and God save me from further connections with such generals."[40]

Sherman declined Porter's invitation, preferring instead to take Wilmington from the rear, after his march through South Carolina. It did not matter. The previous day, Secretary of the Navy Gideon Welles showed Grant the message traffic he had received from Porter. Butler had failed wretchedly, and the admiral insisted that a combination of army and navy forces under a good general officer could take the fort. Grant sided with his old friend. "I know Admiral Porter to be possessed of as fine judgment as any other officer and capable of taking as great risks," the lieutenant general informed the secretary of war. That day, Grant urged the admiral to hold fast. He would send the same troops, reinforced by a brigade. Maj. Gen. Alfred H. Terry would command.[41]

With Grant's involvement, the new expedition functioned superbly. Grant handed Terry sealed orders. Not until he and his force had lost sight of land did they know their destination. Terry's written instructions could not have been more explicit. "It is exceedingly desirable that the most complete understanding should exist between yourself and the naval commander," Grant explained. "I suggest, therefore, that you consult with Admiral Porter freely, and get from him the part to be performed by each branch of the public service, so that there may be unity of action." After directing Terry to prepare a written plan of attack, the lieutenant general ordered Terry to subordinate himself to Porter. "I have served with Admiral Porter, and know that you can rely on his judgment and his nerve to undertake what he proposes. I would, therefore, defer to him as much as is consistent with your own responsibilities." To avoid any misconceptions, the lieutenant general also prepared a letter to Porter, introducing Terry and informing him that "General Terry will show you the instructions he is acting under." He went on to discuss reinforcements that he held on alert in Baltimore and proposed some options for an attack. Then Porter's old friend concluded with the statement, "General Terry will consult with you fully, and will be governed by your suggestions as far as his responsibility for the safety of his command will admit of." Grant had established a unified command.[42]

Between Porter and Terry, they conceived and executed a brilliant operation. Porter reworked his gunfire plan, and on January 13, 1865, after an extensive naval bombardment, Terry and his men, augmented by more than 1,000 marines and sailors under Captain Breese, landed and dug into the beach. The innovative Porter had requested Terry to assign a signal corpsman to his flagship. Thus, when the landing and attack took place, Terry and Porter had ship-to-shore communications. As the amphibious force maneuvered its way up to the Confederate fortifications, Terry and Breese could direct close naval gunfire support through the wigwag system. By mid-afternoon the following day, Terry gave the signal, and the ground troops stormed the walls. For nearly seven hours they battled, sometimes hand to hand. Finally, at 10:00 p.m., Terry lofted a signal flare into the sky. The Union had secured Fort Fisher.[43]

For his role in the victory, Porter praised Terry effusively. "General Terry is entitled to the highest praise and the gratitude of his country for the manner in which he has conducted his part of the operations," the tough-minded admiral commented to the secretary of the navy. "He is my beau ideal of a soldier and a general." Porter probably did not know that Terry, like Butler and Banks, was a citizen soldier.[44]

Returning to Washington in failure, Butler placed the entire blame squarely on Porter's shoulders. The politician turned general convinced some congressional friends to hold hearings on the matter, but the triumph at Fort Fisher with essentially the same resources pulled the rug out from beneath any damaging investigation. On January 7, 1865, at Grant's request, Lincoln relieved Butler of command of the Department of North Carolina and Virginia and ordered him to return to Massachusetts and await orders. As Sherman crowed to Porter ten days later, "I am rejoiced that the current of events has carried Butler to Lowell, where he should have stayed and confined his bellicose operations to the factory girls." Butler acted as a thorn in Porter's side for the remainder of the admiral's life, attacking him publicly and resurrecting incidents and conjuring up fictitious tales that portrayed Porter in a bad light.[45]

Although the campaign concluded well for both the navy and the army, Porter was steamed at Grant. Twice in a row on major operations political generals had caused disasters and squandered the lives of many fine soldiers and sailors. Grant knew of Butler's incompetence before the first attempt, yet he refused to intervene and replace him with someone of talent, fearful of taking on a general with political clout. Porter and the men of the joint campaign suffered as a consequence. Worse, Washington rumors falsely indicated that Grant and the army had assumed credit for initiating the expedition. In a war fought predominantly on the ground, army achievements vastly overshadow navy heroics. This stung high-ranking officers and political heads of the Navy Department, and they were particularly tender about the army stealing the applause for navy valor and success. In a confidential letter to Welles, Porter foolishly blasted Grant with broadside after broadside. He accused Grant of being "always willing to take the credit when anything is done, and equally ready to lay the blame of the failure on the navy." Porter reminded the secretary, "I have served with the lieutenant-general before, where I never worked so hard in my life to make a man succeed as I did for him." Grant paid little more than lip service to the navy's efforts. "He wants magnanimity, like most officers of the army, and is so avaricious as regards fame that he will never, if he can help it, do justice to our department." Grant displayed "indifference" toward the operation "until he found his reputation at stake." Meanwhile, Porter had risked his own reputation with the likes of Butler. "His course proves to me that he would sacrifice his best friend rather than let any odium fall upon Lieutenant-General Grant." Grant deserved blame, not credit.[46]

As he had done earlier in the war when he disparaged McClellan and the Army of the Potomac, Porter let emotions rule reason. The invective acted therapeutically, releasing pent-up frustration and stress from the two ventures, and in a short time Porter felt as warmly as ever toward Grant. The letter, however, came back to haunt him. In 1870, after President Grant had issued a commission promoting Vice Admiral Porter to the rank of Admiral, someone dug up the letter to influence the Senate vote of confirmation. The harsh words stung the president. Since their days at Vicksburg, Grant had counted Porter among his dearest friends. It was hard for the president to believe Porter had ever harbored such vicious thoughts toward him.

Porter reacted with honesty and speed. He immediately admitted authorship of the letter and publicly condemned himself for it. To demonstrate his true feelings, the admiral turned over his wartime journal to a newspaperman for publication. All of its passages regarding Grant indicated deep affection and admiration for the general and the man. Then he went hat in hand to the White House. Still too hurt to forgive, Grant declined to see him, so Porter wrote him a lengthy letter, explaining why he had acted and felt so foolishly after the battle for Fort Fisher and apologizing for his misdeed. Surely their deep friendship since the event, long before he had any hint that Grant would seek the presidency, indicated his genuine sentiments toward him, Porter contended. Nearly three weeks later, Porter received an invitation to visit the White House. The president and the admiral cloistered for an hour, and when they stepped from the room, all had been forgiven. Grant had accepted Porter's explanation, and the two friends put the letter behind them.

In the decades following the war, Porter retained a rich relationship with both Grant and Sherman. As president, Grant had promoted Porter and even wanted him to serve as his secretary of the navy. Grant's fondness for the man and respect for his talents never diminished. Late in life, Grant wrote, "Among naval officers I have always placed Porter in the highest rank. I believe Porter to be as great an admiral as Lord Nelson." Grant was the first of the triumvirate to pass away, succumbing to cancer in 1885.

Sherman and Porter, the ranking officers of their respective services, led the drive toward professionalism in the armed forces. Their intimate relationship, founded at the base of Haynes' Bluff, retained its strength throughout their declining years. A chemistry existed between Sherman and Porter that bonded them forever. "Lord High Admiral of the U.S. Navy" was Sherman's pet name for Porter. Sherman retired in 1884.[47]

Porter, the eldest of the trio, outworked them all. In the summer of 1890, he sustained a massive heart attack. The tough old admiral hung on for some time, but his faculties degenerated. On February 13, 1891, he expired. A naval officer to the end, Porter died in an upright, seated position.

Sherman outlived his friend Porter by a single day.

Poster of Lincoln surrounded by his key military personnel,
with Grant at the top
(National Archives)

7

"I cannot spare this man. He fights."

Lincoln, Grant, and Ultimate Success

A braham Lincoln positioned a sheet of paper on his desk. His long, bony fingers, once calloused and muscular from manual labor but now softened from years of shuffling documents, snatched a pen, plunged it into an inkwell, and began scripting. It was a personal note to Maj. Gen. Ulysses S. Grant. Despite some anxious moments, Lincoln stuck with this fellow, partly from acquiescence, partly from his deep sense of curiosity, and partly because he had no one else with whom to replace him. In any event, Lincoln had come upon the right decision. Just nine days earlier, Grant had won the most complete victory in the entire war, the capture of Vicksburg and its garrison of almost thirty thousand men.

"I do not remember that you and I ever met personally," commenced the President of the United States to Grant. "I write this now as a grateful acknowledgment for the almost inestimable service you have done the country." Lincoln explained how all along he had preferred Grant's eventual course of action—to march his troops down the west bank below Vicksburg, run gunboats and transports passed the batteries, and shuttle his army across the

191

Mississippi River. He had had little confidence in the Yazoo River schemes and the like, "except a general hope that you knew better than I." When Grant swung to the northeast after the capture of Grand Gulf, rather than reinforcing Banks at Port Hudson, "I feared it was a mistake." In candor and humility, Lincoln concluded with choice words, "I now wish to make the personal acknowledgement that you were right and I was wrong."[1]

As a man who had lived his entire life in Kentucky, Indiana, and Illinois, Lincoln grasped the vital importance of controlling the Mississippi River. During more youthful times he had poled down-river on a flatboat to New Orleans, and in the presidential election of 1860, Lincoln had swept the states that comprised the Old Northwest, nearly all of them linked economically to the "Father of Waters." With such longstanding personal and professional interest, it is not surprising that both the campaign and the general who commanded it piqued his interest.

Prior to this congratulatory letter, Lincoln and Grant had very little contact. Nonetheless Lincoln had scrutinized Grant's operations and, from a distance, Grant himself for nearly a year and a half. After Grant's victories at Forts Henry and Donelson in early 1862, promotion came, but no statement of appreciation from the president. Two weeks later, when Maj. Gen. Henry W. Halleck accused Grant of insubordination and incautiously suggested that the general had embarked on a drinking binge to the neglect of his army, the president and secretary of war demanded an investigation. Although Halleck's probe cleared Grant, the charges had conjured up old ghosts and exposed Lincoln to a most unsavory episode in Grant's past. In the aftermath of the two bloody days at Shiloh, waves of gossip surged throughout Washington's alleys and thoroughfares that alcohol had undone Grant again. To a complainant who visited the White House, the president replied, "I cannot spare this man. He fights." Through official channels, though, Lincoln wondered "whether any neglect or misconduct of General Grant or any other officer contributed to the sad casualties that befell our forces on Sunday." The rumors had predisposed the president to doubt Grant's talents and question his conduct.[2]

Strangely enough, the ascension of Grant's old accuser, Halleck, to general in chief in the summer of 1862 improved Grant's standing with authorities in Washington. Months of service with Grant had exposed Halleck to no alcohol problems or serious character flaws, and the new commanding general arrived in the nation's capital as a moderately strong Grant proponent. Halleck publicly exonerated him at Shiloh; privately, he expressed dismay over Grant's organization of forces before battle and his inability to "conduct the operations of a campaign." Yet that was before Halleck himself had ever directed an army in the field. His experiences during the advance on Corinth, Mississippi, in which Grant acted as second in command, and his elevation to commanding general of the U.S. Army evidently softened that opinion. Although he "is careless of his command," Halleck commented to Secretary of the Treasury Salmon P. Chase, he evaluated Grant "as a good general and brave in battle."[3]

Clearly, Lincoln did not share Halleck's assessment. That fall he authorized an old political friend, John A. McClernand, to raise an army of recruits in the Midwest and to lead it in a campaign against Vicksburg, which rested in Grant's Department of the Tennessee. Neither Secretary of War Stanton nor Halleck held McClernand's military aptitude in high esteem, and through some shrewd backroom maneuvering, they enticed Grant into assuming command over him. Somewhat disgruntled, Lincoln absorbed the lesson and yielded. He also kept a watchful eye on this fellow Grant.[4]

With considerable patience, Lincoln observed Grant attempt scheme after scheme to bypass the city's batteries or position his army on the high ground above Vicksburg. Untrained in military matters, Lincoln nevertheless possessed what his secretary of the navy called "a sort of intuitive sagacity," an ability to read individuals and situations and gain insight when others could sense nothing. Perhaps Grant's creativity prevented the president from acting decisively. Certainly the plan to construct a canal on the western bank across from Vicksburg intrigued the president, and Grant's other attempts exhibited an impressive degree of resourcefulness, if nothing else. Unlike other Union generals, McClellan in particular, Grant actively worked to subdue Vicksburg and refused to demand additional manpower. He took the troops and materiel at hand and labored day and night, without complaint. This refreshing change of pace comforted Lincoln. But public pressure for success weighed mightily on Lincoln's shoulders.

By mid-March 1863, Lincoln decided to bring the matter to a

head. Too many rumors and reports of Grant's drunkenness had reached the president's ears, and he and Secretary of War Stanton needed an unbiased individual to obtain firsthand information, a "spy" for the administration. They selected Charles A. Dana. A newspaperman who had sacrificed a job for his prowar stance, Dana had aided the government once before as an investigator. From Cairo and Memphis, Dana gleaned stories and pieced together details from a variety of sources, but with a journalist's passion for the truth, he insisted on visiting the army. Fortune, it seemed, smiled on Grant that day. From Grant's headquarters, Dana held extensive conversations with the army commander, Sherman, Porter, McClernand, and McPherson, among others. Everyone believed in Grant except the self-confident McClernand, whose competence and judgment Dana questioned openly in his reports. In Grant, so Dana implied, the Union had a leader of industry, imagination, and talent.[5]

The richness and volume of Dana's accounts, over seventy in three and a half months, provided Lincoln with the sort of information on Grant that he had long sought. They also coincided with Grant's lightning strikes up toward Jackson and then back on Vicksburg, fighting five battles and winning every one. The president's sentiments changed swiftly, as his doubts about this man and his ability dissolved. In late May, before the fall of Vicksburg was assured, he lauded Grant's conduct of the campaign. "Whether Gen. Grant shall or shall not consummate the capture of Vicksburg," Lincoln notified a friend, "his campaign from the beginning of this month up to the twenty-second day of it, is one of the most brilliant in the world."

About the same time, a story circulated that a delegation had visited Lincoln and demanded Grant's removal for excessive inebriation. Lincoln, so the story went, responded by querying them about the brand of whiskey the general consumed. Quizzically, they asked what that had to do with anything. Lincoln replied that if he knew, he would "send every general in the field a barrel of it." Lincoln himself roared when he heard the tale, and wished very much that he had said it.[6]

The surrender of Vicksburg on the Fourth of July in 1863 vindicated Lincoln's decision to stick with Grant in the face of protest.

His candid confession of error, written barely a week later, not only pertained to the decisive moment of the campaign; it also reflected his newfound faith in Grant as a general. Throughout much of the long and exasperating campaign, Lincoln had entertained doubts about his army commander. Grant's brilliant execution had scrubbed them away.

Over the course of the next eight months, Grant continued to win Lincoln's confidence. The president had struggled to find a commanding general who could utilize the Union's resources efficiently, campaign actively, and serve dutifully within the political parameters that the government established. By early 1864, Grant proved to be that man. His military exploits, sensitivity to political necessities, and wholehearted implementation of government policies distinguished Grant from all other Union generals in Lincoln's mind.

Just two weeks after the fall of Vicksburg, Grant reinforced his high standing by his sending trusted Assistant Adjutant General John A. Rawlins to Washington with the after-action reports and to answer any questions about the campaign. The general requested that Lincoln grant Rawlins an interview, and assured the president that "you will feel relieved when I tell you he has not a favor to ask for himself or any other living being. Even in my position," Grant admitted, "it is a great luxury to meet a gentleman who has no axe to grind, and I can appreciate that it is infinitely more so in yours." No doubt, Grant sent his emissary for a purpose, to explain in person why he had replaced Lincoln's friend McClernand at the height of the campaign. Rawlins, an earnest, unpretentious, loyal man, impressed the president and cabinet with his forthright presentation, which included a thorough and convincing justification for McClernand's removal. Here, it appeared, was a general who grasped the subtle politics of power.[7]

Unlike so many Union generals, Grant delved into the political sphere with an extraordinary light touch. Former politicians brazenly flaunted their contacts and aggravated Lincoln with their political machinations, and then either failed to attend to their duties or lacked the ability to command at high levels. Rare indeed were the political generals who devoted their energies to the business of leading men in battle and resolved to worry about their postwar political careers at the proper time, when the war had ended. Professional soldiers, such as George B. McClellan, eagerly played the political game, but did it so ineptly that they lost some of their most ardent supporters. Others, such as Halleck, had gone to Washington reluctantly and the political machine steamrollered them. And then there was Grant's dear friend Sherman, who detested politics, yet seemed to be dragged into them often because his brother was a U.S. Senator from Ohio.

By contrast, Grant possessed enough political savvy to avoid the subject and leave such matters in the hands of the Lincoln administration. Much to Lincoln's delight, Grant understood the role of a general officer in wartime and the delicate relationship between commander in chief and soldier. Military men must subordinate themselves to political authorities. "So long as I hold a commission in the Army I have no views of my own to carry out," Grant explained to Representative Elihu B. Washburne, his sponsor in Congress. "Whatever may be the orders of my superiors, and law, I will execute. No man can be efficient as a commander who sets his own notions above law and those whom he is sworn to obey." Once he donned the uniform of the U.S. Army, he abandoned his political viewpoints. To his father, he asserted, "Whatever may have been my political opinions before I have but one sentiment now. That is we have a Government, and laws and a flag and they must all be sustained." If he found a law too odious to enforce, he would resign.[8]

In dealing with the most contentious issue of the war, slavery, Lincoln found an ally in Grant. Some Union generals attempted to forge their own policies toward the South's "peculiar institution" or dragged their feet in enforcing the official position of the nation, but not Grant. Lincoln adjusted his policies regarding slavery cautiously, to meet wartime needs. Grant the soldier merely accepted those decisions and implemented them.

Ambivalence best described Grant's attitude toward slavery before the war. His wife owned slaves, and he never fought her on it. Yet on several occasions Grant exhibited sympathy toward the plight of men and women in bondage. By his own admission, he was no abolitionist and declined to call himself antislavery, even though he found little redeeming virtue in the institution.[9]

Lincoln, on the other hand, had actively opposed the extension of slavery and publicly declared his distaste for the institution. A student of the Constitution in the prewar years, Lincoln did not believe the president or Congress had the authority to challenge slavery within the states. After war erupted, Lincoln resisted outright proposals and policies that would emancipate slaves, stifling his personal preferences in favor of the nation's welfare. Always astute politically, the president walked a tightrope, attempting to win the war, retain the loyalty of slaveholding states, promote a Union party in the Confederacy, and assuage the demands of the radicals in the North. When he concluded that the Southern Unionists could offer him little effective support and that the war had reached such a pitch of intensity that a true reunion of the states without the destruction of slavery was impossible, Lincoln acted.

Despite some differences in justification, a strange parallel in attitudes toward slavery existed between Grant the military man and Lincoln the politician. The war brought them together. Uncertain about slavery in peacetime, Grant grasped rather quickly its central role in the war. In late November 1861, Grant discussed his views with his father.

> My inclination is to whip the rebellion into submission, preserving all constitutional rights. If it cannot be whipped in any other way than through a war against slavery, let it come to that legitimately. If it is necessary that slavery should fall that the Republic may continue its existence, let slavery go.

At that time Grant perceived emancipation as precipitous, but he saw the link between the war and bondage. In hauntingly similar language, Lincoln justified his approach to the dreaded institution in a letter to newspaper editor Horace Greeley.

> My paramount object in this struggle *is* to save the Union, and is *not* either to save or destroy slavery. If I could save the Union without freeing *any* slave I would do it, and if I could save it by freeing *all* the slaves I would do it; and if I could save it by freeing some and leaving others alone I would also do that. What I do about slavery and the colored race I do because I believe it helps to save the Union; and what I forbear, I forbear because I do *not* believe it would help save the Union.[10]

As administration policies pertaining to men and women of African descent changed, Grant the soldier implemented them promptly and efficiently. Direct orders, he insisted, must be obeyed.

"I do not believe even in the discussion of the propriety of laws and official orders by the army. One enemy at a time is enough and when he is subdued it will be time enough to settle personal differences." Each step in the process of emancipation placed considerable burdens on generals in the field. In the First Confiscation Act, endorsed by Lincoln in August 1861, the government authorized the military to seize slaves employed on Confederate military projects as "contraband of war." Later, the Lincoln administration specified that officers should not employ their troops in returning runaway slaves. The Second Confiscation Act, signed into law in July 1862, authorized military forces to take all property of rebels, including slaves. Over the next two months, Lincoln initiated the controversial policies of creating black regiments and emancipating the slaves. Grant complied with alacrity.[11]

For Lincoln, the Emancipation Proclamation was the proper moral decision, made legal by his powers in wartime as commander in chief of the armed forces. The Confederate people used slaves to grow food and produce materiel that aided their armies. In the conduct of war, the commander in chief had the power to authorize the seizure of anything that directly assisted the Rebel war effort. Slaves certainly did.

Grant, deceptively perceptive, realized that he need not immerse himself in the debate over the constitutionality of Lincoln's proclamation. Politicians must sort out the delicate interrelationship of politics, society, and the military, not him. His superior had declared it a war measure. As a commander in the field, he would employ that tool to help bring this war to a speedy conclusion. He had seen firsthand how slavery benefited Confederate soldiers, and he had no doubt that its destruction would hurt the Confederacy and aid the Union. Grant said so to Dana, who passed on the general's sentiments to the president.[12]

Even more controversial within the army was black enlistment. Recruitment of whites had slowed to a trickle, and Lincoln, in an effort to beef up troop strength, tapped his most valuable untried resource, black manpower. Again, Grant supported the president's policies. During the Vicksburg Campaign, Lincoln sent Adjutant General Lorenzo Thomas to the Mississippi River Valley to encourage the organization and recruitment of black regiments. Grant cooperated in the endeavor. After the fall of Vicksburg, Lincoln revived the issue, emphasizing to Grant that "it works doubly—weakening the enemy and strengthening us." The general took up the cudgels on behalf of black military service. "I have given the subject of arming the negro my heartiest support," he proclaimed to Lincoln. "This, with the emancipation of the negro, is the heavyest blow yet given the Confederacy." Grant pledged his full support for Thomas's work. "I would do this," he explained further, "whether the arming of the negro seemed to me a wise policy or not, because it is an order that I am bound to obey and do not feel that in my position I have a right to question any policy of the Government." In conclusion, though, Grant professed his honest opinion, that "by arming the negro we have added a powerful ally. They will make good soldiers and taking them from the enemy weaken him in the same proportion they strengthen us."[13]

Several weeks after Grant articulated his position on emancipation and black recruitment, the Union Army of the Cumberland suffered a rout at Chickamauga. By mid-October, the War Department created the Military Division of the Mississippi, uniting all commands west of the Appalachian Mountains, and placed Grant in charge. It then ordered Grant to Chattanooga, to supervise relief of the beleaguered forces there.

As he had done throughout the war, Grant took charge of the situation. He replaced the commander of the Army of the Cumberland with another of its officers, Maj. Gen. George H. Thomas, brought Sherman with reinforcements from the Army of the Tennessee, and opened a supply line. Once he had accumulated enough manpower, Grant unleashed a vicious assault. Troops from the Army of the Potomac rolled up the left flank, Sherman struck the Rebel right and Thomas's men, bent on retrieving their reputation, stormed the works on Missionary Ridge, shattering the Rebel line. "The specticle was grand beyond anything that has been, or is likely to be, on this Continent," Grant gloated to his patron Elihu Washburne. "It is the first battle field I have ever seen where a plan could be followed and from one place the whole field be within one view." Pursuit carried the Federals into northern Georgia. Sherman then completed the campaign by driving northeast to Knoxville to free Burnside's besieged command. In little more than one month, Grant had restored Union fortunes in central and eastern Tennessee. Again, Lincoln proffered his "profoundest gratitude" for the success.[14]

Instead of enjoying his laurels, Grant proposed an active winter campaign season to sustain the initiative. Deep mud in Tennessee and northern Georgia would preclude any effective, large-scale operations there by either side. In the spring, once the roads dried, the Army of the Cumberland should resume its advance. As his next target, Grant eyed Mobile. Since the fall of Vicksburg, he had lobbied authorities in Washington for a landing at Pascagoula, Mississippi, and an overland march on the major Alabama port city. The experiment of cutting loose completely from a supply base and drawing essentials from the land had proven so successful that Grant felt sure he and Sherman could employ their raiding strategy on lengthy campaigns. That summer, the Lincoln administration preferred an invasion of Texas, to discourage any French incursions in territory that Lincoln claimed as United States domain.[15]

This time, Grant sent Charles A. Dana to present his views to the administration, while he forwarded a direct communication to Halleck. From New Orleans and Pascagoula, he would march on Mobile with a large force in January 1864. If the Confederates refused to surrender, Grant proposed to leave a portion to hold the Mobile garrison tightly, and with the bulk of his command launch a massive raid into Alabama and Georgia. Meanwhile, the army near Chattanooga would drive toward Atlanta. The campaign would slice off a chunk of the Confederacy stretching from Chattanooga to Mobile, with Atlanta and Montgomery, Alabama, as vital intermediate points. Unless Lee evacuated Virginia and transported the Army of Northern Virginia south to oppose him, "the enemy have not got army enough to resist the army I can take."[16]

After conversations in Washington, Lincoln, Stanton, and Halleck responded faintheartedly. Before undertaking the bold venture against Mobile, the trio preferred that Grant remove the Confederates from East Tennessee, stifle some guerrilla unrest in Mississippi and West Tennessee, drive the Rebel army in northern Georgia deeper into the interior, and assist Banks in expanding his control of Louisiana. The administration seemed bent on a trivial employment of manpower and resources, rather than a bold effort to follow up the success around Chattanooga. For the second time in less than six months, the campaign for Mobile never got off the planning table.[17]

As Grant's next major expedition, the Lincoln administration countered with a proposed invasion of Texas. The president was worried about Napoleon III's occupation of Mexico, and he sought a Union presence in Texas to prevent French penetration there. The problem was that an expedition into Texas would not diminish Rebel power materially, which should have been the administration's paramount concern. A raid that disrupted parts of Mississippi, Alabama, and Georgia, and captured Mobile, one of the Confederacy's most prized ports, would have inflicted much more serious damage to the Confederate war effort. Nevertheless, Halleck refused to challenge the president on the idea, precisely why Lincoln had brought a man of his expertise to Washington originally. "The President so ordered, for reasons satisfactory to himself and his cabinet," the general in chief explained unconvincingly to Grant, "and it was, therefore, unnecessary for us to inquire whether or not the troops could have been employed elsewhere with greater military advantage." There was no fight left in Halleck. Had someone like Grant, whose opinion now carried weight with the president, pointed out that if they did not defeat the Confederacy, it would matter not a whit whether the French crossed into Texas, Lincoln might have adjusted his priorities. But Grant, as subordinate officer with no direct access to the commander in chief, dutifully accepted the decision of his superiors.[18]

As the winter cold thawed into spring, Grant had achieved limited results. Sherman directed a march on Meridian, Mississippi, which demonstrated the efficacy of the raiding strategy on a smaller scale; otherwise, Grant and the Federals did not conduct a major expedition that winter.

At Halleck's request, Grant submitted another plan in mid-January 1864, this one focusing on the Eastern Theater. As an alternative to the bloodbath of Virginia, Grant suggested a massive raid, some 60,000 troops, from Suffolk, Virginia, into North Carolina. The army would destroy the Weldon Railroad, one of Lee's principal means of supply, and drive on to Raleigh, wrecking anything of military value, consuming foodstuffs and forage, confiscating slaves, and wholly disrupting life in the region. This campaign most likely would compel Lee to evacuate Virginia due to supply problems, and the chaos in North Carolina would lead to massive defections and desertions in the state. From Raleigh, the army had a viable escape route and supply base at New Bern, or it could attack Wilmington, still an open port, from the rear.[19]

Halleck dismissed the scheme before he even presented it to the president. In a clouded response that was uncharacteristic of the scholarly general in chief, Halleck insisted that he had not designated Richmond the primary target for the Army of the Potomac; rather, "that point is Lee's army. I have never supposed Richmond could be taken till Lee's army was defeated or driven away." Citing Napoleon Bonaparte as his source of authority, Halleck argued that taking the direct overland route from Washington toward Richmond and targeting the Confederate Army of Northern Virginia offered the best prospects for success. Presently, he doubted that the Union could generate a force of 60,000, which in any case might not be strong enough to accomplish the mission. "Our main efforts in the next campaign should unquestionably be made against the armies of Lee and Johnston," he persisted.[20]

Neither Lincoln nor Stanton nor Halleck seemed to comprehend the merits of Grant's proposals. Both the North Carolina and Mobile plans were so contrary to the traditional notions of warfare that had emerged from the Napoleonic era, so rooted in actual experiences in the Mississippi River Valley, that the leadership in Washington had no basis from which to evaluate their strengths and weaknesses. Other than the idea of fighting all year long, they found little redeeming value in the concept of a raiding strategy.[21]

Lincoln, the Black Hawk War veteran, had undergone a rude introduction to military affairs as president. The aged Winfield Scott had coached him a bit, as did another old soldier, Ethan Allen Hitchcock. With his gifted intellect, Lincoln devoured military books from the Library of Congress. And the president certainly learned some hard lessons from his experiences with McClellan. Since then, Halleck had taught him much through explanations, and careful perusal and contemplation of message traffic at the telegraph office rounded out his knowledge.

To expect Lincoln to grasp this bold approach to the war without extensive explanations of its merits, though, was asking too much of the man. It had taken the collaborative efforts of Grant and Sherman months and months of deep thought and conversation, as well as the invaluable experience of wrestling day to day with the problem, before they arrived at a viable solution. Lincoln, juggling dozens of distinct issues simultaneously, could allocate no time for such deep reflection, nor did he possess a corpus of experience in military affairs to guide him.

Secretary of War Stanton, like Lincoln, was a lawyer by profession. Prior to heading the War Department, he had no military experience. An excellent administrator with an abrasive personality, he could galvanize the war effort by sheer force of character, driving the military bureaucracy to new heights of efficiency through his mastery of detail. But Stanton exhibited no particular flair for military strategy or operations and his duties, which immersed him in the day-to-day affairs of the War Department, provided scant time to grapple with these issues.[22]

Halleck, nicknamed "Old Brains" for his cerebral ways, had comparatively little actual campaign experience. His knowledge derived primarily from scholarship, and though deep, it was conventional. Political infighting and the stress of the job as general in chief had worn Halleck to a frazzle. As Lincoln explained to his private secretary, he had served the president well until the defeat at Second Manassas, "when he broke down—nerve and pluck all gone—and he has ever since evaded all responsibility." Lincoln's disappointment clearly in evidence, he overstated the case when he described Halleck's role as "little more since that than a first-rate clerk." Unwilling and unable to battle the politicians, the generals, and the public simultaneously, Halleck lacked the stamina to fight Lincoln and Stanton, even if he believed in Grant's plans.[23]

Accustomed as the three were to military incompetence or indecisiveness, they intruded into martial affairs, sometimes counterproductively. At the critical moment of the Vicksburg Campaign, for example, Lincoln and Welles ordered Porter to patrol the Mississippi River between Vicksburg and Port Hudson, rather than cooperate with Grant. In the end, Grant and Porter circumvented the impeding directive, but it caused them excessive work and resulted in the loss of valuable equipment when they had to run the Vicksburg batteries twice instead of once. At other times the top leadership forced narrow approaches and misguided priorities on field commanders. With McClellan and a host of others who proved incapable of acting effectively, it made good sense to intervene at the necessary moment. But Grant and Sherman were no ordinary generals. And even after they rose to positions of great power, it took Lincoln, Stanton, and Halleck time to believe in them and their methods of warfare.[24]

Employing the fundamental principles of speed, surprise, maneuverability, economy of force, and concentration of power at the decisive point, the raiding strategy struck deep into the vulnerable enemy rear. It damaged Southern will to resist and sapped the strength of the principal Rebel armies indirectly, so that when Federals engaged them in major operations, the Rebel forces entered combat from a position of weakness. By demolishing the railroads, Grant and Sherman prevented valuable supplies from reaching Confederate troops, worsening the plight of the men, promoting desertion, and limiting the ability of Rebel armies to operate effectively. It eschewed the occupation of territory, which squandered the might of an army by siphoning off valuable manpower. "A large army," Sherman asserted, "is wasted in detachments." Without garrisons and supply lines, Federals removed primary targets from Rebel cavalrymen and guerrillas. As the raiding force penetrated a region, it dismantled railroads, burned bridges, destroyed any manufacturing facilities, consumed food, confiscated livestock, liberated slaves, terrorized civilians by the mere presence of the enemy, and wholly disrupted the lives of Confederate citizens. In turn, the raiding strategy demoralized the Rebel troops, who could not shield the folks at home from Yankee ravages, and spurred desertion, as soldiers abandoned the army to look after the needs of loved ones.[25]

Long suffering with Union commanders who sought to occupy territory as opposed to defeating the Confederate armies, Lincoln, Stanton, and Halleck had difficulty understanding the merits of the raiding strategy. Instead of bearing down on enemy forces and fighting to destroy them, Grant and Sherman urged a strategy that intentionally avoided them. But they also refused to occupy portions of the Confederate States that fell to their armies. Grant and Sherman concentrated on wrecking the Confederate logistical base and disrupting the lives of Confederates who resided along their swath.[26]

Lincoln and his key advisors confused "ways" with "ends" in their strategic formulation. Defeat the Confederate armies, they believed, and you defeat the Confederacy. By comparison, Grant and Sherman argued that the "end," or what the Union hoped to accomplish by this war, was to compel the secessionists to return peacefully into the Union. Whipping the Rebel armies was only part of the equation; the Federals had to make war on the Southern people, to convince them that life within the Union far exceeded the quality of existence outside it. The Union needed to crush the secessionist spirit from the Southerners. Thus, the raiding strategy operated well in conjunction with a more traditional strategy that sought the destruction of Confederate armies. As Sherman had attempted to explain to Halleck, "We are not only fighting hostile armies, but a hostile people, and must make old and young, rich and poor, feel the hard hand of war, as well as their organized armies."[27]

Despite difficulty winning approval for his schemes, or convincing the Union hierarchy of the merits of raiding, Grant's star was in the ascendancy. Rumored bouts with alcohol and a reputation for sloppy supervision aside, Grant had achieved a level of success that no one in the Union Army could approach. He did so, moreover, with the resources at hand. Unlike McClellan and sundry other commanders, Grant functioned on a fundamental assumption that if the president had more men for his army, he would give them. No doubt, Lincoln needed this man to direct the war effort.

But Lincoln, the consummate political being, wanted assurances that Grant did not have his eye on the highest post in the land. From George Washington to Zachary Taylor, military success had long been a vehicle for the presidency. During McClellan's tenure as commanding general, he never discouraged talk of his candidacy and explicitly distanced himself from administration policies. The presidential bug bit him in 1864, and he actually ran as Lincoln's opponent on the Democratic ticket. Maj. Gen. Joseph Hooker, one-time commander of the Army of the Potomac, called for a dictatorship during the war. Lincoln, with his wonderful sense of humor, made light of the remark, encouraging the general to win a victory and he would risk the dictatorship. Still, the 1864 presidential election was pivotal in the nation's history. And while Lincoln could chide Hooker for his undemocratic opinions, he knew that only re-election offered political survival. Of all the personages in the North, the nation's newest hero, Grant, posed the greatest threat to a second term for Lincoln. After the fall of Vicksburg, and even more so after the victory at Chattanooga, Democrats and Republicans alike wondered about Grant's political desires and affiliation.

Grant had already passed two litmus tests for Lincoln: one on his military skills and another on his willingness to implement controversial policies. On the third one, his political aspirations, Grant scored brilliantly. In December 1863, in response to an inquiry from a Democratic Central Committee member, Grant declared, "Nothing likely to happen would pain me so much as to see my name used in connection with a political office." He much preferred to remain in uniform, "supporting whatever Administration may be in power, in their endeavor to suppress the rebellion and maintain National unity." One month later, Rawlins reiterated to Elihu Washburne that Grant "is unambitious for the honor." Lincoln had finally found his general.[28]

That winter, Grant's congressional friend Washburne sponsored a bill to revive the position of lieutenant general, with Grant as the obvious choice to assume the rank. Once Lincoln learned of Grant's lack of interest in challenging the incumbent president, he endorsed the legislation, and it sailed through Congress in late February. By early March, Grant arrived in Washington with his fourteen-year-old son in tow to assume his new post as lieutenant general, commanding all Union armies. At the Willard Hotel, he registered unpretentiously as "U.S. Grant and son, Galena, Ill." During dinner, crowds applauded him. Later that night, he attended the president's weekly reception, sans progeny. His entry caused quite a stir. Lincoln, his six-feet-four-inch frame projecting well above the crowd, spotted Grant and approached him. "Why, here is General Grant! Well, this is a great pleasure," pumping the general's hand as he spoke. Grant appeared uncomfortable in such a gathering, but Lincoln's warmth made him feel more at ease. Soon Secretary of State William Seward whisked Grant away to introduce him to Lincoln's wife and then into the East Room, where the crowd cheered and forced the diminutive Grant to stand on a piece of furniture so that all could view him. The next day, Lincoln presented Grant with his commission as lieutenant general.[29]

Grant had intended to stay in Washington briefly, just long enough to prepare campaign plans for the spring and clear up various command issues. Sherman implored him to return west for the offensive season, and he tended to agree with his friend. He could accomplish more in the field than in the political snake pit of Washington. For proof of its dangers, Grant need look no further than Halleck.

Within a few days, though, he realized that was impossible. Authorities in Washington expected him to remain in the East, where Lee had stymied the Army of the Potomac for three years. Public and political opinion demanded that he decisively defeat Lee's forces in Virginia. In a way, that dogged Rebel army had come to symbolize the secession movement, and only after Grant had crushed it could reunion become a reality. Yet he could not survive in that political minefield. Washington offered too many distractions and demanded too many obligations for him to devote the energy required to win the war.

In the end, Grant jerry-rigged a solution. He would remain in the East, but not in Washington. Instead, he planned to travel with the Army of the Potomac, keeping an eye on its operations while leaving its command in the hands of Maj. Gen. George G. Meade. With telegraphic communications, Grant could keep abreast of military news throughout the nation readily. Sherman assumed stewardship of the Military Division of the Mississippi, and McPherson took charge of the Department and Army of the Tennessee. Grant elected to retain Halleck, giving him the title of chief of staff, although he hardly functioned as one. Commanders in the field communicated to Halleck, who culled their messages and summarized important information for Grant. Sometimes Halleck offered advice; at other times he relayed Grant's decisions or new government policies; and occasionally he formulated his own orders. Halleck's amorphous position bore little resemblance to the modern chief of staff; if anything, his duties corresponded to a chief of staff on a general's staff. Perhaps unsound systemically, Grant's command structure worked well in most instances because it best utilized the abilities of the individuals.[30]

The campaign plan for 1864, which Grant had devised with the able assistance of Sherman, called for all parts to work as a whole and concentrate on a common center. He ordered Banks to extricate himself from Texas, strip most of the manpower from the Mississippi River Valley, and launch a campaign against Mobile. Sherman, with the Armies of the Cumberland, Ohio, and Tennessee, received general instructions to advance on the Confederate Army of Tennessee. While Meade moved against Lee's Army, Grant directed Butler's columns to march on Richmond from the south side of the James River and another Federal command in the Shenandoah Valley to push southward.[31]

Grant sought to mount simultaneous advances and to apply continual pressure in order to prevent the Confederates from shifting reinforcements back and forth. As Sherman explained to Banks in late April, "we must all soon pitch in, and for weal or woe battles must ensue more bloody than any which have characterized this war." The lieutenant general wanted everyone to act boldly and energetically. No doubt in the back of Grant's mind, and in the forefront of Lincoln's, lay the presidential contest of 1864.[32]

Although his plans for the spring offensive called for unified action in conventional advances, Grant did not abandon the underlying precepts of the raiding strategy. Once Sherman broke up Joseph E. Johnston's army, both Grant and Sherman hoped that he could penetrate into the interior, destroying the Confederate war resources in a massive raid. Grant, moreover, had the secretary of war issue express orders to all Union commanders to "take proper measures to supply, as far as may be possible, the want of their troops in animals and provisions from the territory through which military operations are conducted." Officers were to provide receipts to civilians for confiscated property. "Special care will be taken to remove horses, mules, live-stock, and all means of transportation from hostile districts infested or liable to be infested by guerrilla bands of rebels." War against the resources of the Confederacy had become the official policy of the U.S. Army.[33]

The plan absolutely delighted Lincoln. Since early 1862, he too had urged simultaneous advances. With flawless logic, Lincoln determined that continuous pressure along every front enabled the Union to employ its numerical superiority best and to limit the Confederate advantage of interior lines of communication and transportation. By being pressured everywhere, the weak Confederate forces inevitably must lose some important positions. Much to the president's chagrin, none of his generals-in-chief could coordinate the various armies well enough to execute the concept.

Grant took the Lincoln program one step beyond that by requiring his designated defenders to advance into Confederate territory as well. Union forces need not protect railroads and bridges in the North by remaining at those sites; in many instances, they could shield them just as well by advancing onto Rebel soil. In his colloquial way, Lincoln honed in on the plan's fundamental strength when he declared to Grant, "Those not skinning can hold a leg."[34]

A few days before the campaign began, Lincoln lauded Grant for the way he had taken charge of the war effort. Expressing his "entire satisfaction with what you have done up to this time," Lincoln neither knew nor cared to learn all the details. "You are vigilant and self-reliant; and, pleased with this, I wish not to obtrude any constraints or restraints upon you." He concluded with some words of support, offering, "If there is anything wanting which is within my power to give, do not fail to let me know." In the hands of others, this blank check could have come back to haunt Lincoln. But the president understood his general in chief. Grant would only call on him when he truly needed assistance.[35]

Grant, in reply, thanked the president for his recent help and assured him that the government had always supported his military endeavors. Since his elevation to lieutenant general, "I have been astonished at the readiness with which every thin[g] asked for has been yielded without even an explaination being asked." In stunning contrast to McClellan and numerous others, Grant declared: "Should my success be less than I desire, and expect, the least I can say is, the fault is not with you." Lincoln, no doubt, was impressed. In a refreshing change of pace, here was a general who assumed full responsibility for the outcome of his campaign.[36]

Across the Rapidan River, Grant plunged the massive Army of the Potomac into the dense woods and thickets called the Wilderness. Lee rocked the Union army with a surprise attack. In times past, Federals had retreated after such a blow. Under Grant's supervision, the army recoiled, then slipped around the left flank for the next encounter. Lincoln approved. "How near we have been to this thing before and failed," the president commented to his private secretary.

"I believe if any other general had been at the head of that army it would have been on this side of the Rapidan. It is the dogged pertinacity of Grant that wins."[37]

Grant continued to press Lee's army, slamming his forces against Rebel positions whenever he detected weakness. Casualties mounted in staggering numbers, as Lee parried blow after blow. But the Confederate master could not regain the initiative he had lost after the Wilderness. Grant directed Meade to retain close contact with the Army of Northern Virginia at all times, to prevent Lee's famed sweeping flank attacks. Each time Lee blocked Grant's path, the Union general shifted to the southeast, where he could draw supplies from the water and bring his army closer to the forces of Benjamin Butler, in whom Grant lacked confidence. The lieutenant general hoped to interpose his army between Lee and Richmond and compel the Confederate commander to attack him. But in test after test, Lee's men beat Grant to the decisive point.

Then, in mid-June, Grant outfoxed Lee. He pulled back his troops, slipped across the James River undetected, and struck for Petersburg, a vital railroad junction some thirty miles south of Richmond. Lincoln, who scrutinized military message traffic as a miser pores over money, grasped the plan's merits. "I begin to see it," he wired Grant. "You will succeed. God bless you all." Lincoln divined wrong. A brilliant defense by Confederate General P. G. T. Beauregard's troops, and the unresponsiveness of the Federal attackers, saved the city. Both armies fortified their positions and settled into trenches.

With inferior manpower and inadequate resources, Lee realized that if the siege continued, eventually he would lose Richmond and much of his army. Only through maneuver could he nullify the Union strength. From his main army Lee detached Lt. Gen. Jubal Early to halt a Union advance on Lynchburg. Early accomplished this successfully, and Lee followed up the victory by directing Early to march northward. Harking back to Jackson's achievements in the Shenandoah Valley in 1862, Lee hoped to threaten the Yankee capital and perhaps draw sufficient resources from Grant to permit the Confederates to assume the initiative once more.

Lee had chosen his mark well. During the Union advance southward, the Army of the Potomac covered Washington, and most of the capital's garrison became superfluous. To replace his campaign losses, Grant commandeered all of its field-ready troops, leaving only a meager contingent of invalids to occupy the defenses. Thus, when he shifted below Petersburg, Grant invited a Rebel advance on the Union capital. Early's movement caused such a stir among Washington authorities that Grant sent back the Sixth Corps, a division of the Nineteenth Corps, and 3,000 dismounted cavalry. At the same time, Meade studied how long it would take his army to remove all heavy guns from around Petersburg in the event of a Union retreat.[38]

While the Confederate raid flustered numerous military and civilian officials, Lincoln remained relatively calm; he had been through much worse than this. The president, at the core offensive minded, viewed the crisis as an opportunity, not a disaster. Skillful military leadership, he insisted, could bag Early's entire invasion force.

Instead, confusion reigned supreme. Four separate military departments, the arrival of reinforcements, intervention by Halleck and Stanton—both men worried more about saving Washington than about defeating Early—and temporary telegraphic delays between Grant and the War Department muddled the Union response. By mid-July, Early's command stood just outside the city as fresh Yankee troops hastily manned the works at Fort Stevens.

The implacable Union lieutenant general refused to be stampeded as were the personnel in Washington. Although he may have underestimated the Federal strength and the caliber of soldiers in the capital fortifications, he did not undervalue the quality of the city's defensive works. Grant, like Lincoln, viewed Early's raid in offensive terms. Along with reinforcements, he responded to the crisis by advising Halleck to position Union forces south of Early's command and "follow him up sharply." He even offered to return to Washington and take charge personally, if Lincoln wanted him to do so.

The president did. "Now, what I think is that you should provide to retain your hold where you are, certainly, and bring the rest with you personally, and make a vigorous effort to destroy the enemy's force in this vicinity," Lincoln counselled Grant. "I think there is really a fair chance to do this if the movement is prompt." The president, always diplomatic, closed with the words, "This is what I think, upon your suggestion, and is not an order." The president wanted Grant to take charge of the situation.[39]

Grant mulled over the matter and elected to remain at his City Point, Virginia, headquarters. "I think, on reflection, it would have a bad effect for me to leave here," he explained to the president. All three Union field commanders there, Major Generals David D. Hunter, E. O. C. Ord, and Horatio Wright, impressed Grant, and the commanding general possessed "great faith that the enemy will never be able to get back with much of his force." Lincoln replied that Grant's plan was "very satisfactory." Nonetheless, Early eluded them, as Wright and Hunter closed too hesitantly. Lincoln, according to his secretary, was "evidently disgusted," complaining sarcastically that Union commander Wright had pursued lazily "for fear he might come across the rebels & catch some of them."[40]

Early's raid forced Grant to choose between top priorities. Since the Confederate general had escaped with his command intact, Grant felt pressure to keep the Sixth Corps near the nation's capital. He could not risk the fall of Washington or even its partial occupation for a second time. With the presidential election just four months away, the political repercussions of another invasion or the capture of Washington would be enormous. Tugging him in the other direction was Lee's army, which loomed larger and larger in his mind. For three and a half months, Grant had failed to damage it significantly. As Early advanced toward Washington, Grant had almost completed preparations for an attack on the Weldon Railroad, one of Lee's primary supply lines. Its capture and destruction could inflict serious damage to the Confederate war effort in Virginia. In Grant's mind, those troops he had transferred north might provide the margin for success in the operation, and he was sorely tempted to recall them.

The president, for his part, refused to intervene. Since Lincoln's selection of Grant, the lieutenant general had done all the right things to gain his confidence. By midsummer, the president had linked his political fortunes to Grant's military performance. Grant alone, so Lincoln insisted, could judge whether to reinforce the Army of the Potomac or break up Early's Corps. In a classic case of a military dilemma with massive political repercussions, Lincoln, wholly committed to victory on the battlefield and confident in his general's decision-making capacity, yielded to him as the principal martial authority. This signified tremendous faith in his general. After extensive ruminations, Grant elected not to recall the Sixth Corps. Those soldiers could accomplish just as much by striking at Early, driving him from the Shenandoah Valley, and wrecking the railroad from Charlottesville to Gordonsville, Grant concluded.[41]

All the troops in the Washington area, however, would achieve little without a more effective command structure. Early's raid exploited a complex arrangement of small departments and pinpointed a defect in Grant's command organization, with Chief of Staff Halleck in Washington and him in the field. Operations around the nation's capital lacked effective coordination and direction in Grant's absence. Lincoln had appointed Grant lieutenant general because he had demonstrated an ability to assume responsibility and gain victories. In this case, no one on the scene had taken charge, and Grant was too distant to assume complete control.

As a solution, Grant proposed the reduction of three departments into districts and their merger into a larger department with a single head. He recommended Maj. Gen. William B. Franklin, a former corps commander, for the assignment. The War Department stalled. Stanton exhibited little interest in the reorganization, and Grant's choice for the position was unacceptable. Earlier in the war, Franklin had fallen from grace for his dilatory ways.

Halleck apparently favored Maj. Gen. C. C. Augur, head of the Department of Washington, whom he described as "capable and efficient." Disturbed by the denuding of Washington's defenses and upset over the intrigues of Grant's staff against himself, Halleck announced to the lieutenant general that he had "no good reason for removing or superseding" Augur. In effect, if Grant wanted Augur removed, he would have to order it himself. Whether it was the man himself or because he was Halleck's choice, Augur would not do for Grant.[42]

The lieutenant general had reached an impasse with Stanton and Halleck, and he immediately appealed to Lincoln. His trusted chief of staff, John Rawlins, carried a letter and spoke on Grant's behalf, explaining the entire situation and proposing the creation of a "Military Division," with George G. Meade, commander of the Army of the Potomac, as its head. "With Meade in command of such a division," Grant's letter affirmed, "I would have every confidence that all the troops within the military division would be used to the very best advantage from a personal examination of the ground, and [he] would adopt means of getting the earliest information of any advance of the enemy, and would prepare to meet it." Rather than act immediately, Lincoln preferred to wait for a face-to-face meeting with Grant.[43]

But before the two could gather, Early's Corps stirred up trouble. After carrying off his booty to a more secure location, Early struck camp and advanced north through the Valley. Grant, too distant to direct specific courses of action, exhorted authorities in Washington to coordinate the response while he loaded the remainder of the Nineteenth Corps on transports to reinforce them. Lincoln attempted to fill the power vacuum by ordering Halleck to assume command of all forces in the four departments—Susquehanna, Washington, West Virginia, and Middle. "You will be expected to take all military measures necessary for defense against any attack of the enemy and for his capture and destruction," the president instructed Halleck through the secretary of war.[44]

By the time Lincoln met Grant at Fort Monroe, Early's forces had crossed the Potomac River and penetrated into southern Pennsylvania, torching Chambersburg and occupying Hancock, Maryland. The situation required prompt action. Convening for just a few hours, the commander in chief and his general in chief evidently ruled out Halleck and Meade to head the unified forces against Early. The emergency warranted a field commander, not someone who would direct operations from Washington. Halleck's current role as chief of staff, however distasteful to him personally, was too vital for Grant to sacrifice for such an assignment. He also lacked the aggressive qualities that Grant sought. Lincoln most likely opposed Meade's selection, recalling his failure to pursue Lee after Gettysburg. A violent temper that flared all too often may have convinced Grant, too, that Meade lacked the proper attributes for the job. What Lincoln and Grant needed was a hard-driving commander who would fight relentlessly and seek the destruction not only of Early's troops but of the resources of the Valley as well. It was a perfect job for the feisty cavalry commander, Maj. Gen. Philip Sheridan.

"I am sending General Sheridan for temporary duty whilst the enemy is being expelled from the border," Grant notified Halleck. "Unless General Hunter is in the field personally, I want Sheridan put in command of all the troops in the field, with instructions to put himself south of the enemy and follow him to the death." Along with Sheridan, Grant transported enough cavalry from the Army of the Potomac to match the strength of Early's horsemen.[45]

Despite Grant's specific instructions, Federal efforts to block Early's escape failed to gel. The power and authority that Grant intended to bestow on Sheridan never seemed to materialize; the wheels in the upper echelons of the War Department did not turn rapidly in Sheridan's favor. Secretary of War Stanton believed the tough little cavalryman with the flowing black mustache and coal eyes lacked the maturity to direct such a campaign. He refused to lift a finger for Sheridan. Since Hunter commanded in the field, he retained control of the operation, and the aggressive Sheridan lapsed to a position as head of the cavalry force. Halleck thought little of Hunter but refused to intervene on Sheridan's behalf. This was Grant's decision to make, not his, the chief of staff contended.[46]

For two days Lincoln observed from the sidelines as the War Department gears grounded. Yet nothing emerged. Almost two years ago, Stanton and Halleck had outmaneuvered Lincoln to ensure that Grant, not McClernand, commanded the Vicksburg expedition. The president had ordered McClernand's assignment, but never followed up to assure compliance. In retrospect, Stanton and Halleck clearly circumvented Lincoln's will for the best interest of the nation. Nonetheless, Lincoln carefully stowed away the lesson. Now, the sage president coached his commanding general, offering to share this hard-won knowledge. To Grant, he telegraphed that the orders placing Sheridan south of Early with instructions to pursue the Confederates until his columns destroyed them "is exactly right as to how our forces should move." He then warned Grant that directives and implementation were two distinct matters. "Please look over the dispatches you may have received from here even since you made that order, and discover, if you can, that there is any idea in the head of any one here of 'putting our army south of the enemy,' or of 'following him to the death' in any direction." With words of wisdom, earned through nearly four years of political bat-

tles in Washington, Lincoln counseled, "I repeat to you it will neither be done nor attempted, unless you watch it every day and hour
and force it." Two hours after receiving Lincoln's advice, Grant
boarded a steamer headed north. At Monocacy, Virginia, he consulted with Hunter, who requested that Grant replace him. Sheridan
finally assumed command.[47]

Grant awarded his subordinate extensive powers to remove
incompetent or uncooperative officers, regardless of rank. This time,
the lieutenant general demanded results. "What we want is prompt
and active movements after the enemy," he explained.[48] And
Sheridan fulfilled Grant's expectations. By the time he assumed
command, Early and his band of raiders had slipped back across the
Potomac River into Virginia. Grant kept Sheridan on a short leash
for five weeks, assuming that Early and his reinforced corps outnumbered the Federals. When Lee recalled a portion of the command, Grant, in person at Sheridan's headquarters, endorsed the
plan of action. At Winchester, in mid-September, Sheridan delivered
a powerful blow, followed up by the rout of Early's depleted ranks at
Fisher's Hill. Mission accomplished, Sheridan began to withdraw
his army, gobbling up food and livestock and torching barns and
mills as he marched. A month earlier, Grant had urged him to
destroy all war resources, insisting "If the war is to last another year,
we want the Shenandoah Valley to remain a barren wasteland." So
effective were Sheridan's troops at stripping the countryside of valuable provender that soldiers joked of crows flying over the Valley
toting haversacks.[49]

But the report of the demise of Early's Corps was premature.
Reinforcements from Lee enabled the Confederate general to attack
once more, in mid-October, at Cedar Creek. In the morning hours,
Early whipped the Federals, but by afternoon the tide turned.
Sheridan, absent from the command that morning, rallied his troops,
and in the late afternoon, he struck with fury. The Confederate line
crumbled. Not only did Sheridan reverse the day's fortunes, he captured much of Early's artillery and wagon train. Grant's confidence
in Sheridan, and Lincoln's in Grant, had paid great dividends during
the closing weeks of the presidential campaign. Coupled with the
fall of Atlanta to Sherman in September, the triumph over Early in
the Valley secured Lincoln's re-election.

Over the course of his eight months as lieutenant general, Grant's relationship with Lincoln blossomed. Affable, witty, and always willing to please, Lincoln was a very likable individual who readily won over Grant, as he did so many others. The president, so Grant reasoned, "gained influence over men by making them feel that it was a pleasure to serve him." Grant, by nature introverted, bore an agreeable countenance and possessed a deceptively clever mind and a listener's ear that appealed to the gregarious Lincoln. Yet at the heart of their association rested an understanding and respect by each for the position and responsibility of the other. Unlike many Civil War generals, Grant comprehended fully his rank and authority within the command structure. He worked for the commander in chief. To any of Lincoln's requests, demands, or inquiries, Grant responded promptly and properly. Nor did he ever underestimate Lincoln or undervalue his talents. For his part, Lincoln admired the general and his abilities. He trusted Grant to act in the best interests of the nation.[50]

Thus, they complemented one another well, Grant the skilled soldier and Lincoln the savvy politician. Success for one spelled success for the other. If Lincoln failed at the polls, it could mean doom for Grant as a military man. By the same tune, Grant's achievements on the battlefield would translate directly into ballots for Lincoln. The two men had hitched their horses to one another's wagons. They had faith in each other, which, in turn, bred security and confidence in their relationship. Lincoln and Grant could always approach one another candidly, because an honest disagreement would never founder the rich alliance they had forged. The president and the commanding general had learned to rely on one another.

Amid this excellent working atmosphere, Grant felt comfortable approaching Lincoln on exceedingly delicate matters, and the president reciprocated with responses in the same spirit of goodwill. In mid-July 1864, after the calamitous losses against Lee's army had depleted his ranks, Grant suggested the president call for 300,000 volunteers or draftees. "The greater number of men we have the shorter and less sanguinary will be the war," Grant predicted. They would strengthen the field armies, reduce guerrilla raids, and promote enemy desertions. "I give this entirely as my views and not in any spirit of dictation," the general justified gingerly, "always holding myself in readiness to use the material given me to the best advantage I know how."[51]

Grant was asking a great deal. With the presidential election just a few months away, implementation of the general's request could cause serious political damage to the president. Lincoln replied that he received Grant's proposal for 300,000 more troops. "I suppose you have not seen the call for 500,000 made the day before, and which I suppose covers the case." Then, with a touch of wryness, Lincoln closed, "Always glad to have your suggestions." Grant and Lincoln communicated well.[52]

Later, as draft day approached, Halleck feared riots and advocated preparation for the removal of troops from the field to quell civil disturbances. "Are not the appearances such that we ought to take in sail and prepare the ship for a storm?," he questioned. Grant countered that there should be no delay of the draft and governors should organize state militia to quash rioters. "My withdrawal now from the James River would insure the defeat of Sherman," the lieutenant general rejoined, and with 20,000 more men Sherman would crush Hood's army around Atlanta. Lincoln, who caught a glimpse of the exchange, threw his weight behind Grant. "I have seen your dispatch, expressing your unwillingness to break your hold where you are," the president telegraphed. "Neither am I willing." Then, in blunt words, Lincoln advised, "Hold on with a bulldog grip, and chew and choke as much as possible."[53]

In certain instances, the general did not hesitate to decline Lincoln's overtures. When the president suggested a captain for Grant's staff, he passed on the offer, stating firmly that he did not accept anyone for his military family whom he did not know personally to possess the qualifications for the post. Yet Grant employed discretion. Late in the war, Lincoln requested, as a personal favor, that he extend a staff position to the president's son. Lincoln offered to furnish all expenses and give him a nominal rank. Grant readily accepted, and on Grant's recommendation, Robert Todd Lincoln received a commission as captain.[54]

Lincoln, too, did not acquiesce to Grant's judgment universally. Too many times earlier in the war the president had accepted the opinion of military leaders when his own sound judgment told him otherwise. And events usually bore out Lincoln's original opinion.

Often professing scant military knowledge, the president nonetheless screened War Department telegrams carefully and had no qualms about firing off queries or suggesting reconsideration of decisions to the lieutenant general. After perusing a message from Grant to Sherman that loosely proposed a "desperate effort" to hold Lee's army at Petersburg without utilizing so many Federal troops, and forwarding the excess manpower to Georgia, Lincoln interceded. He appreciated Grant's enterprising attitude as the election neared, but expressed "hope you may find a way that the effort shall not be desperate in the sense of great loss of life."[55]

Several months later, the president voiced strong opposition to Sherman's march on Savannah. When Sherman suggested the drive through Georgia, leaving Thomas in Tennessee to tend to Hood's army, Halleck voiced objections. Grant, too, questioned the wisdom of the campaign with Hood's army intact. Sherman, drawing on his intimate knowledge of the commanding general and his newfound prestige after the capture of Atlanta, swayed his friend with carefully chosen words about offensive and initiative. Lincoln, who again pored over the messages, still did not like the plan. Fixed as he was on the destruction of the enemy army through battle, he could not comprehend the value of such a march, especially when he weighed it against the perils, perhaps the loss of an entire army and Hood's consequent advance northward. "The President feels much solicitude in respect to General Sherman's proposed movement and hopes that it will be maturely considered," Stanton alerted Grant. A "misstep by General Sherman might be fatal to his army," Lincoln feared. Grant, "on mature reflection," endorsed Sherman's operation, and Lincoln refused to overrule the designs of his two best generals. But several days later Stanton paid Grant a visit at City Point, no doubt at Lincoln's urging, to explain the president's reservations and receive assurance that Sherman could fulfill all his intentions without incurring excessive risk. Only after Sherman reached Savannah safely did Lincoln grasp the essence of the raiding strategy. Piecing together Confederate newspaper reports and snippets from Sherman, Lincoln finally visualized just how disruptive to Confederates and productive to Federals these raiding campaigns could be. In a congratulatory letter, the president confessed, "When you were about leaving Atlanta for the Atlantic coast, I was anxious, if not fearful; but feeling that you were the better judge, and remembering that 'nothing risked, nothing gained,' I did not interfere. Now, the undertaking being a success, the honor is all yours; for I believe none of us went further than to acquiesce."[56]

With the November 1864 re-election behind them, Lincoln and Grant concentrated on closing out the war. Neither man forgot the responsibilities of his position or the underlying strengths and fundamental needs of the other. When Thomas delayed his attack on Hood at Nashville to complete minor details, and the War Department hesitated to order his removal, Grant steamed north and then boarded a train for Nashville. Lincoln had appointed him to take charge of the war, and in situations like this, Grant simply assumed the president wanted him on the scene. Before Grant arrived in Nashville, Thomas routed Hood's army, and the lieutenant general never had to act. Nonetheless, Grant had learned the lesson of Sheridan's appointment well. A few weeks later, Grant requested that Lincoln shelve Maj. Gen. Benjamin Butler, a powerful Democrat but a military incompetent, who would ascend to the command of all operations around Petersburg if anything happened to Grant. Now that the election had passed, Lincoln willingly incurred the wrath of loyal Democrats for the benefit of the Union Army. Grant stood up for Lincoln's interests, and Lincoln looked out for his general's welfare.[57]

Even though both men could see an end near, Lincoln the military watchdog remained ever vigilant. In late February 1865, as Sheridan commenced a campaign to capture Lynchburg, an important railroad junction for Lee's army, Lincoln snatched at a telegram from Sheridan which implied that only a token force would protect the northern Shenandoah Valley. "General Sheridan's dispatch to you of to-day, in which he says he 'Will be off on Monday,' and that he 'will leave behind about 2,000 men,' causes the Secretary of War and myself considerable anxiety," he notified Grant. "Have you well considered whether you do not again leave open the Shenandoah Valley entrance to Maryland and Pennsylvania, or at least to the Baltimore and Ohio Railroad?" Grant explained to Lincoln's complete satisfaction that Sheridan had designated his entire infantry and 3,000 cavalrymen as the protecting force, and his route of advance would also shield these vital areas. Sheridan's telegram merely informed Grant that an additional 2,000 horsemen would remain.[58]

At the beginning of March, during an exchange of civilian prisoners and improperly captured prisoners of war, Confederate General Longstreet and Union General Ord conversed about the possibility of a military convention to seek a termination of hostilities. With the Confederacy tottering on the brink of collapse, Lee immediately seized the opening and communicated to Grant that his government had authorized him to discuss the prospects for such a meeting. A month earlier Grant had become involved in a sticky problem over Confederate negotiators who were seeking a conference with Lincoln. Eventually, the president extricated Grant from that mess and met with the group, but nothing came of the gathering. The general wanted no part of repeating such an experience.

Sensibly cautious, Grant requested instructions from authorities in Washington. This time, Lincoln took charge. Preparing the order with his own hand, the president wanted Grant "to have no conference with General Lee, unless it be for the capitulation of General Lee's army or some minor or purely military matter." Grant was "not to decide, discuss, or confer upon any political question. Such questions the President holds in his own hands, and will submit them to no military conferences or conventions." Thus, Lincoln had wisely set clear guidelines for negotiations: Grant could treat only for surrender and nothing else. The next day, the Union commanding general informed Lee that the president alone possessed the authority to undertake such discussions as Lee proposed.[59]

Barely two weeks later, Grant asked Lincoln to visit him in City Point. "I would like very much to see you, and I think the rest would do you good," he telegraphed. Grant appreciated the sacrifices Lincoln had endured over four years of war, as well as the unflinching support he had exhibited toward Grant the past year, and he wanted the president nearby for the breakthrough.

Lincoln suspected something big was up. On March 24, the day Sherman's army closed the Carolinas Campaign, Lincoln's ship docked at City Point. The next day, Lee desperately attempted to crack through the Union line and failed. Lincoln's son, Capt. Robert Lincoln, referred to it as "a little rumpus up the line this morning." The engagement was more than that; it was Lee's last hope of saving

Richmond. Sherman visited on March 27 and 28, describing his campaign, entertaining Lincoln, Grant, and Porter with tales from his almost legendary army, and discussing the prospects of peace. Then dress parades and visitors occupied Lincoln's time the next day.[60]

On March 29, Grant launched a powerful turning movement around Lee's right flank, threatening the Southside Railroad. Grant headquartered near the action; he relayed telegrams regularly to the president, who analyzed and assessed each tidbit of information as it arrived. Grant was right. Lincoln relished every moment of it. After four years, he truly felt a part of the ultimate conquest.

The president felt guilty over his absence from Washington for such an extended period. "I begin to feel that I ought to be at home," he notified Stanton in Washington, "and yet I dislike to leave without seeing nearer to the end of General Grant's present movement." Stanton replied that Lincoln should witness the fall of Petersburg and Richmond at the least. "No other duty can weigh a feather" compared to urging the army onward. "A pause by the army now would do harm; if you are on the ground there will be no pause."[61]

On the morning of April 3, Lincoln caught a train to Patrick's Station, where an escort took him to Grant's field tent. The two men galloped into Petersburg, to examine the city that had resisted Grant's onslaught for nine months. A delighted Lincoln thanked his general warmly for a job well done. That day, Federal troops occupied Richmond.[62]

Lincoln, with a hankering to visit the Confederate capital, boarded a gunboat and chugged up the James River, escorted by Admiral Porter in his flagship. As he climbed on the docks, throngs of joyous freedmen and freedwomen crowded around him and cheered their hero. Through the streets he wandered, touring the town and examining the debris from a recent fire. Perhaps for him the highlight was sitting in Jefferson Davis's chair at the Confederate White House.[63]

Soon back in City Point, Lincoln resumed his job of scrutinizing telegrams from Grant. He could not resist them. Lee had broken for Lynchburg, with Grant in hot pursuit and Sheridan, in command of cavalry and infantry, swinging wide to box in the Confederates. At Burke's Station, Sheridan carved out a sizable chunk of Lee's army.

To Grant, the victorious "Little Phil" observed, "If the thing is pressed I think Lee will surrender." Lincoln, after scanning the telegram, pointedly cabled Grant, "Let the *thing* be pressed." It was. On April 9, 1865, Lee surrendered his army at Appomattox Court House.[64]

That afternoon, Grant caught a train for City Point, where he boarded a steamer for Washington. Lincoln had landed at Washington on the evening of April 9. Stanton met him on the dock with Grant's telegram proclaiming Lee's surrender. The nation's capital erupted in euphoria at the news.

For a few days, the lieutenant general plowed through paperwork, racing to finish so that he could spend a few well-deserved days of rest with his family in New Jersey. On April 14, Grant attended a cabinet meeting. In a casual moment, Lincoln predicted some major favorable event, perhaps Johnston's surrender to Sherman. The previous night, he had a dream that he was on some fast-moving vessel traveling toward an "indefinite shore." Throughout the war, the dream had recurred on the verge of some significant event or battle.[65]

That night, the president and his wife planned to attend *Our American Cousin* at Ford's Theater. He asked the Grants to accompany them. The general begged off, pleading a long-awaited visit to his children as the top priority. It was Lincoln's final request of Grant, and he declined it. By 7:22 a.m. the following morning, the president was dead.

8

Partners in Command

At the outbreak of hostilities, the Confederates possessed an overwhelming advantage over the Federals among individual leaders. Never before had a wartime president possessed such a broad military and political background as Jefferson Davis, and a coterie of high-ranking officers—Robert E. Lee, Joseph E. Johnston, and Albert Sidney Johnston—were touted as the best either side had to offer. Yet over the course of the war, superior political and military leadership emerged among Union ranks, men who worked together more effectively than did their Confederate counterparts. Through the collaborative efforts of Lincoln, Grant, Sherman, Porter, and others, the Union utilized its military talents and resources better than did the Confederacy, contributing significantly to ultimate victory. Lincoln provided the vision and the essential men and materiel, directing mobilization and shielding his officers from the worst hazards of politics so that they could concentrate on fighting the war. In an open atmosphere that encouraged the frank interchange of ideas, the commanders thrashed out concepts and strategies, skillfully employed the manpower and equipment at hand, and cooperated fully in execution. Thus, Union political and military leaders wrestled more effectively with the massive and complex problems of warmaking in an age of industrialization and nationalism because they functioned better as a team. Together, they established unsurpassed command relationships that aided them in winning the war.

Davis undertook the position of Confederate president with a wealth of experience in the military and political world. A graduate of West Point, Davis had served in the Regular Army and valiantly commanded volunteers in wartime. In government, he sat on the Military Affairs committees of both houses of Congress, and held the post of secretary of war. These years in and around the military establishment acquainted him personally with many of the high-ranking officers in both armies, and he felt at ease delving into the military world.

With the preservation of Confederate independence as his objective, Davis adopted a military strategy that called for defense as close to the borders as possible. In a democratic republic, the Confederacy could not afford to sacrifice the homes of its citizens; the political repercussions would have been too great. Yet the Confederacy lacked the resources to protect every point along its mammoth geographic borders. Instead, Davis positioned armies along logical routes of invasion, to deter or repel Union advances and seal off penetrations elsewhere. To cope with the overwhelming Yankee manpower and resources, the Confederate president created vast military departments under single leaders. He hoped that when Federals launched large-scale offensives, two or more armies would concentrate to defeat the attackers.

No strategy could protect against all eventualities, particularly against a foe with superior strength. The weakness of Davis's plan lay in its inability to defend against simultaneous advances. Alternative strategies, however, offered even greater problems. Joseph E. Johnston's insistence on concentration of forces would have exposed huge areas of the Confederacy to Union invasion, a political sin that would have condemned Davis in the hearts and minds of his fellow countrymen forever. It, too, failed to address the dilemma presented by concurrent offensives. A guerrilla war, yet another proposal, was wholly impractical. Most Confederates were a propertied class. They had seceded over the right to own, remove, and utilize property, specifically slaves, as they saw fit; they took up arms to protect those rights and defend their homes from invasion. Partisan warfare on their home ground would expose their sacrosanct property and families to even greater ravages by Yankee invaders, especially under the Grant–Sherman raiding scheme. The adoption of a strategy that sacrificed their primary motives for establishing and fighting for an independent nation made no sense. In areas such as Missouri where guerrillas campaigned actively, they proved as vexatious to the Confederate government as they did to the Federals. And there, Yankees contended with the issue of ferreting out Rebels among a Unionist majority whose property and welfare they had sworn an oath to protect. Outside the Border States, Union ranks need not trouble themselves over such distinctions.[1]

Davis's primary drawback stemmed from his personality. A man of unswerving honesty and integrity who perceived himself as acting in the best interest of the nation, Davis was stung by criticism. He never brooked opposition well, and in his mind he twisted challenges to his policy into assaults on his character. A brusque, impersonal manner accentuated by stress and the discomfort of physical ailments compounded Davis's difficulties.

In the East, the Confederate president stumbled with Joe Johnston. Miscommunication and Johnston's fixation on both concentration at the expense of territorial defense and his personal command prerogatives shattered the goodwill that existed between them in the first months of war.

Robert E. Lee and his subordinates rescued Virginia from a disastrous fate. Lee reentered the scene as the massive Union war machine rumbled forward in the spring of 1862. With the aid of Thomas J. "Stonewall" Jackson and others, Lee neutralized the overwhelming Federal advantages in manpower and equipment. By autumn, his Army of Northern Virginia had driven the Yankee invaders from nearly all of the Old Dominion.

Among Lee's many great qualities was his ability to utilize the strengths and overcome the weaknesses of those around him. He possessed an unusual talent for adapting his own personality to work well with superiors and subordinates, without selling out his designs or compromising his own dignity. The deferential Lee understood how to operate with the commander in chief better than anyone else. He assumed responsibility for his command, kept Davis apprised of plans, implemented government policies promptly, and offered suggestions delicately. Lee also had the benefit of extraordinary success in combat, but that came well after he had won Davis's confidence and trust. Together, they formed a solid, professional working relationship.

Of all Confederate commanders, none approached Robert E. Lee in ability or accomplishment. Intelligent, mature, and audacious, Lee formulated his own designs with little input from others. Even Jefferson Davis did not tinker with his schemes. There was no need. What Lee's army lacked in execution, it compensated with boldness of operational plan, and in the end, Lee achieved some of the greatest victories in American military history. So successful was Lee in repelling Union advances that his army eventually represented the independent Confederacy in the minds of both Southerners and Northerners.[2]

With "Stonewall" Jackson, Lee established a superb working relationship. Bonded through similar approaches to warfare rather than any intimate friendship, Lee and Jackson designed and executed masterful operations. Jackson's untimely death after Chancellorsville deprived Lee of his finest operational commander. Never again could the bold army commander attempt those sweeping flank attacks and risky turning movements.

During the summer of 1863, Lee's army exhibited a noticeable decline in effective execution. James "Pete" Longstreet, a fine tactician and operational leader who overrated his own ability to conceive strategy, retained a corps and handled it reasonably well, but neither Richard S. Ewell nor A. P. Hill could make the transition from division to corps command. For the remainder of the war, the army reacted sluggishly, particularly after Longstreet's wounding at the Wilderness. Throughout much of the spring campaign of 1864, an ailing Lee acted as both army and corps commander. A paucity of bona fide command talent, as much as anything, undid Lee and his Army of Northern Virginia.

To the west, Albert Sidney Johnston directed Confederate operations. Johnston, Davis's idol and friend, retained strong personal rapport with the Confederate president throughout his service, despite significant defeats. Upon Johnston's premature death at Shiloh in April 1862, Gen. P. G. T. Beauregard held the command briefly, but the general's immaturity had so alienated Davis early in the war that his status was exceedingly tenuous. Eventually, Davis adopted a two-command system, with the prickly Braxton Bragg heading one army and John C. Pemberton the other. When neither man seemed to engender confidence among subordinates or the public, Davis appointed Joseph E. Johnston to oversee both forces.

Joe Johnston never grasped the art of dealing with Davis. Strong-willed, charismatic, sensitive, ambitious, self-righteous, secretive, touchy about command prerogatives—Johnston was all of these. Perhaps Lincoln, with his fixation on goals and his suppleness of personality, might have extracted Johnston's considerable strengths and abated the impact of his weaknesses. Davis, a stiff, formal type, lacked the pliable demeanor to do so. The Davis–Johnston clash, then, was almost inevitable. Johnston never adopted Davis's program for winning the war, and as a result the Confederacy squandered its opportunities and resources in the West.

Other Confederate generals, too, struggled in their relationships with Davis. Samuel Cooper, the Adjutant and Inspector General, was soon ground down under the president's strong personality. Davis relied on him early in the war to institute systems and routine, but as the war dragged on, Cooper acted more and more the role of a low-level functionary. Beauregard never fully recovered from his clashes with Davis in 1861 and 1862, even though he exhibited considerable skill as a commander around Petersburg in 1864. Bragg retained Davis's high regard when others lost faith in him. After Bragg's removal as commander of the Army of Tennessee, Davis salvaged his career by appointing him military advisor to the president. But being too beholden to his protector, Bragg failed to provide Davis with the sort of independent judgment and advice that the president required. Distance from Richmond benefited Edmund Kirby Smith, commander of the Trans-Mississippi Department, in his relationship with Davis. Nevertheless, he too had his share of disputes with the president, mainly over Smith's attempts to fill the decision-making void in the absence of true government authority in the region.

In contrast to the Confederates, outstanding leadership among the Federals began at the top, with Abraham Lincoln. His death at the hands of John Wilkes Booth jolted both the public and the military into realizing just how extensive his contributions had been to the ultimate Union triumph. Through all the carping, the criticism, and the disasters, Lincoln had stood steadfast in his commitment to restore the Union and crush the institution of slavery. In time, he had come to symbolize those causes in the hearts and minds of civilians and soldiers.

The president's genius rested not with mastery of military strategy; rather, it lay in his strategic vision. With razor-like acuteness, Lincoln sliced away all the extraneous concerns until only a single, core issue remained: the reunion of the states. Nothing else mattered. Amid all the confusion and distractions, that dazzling Lincoln intellect somehow maintained its focus on the national objective. He adapted plans, rotated personnel, endured criticism, mourned losses, and initiated drastic, occasionally revolutionary, policies to fulfill his national strategy. Later, by admitting that slavery was the root cause of the sectional crisis and by seeking its destruction, he elevated emancipation from a military policy to a political objective as well. Thus, for Lincoln and the Northern States, restoration of the Union and emancipation became *sine qua non*, the indispensible demands for cessation of hostilities. They were the goals of Lincoln's national strategy.[3]

As a military strategist, Lincoln developed remarkable proficiency. At the beginning of the war, the president knew virtually nothing about the military establishment, other than what he had learned during a handful of weeks in the Illinois militia. But Abraham Lincoln, armed with that wonderful, inquisitive mind, was a quick study. He sucked in information from books, picked the brains of respected officers, and scrutinized message traffic, so that in the late stages of the war Lincoln had accumulated a considerable body of military knowledge. These insights into warfare, along with great good judgment and his muscular thought process, elevated Lincoln into a formidable military talent.

Secure in himself and the direction he designated for the nation, Lincoln adapted his ways to elicit the strengths and compensate for the weaknesses of others. The Union president prided himself on keen interpersonal skills. Gregarious, ingratiating, even self-deprecating, the "country lawyer" Lincoln grasped the value of personal rapport in dealing with others. He could size up people almost instantly, and possessed an ability to alter his ways in order to work well with others.

Toward the superannuated Winfield Scott, Lincoln displayed evident veneration. The once-accomplished general and powerful Whig had seen his best days; nevertheless, Scott still held the key to a wealth of military knowledge that the neophyte commander in chief needed. Lincoln accorded Scott his due respect, and the aged general responded with all the kindness and advice that his ailing body would permit.

Undoubtedly Lincoln's most frustrating relationship of the war was with George B. McClellan. A general of evident intellect and industry, McClellan trained an army superbly and motivated its soldiers splendidly. Then he hesitated to fight it. Lincoln tried everything to compel McClellan to execute. He poked, prodded, pleaded, ordered, and threatened McClellan, to no avail. Despite Lincoln's pliability, he could not overcome McClellan's psychological baggage.

Lincoln appointed Edwin M. Stanton as secretary of war for several reasons. He was a prominent War Democrat, a man respected by the leadership of both political parties. Lincoln also sought an individual who had a reputation for honesty and was an accomplished administrator to head the scandal-riddled War Department. Before his appointment, Stanton held Lincoln in disdain, criticizing his decisions and at one time noting "the painful imbecility of Lincoln." Lincoln deftly co-opted him. Stanton's drawbacks included a lack of military knowledge, a passion for political intrigue, and an abrasive personality. The likable Lincoln buffered the harsher aspects of Stanton's nature, drew heavily upon his extraordinary executive capacity, and listened to Stanton's military advice without necessarily adopting or dismissing it. Edwin M. Stanton never bullied Lincoln into anything.[4]

When Lincoln brought a reluctant Henry W. Halleck east to run the war effort, he expected great things. But the political grind of Washington and the demands of the job chewed up the brainy Halleck in short order. A man lacking in the look or the confidence of a field leader, Halleck lost faith in himself after the Union army suffered a rout at Second Manassas. Much to Lincoln's chagrin, Halleck never seized the reins of the Union war effort. Nonetheless, the commander in chief refused to discard him. Even though he disappointed Lincoln, Halleck could serve a useful purpose, explaining military matters to the president, advising subordinates, and preventing the most egregious blunders in the field. Until a true military leader emerged, Lincoln continued to employ Halleck and attempted to adjust to the general in chief's inadequacies.

In Ulysses S. Grant, Lincoln found a general who fulfilled all his expectations. Grant understood his position within the political–military hierarchy, exhibited enough savvy not to embroil himself in politics, restrained his ambition, and functioned effectively with the available resources. While President Lincoln wrestled with the war's political aspects, he selected Grant as lieutenant general to invigorate the military components as he had done in the West. Grant did just that.

Together, the Lincoln–Grant team functioned exceedingly well. Lincoln adroitly guided Grant through political minefields, and the new commanding general assumed the mantle for army operations. As commander in chief, Lincoln kept a watchful eye on military affairs. After all, ultimately it was the president's responsibility. Whenever Lincoln disagreed with a Grant decision, he merely questioned it, voicing his objections and laying out possible repercussions. But he never overruled his general. With Grant, a man sensitive to the wishes of his superior, Lincoln had a most trustworthy and reliable subordinate.

Yet Lincoln was not without his faults as commander in chief. Occasionally, he interfered with his commanders to the detriment of the armed forces. And while Lincoln grasped certain concepts that eluded some of his generals, such as the destruction of the enemy's armed forces, in the course of his struggles with his military leaders these ideas consumed him to the exclusion of others. He confused military "ends" with "means," viewing the defeat of Rebel soldiers as the objective when it was only part of the equation.

The American Civil War was a revolution, and Union success demanded that the Federals suppress the secessionist spirit in the population. The raiding strategy of Grant and Sherman did just that. It exposed the Confederate population to the hardships of warfare, deprived their armies of valuable resources, wrecked their logistical network, and promoted desertion in the Rebel ranks. By demonstrating the vulnerability of Southerners to such campaigns, these raids damaged the morale of the civilians who escaped their ravages. The raiding strategy, operating in conjunction with more traditional campaigns that targeted Confederate military might, and particularly its armies, finally offered the Union the appropriate "means."

Lacking the experience of military service, Lincoln never witnessed the horror and fear in the faces of civilians as an enemy army marched through their neighborhood, consuming their food, wrecking their resources, and absconding with their slaves. He did not know that military forces could bring him that much closer to fulfillment of his national strategy. Grant and Sherman, inured to the practical aspects of campaigning, grasped this.

No doubt, Grant's collaborationist style proved to be a tremendous asset in coping with the increasing complexities of warfare. During the course of the war, Grant formed an impressive array of symbiotic relationships. Tough-minded and relentless in battle, Grant reassured those around him with his calm and confident temperament. He fortified the nervous, high-strung Sherman, restoring his confidence and reviving the general as an effective commander. He taught Sherman how to prevent the ambiguities and uncertainties of warfare from paralyzing him. The therapeutic Grant, in a peculiar way, instructed his friend Sherman how to live with Sherman. In return, Grant tapped that marvelous creative mind of Sherman's. Spitting out fresh thoughts, perpetually analyzing and reassessing situations and courses of action, Sherman offered Grant a wealth of ideas from a variety of perspectives. Sherman expanded Grant's world. And both men, loyal to the core, found comfort in the notion that in these tumultuous times they could always depend on one another.

The brilliant naval commander David Dixon Porter melded handsomely into the Grant–Sherman team. Just as Sherman did for Grant, Porter broadened Grant's and Sherman's horizons, offering an entirely new perspective from the vantagepoint of the maritime world. Porter's expertise, derived from several decades on the high seas, and his fertile, resourceful mind found a warm reception with the Grant–Sherman brain trust. In contrast to most army officers, who treated navy men with prejudice if not disdain, Grant and Sherman accorded Porter coequal status. They brought the admiral into their inner circle. Grant and Sherman offered him the hand of friendship, listened attentively to his ideas, debated plans with him, and relied on his professional abilities time after time. For Porter, the two shattered the stereotypical mold of army officers and paved the way for true army–navy cooperation. In new and exciting ways, Grant and Sherman aided Porter's development as a naval officer, exposing him to the intricate realm of joint operations. And by the end of the war, Porter had become its master.

With Grant and Sherman, warfare was both an intellectual and an operational enterprise. They established an open headquarters, where ranking officers regularly dropped by during day or night, offering suggestions, kicking around ideas, and grappling with problems. This free and frank exchange of viewpoints not only resolved military issues but also served as an outstanding training ground for officers. Generals James B. McPherson, Philip Sheridan, Oliver Otis Howard, John M. Schofield, and many others honed their skills and enhanced their knowledge as military commanders there. Even more experienced leaders, such as George G. Meade and George H. Thomas, benefited from the "school," as did its founders, Grant and Sherman.

The program worked magic with younger officers. McPherson, a protege of the Grant–Sherman collaboration, fell under their spell in 1862 and rose to lead the Army of the Tennessee. Both Grant and Sherman viewed his death in July 1864 as a great tragedy to the Federal cause. In the East, Howard suffered a disappointing career at the head of a corps, suffering badly at both Chancellorsville and Gettysburg. Schofield, a respected and intelligent officer, had achieved nothing appreciable as a commander before he joined fortunes with Sherman. Likewise, the aggressive Sheridan offered little more than raw ability when Grant took a liking to him. By the late stages of the war, Grant and Sherman had elevated the talents of these men, so that Howard led an army well and Schofield and Sheridan regularly and effectively directed large expeditionary forces. And each of them mentored his own class of promising junior officers. The "open headquarters" system, then, paid great dividends for the Union Army.[5]

When Grant assumed the post of lieutenant general early in 1864, he soon discovered that his agenda and approach to the war conflicted with the wishes of the Northern populace and its elected servants. He planned to replace Meade, the commander of the Army of the Potomac, most likely with William F. "Baldy" Smith, and he intended to return west, to direct operations there. Conspicuous in his designs would be the raiding strategy that he and Sherman had formulated and refined in recent months. Political forces and public sentiment, however, demanded that he remain east and fight Lee's command. Lincoln, Stanton, and Halleck called for war that targeted Rebel troops. Not until Union forces shattered the invincible

Army of Northern Virginia, so they and many others believed, could the Federal government achieve victory. Neither he nor Sherman preferred such a policy, but within those confines, they had no alternative. Public and political perception dictated such a course of action.

Grant's plan that spring was a sound one, to pressure the Confederates on all fronts, using superior Federal resources most expeditiously. All Union forces would employ the essence of the raiding strategy, to make a concerted effort to consume the food and damage the war resources of the Confederacy as they advanced. He and Sherman would oversee the main thrusts, one against Lee's army, the other toward Atlanta against the Army of Tennessee under Joe Johnston. Both men knew that they would not likely win the campaign in a single decisive battle. Civil War armies were too large, too resilient, and pursuit too difficult to hope for one climactic engagement. Only if their opponents committed some grave blunder, as the Rebel commanders had done at Fort Donelson and at Vicksburg, could they hope for instant success. Lee and Johnston were too wily for that.

Grant and Sherman thought on the operational level. Through extended maneuvering and fighting—attempting to gain critical positions that would compel the Confederates to assault them, seeking opportunities to bore holes in enemy lines, or damaging them with flank attacks—they intended to break up their opponent's army, to deliver a series of blows that would deprive it of its offensive capabilities. Then Grant, Sherman, and others could concentrate on the raiding strategy. They must keep in constant contact with their prey, in order to prevent the Confederates from assuming the initiative and bar them from sending reinforcements elsewhere. Although Grant rightly assumed that Lee's forces would be the tougher nut to crack, he did not single out Sherman to gain the victory while he sat tight. Not until he locked into siege with Lee around Petersburg, and Sherman pushed to the gates of Atlanta, did Grant adopt specific measures to hold Lee's army in place and aid Sherman's endeavors. By the time Atlanta fell to "Uncle Billy," the remnants of the Confederate Army of Tennessee no longer posed a threat to the safety of his command. Ten weeks later, Sherman detached a portion under Thomas to deal with the remains of John

Bell Hood's battered army, while he took over 60,000 men on his march through Georgia. Grant would hold Lee fast as Sherman roared through the heart of the Confederacy, confiscating food, wrecking railroads and factories, disrupting civil life, promoting desertions, closing in on Lee, and convincing the Southerners of the hopelessness of their cause.[6]

The key to successful command relationships, then, rested in the ability of leaders to understand strengths and weaknesses. They had to know themselves, to know their own assets and liabilities as well as the qualities and characteristics of critical subordinates. They also needed the capacity to elicit those skills from their underlings. It was imperative for leaders to assemble personnel who complemented rather than supplemented their own capabilities, so that they could draw from a wide range of talents to tap into and employ resources most effectively to meet the increasingly complex demands of the war. Compatibility and intimacy were advantageous but not necessary. Professional attitudes, more than amicable personalities, lay at the interactive bedrock of these successful military partnerships.

Despite overwhelming resources—manpower, industrial might, and a powerful agricultural base—the Union struggled during the first years of the conflict. The mere possession of these assets by no means ensured a Union victory. Not until its political and military leaders learned to harness that power and focus it on the enemy's source of strength, what Clausewitz called the center of gravity, did the war shift decisively in the Union's favor. Lincoln, Grant, Sherman, and Porter, all partners in command, did just that.

APPENDIX:
MCCLELLAN'S TRAGIC FLAWS IN
THE LIGHT OF MODERN
PSYCHOLOGY

*E*ver since the days of the Civil War, participants and historians have grappled with the question of why George B. McClellan failed as commanding general and commander of the Army of the Potomac. A man of undeniable intellect and charisma, an unsurpassed talent in the creation and organization of an army, McClellan unexpectedly floundered in his role as war leader.

Perhaps an exploration into what psychiatrists and psychologists term "paranoid personality disorder"[1] will provide some valuable insights into McClellan's private world. According to the *Diagnostic and Statistical Manual of Mental Disorders* of the American Psychiatric Association, individuals who suffer from this affliction interpret actions of other people as deliberately threatening or demeaning. They ponder innocuous and insignificant remarks and find hidden, unintended meanings that affront them.

Mistrust rests at the core of paranoid personality disorder. Without justification these individuals question the loyalty of others, assigning to them the worst possible motives. They are excessively suspicious by nature. Easily feeling slighted, they bear grudges deeply and often are wholly unforgiving. Only those who have gained their absolute trust can achieve a level of intimacy with them; thus, they have few true friends.

Paranoid personality disorder causes its sufferers to become extremely secretive. They hesitate to confide in others for fear the information will be used to their detriment. A lack of sufficient trust induces them to doubt the reliability of others. Seldom if ever do they delegate responsibility, instead overseeing the minutest details personally.

The need to dominate is prevalent among individuals with paranoid personality disorder. In conjunction with mistrust of others, a heightened fear of losing the ability to influence and shape events compels them to seek control of relationships and situations. They are hypersensitive to rank and power. Those afflicted by the illness actively seek authority positions. They struggle in roles of inferiority, often alienating or aggravating superiors in an effort to dictate the flow of the relationship. They hold those whom they deem weak in particular disdain. There is, then, an exaggerated sense of self-importance among individuals with paranoid personality disorder.

Despite self-perceptions as being objective and rational, they are nothing of the sort. When fresh problems or events confront them, they block out information that runs contrary to their initial or pre-conceived expectations. They embellish difficulties and overreact to them. Magnifying obstacles well beyond their true merit or strength, they take excessive precautions against any perceived threat and cling rigidly to their views even in the face of contrary evidence. They cannot cope with failure and avoid blame at all costs. Although these people are highly critical of others, they react harshly to any criticism received and are quick to justify themselves.

Some view them as "keen observers who are energetic, ambitious, and capable," but most come to see them as "hostile, stubborn, and defensive."[2] Psychiatrists and psychologists speculate that "these individuals were subjected as children to parental antagonisms and harassment [sic]. Many served as scapegoats for displaced aggression."[3] Extreme stress exacerbates their affliction, which usually appears for the first time in late adolescence or early adulthood.

Frequently individuals who suffer from paranoid personality disorder also display features of another psychological debility, narcissistic personality disorder. Narcissistic personality disorder consists of "grandiosity, lack of empathy, and hypersensitivity to the evaluation of others." Such individuals react harshly to criticism. These people hold majestic views of their own talents and accomplishments, but without the requisite achievement. In their minds, they convert minor successes or even failures into sensational accomplishments. Often consumed with visions of power, sufferers consider their "rare status" as entitling them to preferential treatment or disproportionate resources to fulfill tasks. They demand continual attention and admiration and react bitterly when they do not receive them. Deeply envious, they express insensitivity to others. Thus, paranoid and narcissistic personality disorders recurrently operate hand in hand.[4]

What little information about McClellan's youth that exists is by no means inconsistent with the formation of paranoid personality disorder. He was born in Philadelphia, third among five children, in 1826. His mother came from a well-connected family in Philadelphia, which provided George with entrée into the local aristocracy. His father was a highly intelligent, extremely principled physician who founded Jefferson Medical College and was ousted for his unyielding ways. A man of unusual energy, he demanded much of himself, at one time running the medical school, practicing as a physician, editing a medical journal, and raising a family. According to his eulogizer, Dr. McClellan's "feelings were quickly excited and warmly expressed at the sense of unkindness or injustice." He "was hurried into controversy" and possessed a penchant for rigidity in thought.[5] Despite his mother's money and his father's stature in the city as a prominent physician, the McClellans socialized beyond their means. Hobnobbing with the aristocracy, an expensive stable of horses, and lavish spending on their children's education dried up their funds. When Dr. McClellan died unexpectedly in 1847, he had incurred considerable debts.[6]

From a young age, George exhibited a marvelous mind. His capacity for knowledge, coupled with a first-rate education, transformed McClellan into a true intellectual force. By age twelve, he had mastered Latin, French, and the classics, and at fourteen he enrolled in the University of Pennsylvania. Two years later, he entered West Point, where his academic excellence continued. At nineteen and a half years of age, McClellan graduated second in his class. Academic success came easily to McClellan; none of his classmates ever accused him of being an overachiever.

Even during his eleven-year Regular Army career, where most officers' minds languished, his reputation for cerebral prowess expanded. An engineer officer, he prepared two papers for the Napoleon Club at West Point (one of them 111 pages long), invented a cavalry saddle, and translated a bayonet manual from French, all in his spare time. His greatest intellectual feat, though, occurred during a three-month leave after observation of the Crimean War, when McClellan taught himself Russian and translated a 300-page book from Russian into English.

Success had always come easily to young McClellan. Only once did he confront failure. In his first weeks at West Point, the homesick lad of fifteen struggled to keep pace with his older and more physically developed classmates on the drill field. To his sister he even intimated that he might drop out. But that morning he replaced his tight-fitting shoes with a larger pair, and magically he outperformed the others. Later in the day, a jubilant McClellan announced to his sister that all his fears had dissipated. He now possessed no doubts that he would do "as well as anyone who ever did go through here."[7]

From his youth, McClellan clashed with his superiors. When he was a lad of about twelve, he and his teacher, Rev. Samuel Crawford, had a squabble, for which McClellan claimed fifty years later that he was blameless. At West Point, he contended that faculty members demonstrated preference for the student ahead of him in class rank, depriving him of the deserved position of Number One. Upon reaching adulthood, such battles increased in frequency and severity, so that he admitted to his sister-in-law, "I don't think I am of a quarrelsome disposition—but I do have the luck of getting into more trouble than any dozen other officers."[8]

After his graduation, the War Department commissioned him in the Corps of Engineers, with assignment to the Company of Engineers at West Point. The Mexican War, in which McClellan served with distinction, took him away for nearly two years, but afterward he returned to duty at West Point, only to become embroiled in controversy with the superintendent. McClellan resented the superintendent ordering him about like a junior faculty member; then he irritated the superintendent by cutting mandatory chapel; finally, the two fell out over the location of a mere storage shed. In all three instances, McClellan filed protests with the chief engineer of the U.S. Army, Brig. Gen. Joseph Totten, including a seven-page pleading on the outbuilding. To escape West Point, McClellan proposed various schemes to Totten, one of which he toned so impertinently that the letter raised the ire not only of Totten but also of the secretary of war, no small achievement for a second lieutenant. In response, McClellan simply wrote Totten off as an "old lady" and justified his conduct by insisting that he was right and they were wrong.[9]

Over the next six years, McClellan received numerous independent assignments, but whenever he labored under the direct supervision of another officer, trouble erupted. A friend from the Mexican War and now a territorial governor, Isaac Stevens, offered him a post on an exploratory expedition to the Pacific Northwest, assessing possible transcontinental railroad routes through the region. McClellan agreed, although an order arrived from Totten detailing him to that duty before his letter of acceptance reached Washington. Later, the two men clashed when Stevens disagreed with McClellan's judgment. A peevish McClellan refused aid to a reconnaissance party because Stevens issued the order "in direct opposition to my judgment." In his journal, McClellan assailed Stevens, insisting that he would no longer serve under him unless he vowed to interfere no more. Proclaiming his innocence in the controversy, McClellan fortified his conscience by now arguing, "The great consolation is that I was detailed in this service without either my knowledge or consent," revealing what his premier biographer asserts was his "bent for self-deception."[10]

Barely a year later, McClellan won a choice appointment as one of three American observers during the Crimean War. Junior to two majors approximately twenty-five years older, the freshly promoted captain accused his superiors of being "d—d old fogies!! I hope that I may never be tied to two corpses again—it is a hell on earth."[11] Only a clearly defined separation of duties, which granted him some independence, eased his conflict with the two ranking officers, so that near the end of his year in Europe, he noted some improvement in relations.

The single instance during this period when McClellan did not instigate turmoil with his direct superior took place on an exploration up the Red River. McClellan and his commander, Capt. Randolph B. Marcy, worked well together. Of course, McClellan could not refrain from exploding when rumors reached him that Marcy had downplayed his contributions in the after-action report. Once McClellan learned the truth, he restored his high regard for Marcy. Interestingly, McClellan courted Marcy's daughter Ellen for several years and eventually won her hand.

Nor did McClellan's conflicts stem from the confines of military service. In 1857, he resigned his commission to accept an appointment as chief engineer for the Illinois Central Railroad. Within months he and the directors tussled. The Panic of 1857 brought the overextended railroad company to its knees, and entreaties to reduce costs and send all available funds to the New York headquarters evoked a bitter response from McClellan. McClellan refused to cut services and payroll to save money, and when the directors challenged his approach, he personalized their disagreements. "If I fail to comply with any suggestions or orders it will be because I see such good reason for my course that I am willing to risk my reputation & position on the issue," he declared to a director.[12] With McClellan's help, the Illinois Central rode out the storm, and he emerged from the economic crash in a stronger position. Yet disputes with the company president multiplied, and in August 1860, when the Ohio and Mississippi Railroad offered him the superintendency at double his current salary, McClellan accepted. A new job did not free him from discord, though. He was soon at odds with an operating superintendent, and only a call to arms terminated the feud.

Thus, when his relationship with Lincoln crumbled, it was just another in a long line of failed relationships with superiors for George B. McClellan. McClellan's psychological baggage impeded his ability to function as army commander and general in chief. Mistrustful by nature, he discovered deliberately threatening or demeaning remarks in innocuous comments. His excessive secrecy, need to dominate, and hypersensitivity to rank and power inhibited his capacity to labor under Lincoln or anyone else—teachers, immediate commanders, railroad presidents, secretaries of war or generals-in-chief. McClellan formed initial or preconceived expectations and clung to them rigidly, obscuring all information that contradicted the original assessments. He grossly exaggerated the strength of obstacles, took extreme precautions, and in failure blamed everyone except himself. Severely critical of others, he reacted bitterly to criticism and justified himself at every turn. These qualities, all characteristic of paranoid personality disorder with narcissistic tendencies, prevented McClellan from performing his duties as commanding general and general in chief satisfactorily.

NOTES

Preface and Acknowledgments

1. See James M. McPherson, "Lincoln and the Strategy of Unconditional Surrender," in *Abraham Lincoln and the Second American Revolution* (New York: Oxford University Press, 1991), pp. 69–70. Definitions for *military strategy* and *operational art* are straight from U.S. Department of the Army, Field Manual 100-5, *Operations* (Washington, DC: U.S. Government Printing Office, 5 May 1986), pp. 9–10, with slight modification. Lecture of COL (Ret) Art Lykke, 24 Sep. 1991 at the U.S. Army War College (USAWC).

Chapter 2. "He has lost his left arm, but I have lost my right"

1. Quoted in Vandiver, *Mighty Stonewall*, p. 134.
2. Letcher to Lee, 27 Apr. 1861 (*The War of the Rebellion: Official Records of the Union and Confederate Armies* [hereafter OR], Washington, D.C.: U.S. Government Printing Office, 1880–1901), I, 2, p. 784. Also see Lee to Jackson, 27 Apr. 1861. *OR* I, 2, pp. 784–85.
3. For an excellent character analysis of Jackson, see Charles Royster, *The Destructive War: William Tecumseh Sherman, Stonewall Jackson, and the Americans* (New York: Alfred A. Knopf, 1991). The best biography of Jackson is Frank E. Vandiver, *Mighty Stonewall* (New York: McGraw-Hill Book Company, 1957). Also see G. F. R. Henderson, *Stonewall Jackson*

and the American Civil War (New York: Longmans, Green and Co., 1949, originally published 1898).

4. Jackson to Lee, 6 and 11 May 1861. *OR* I, 2, pp. 809–810 and 832. Also see Lee to Jackson, 6 May 1861; Jackson to Lee, 7 May 1861. *OR* I, 2, pp. 806–807 and 814–15.
5. Lee to Jackson, 9 and 10 May 1861. *OR* I, 2, 822 and 824–25.
6. Jackson to Johnston, 24 May 1861. *OR* I, 2, p. 872.
7. Vandiver, p. 152. Also see *OR* I, 2, pp. 185–86.
8. For a superb study on Jackson's first command, see James I. Robertson, Jr., *The Stonewall Brigade* (Baton Rouge: Louisiana State University Press, 1963).
9. Quotation in John Hennessy, *The First Battle of Manassas: An End to Innocence, July 18–21, 1861* (Lynchburg, VA: H. E. Howard, Inc., 1989), pp. 83 and 152; Vandiver, p. 161.
10. Vandiver, p. 166.
11. Quoted in Vandiver, p. 169.
12. See Jackson to Benjamin, 20 Nov. 1861; Johnston to Cooper, 22 Nov. 1861; Benjamin to Loring, 24 Nov. 1861. *OR* I, 5, pp. 965–69.
13. Taliaferro to Staples, 23 Jan. 1862. Jackson to Johnston, 17 Jan. 1862. *OR* I, 5, pp. 1042 and 1036. See Chapter 4 for additional information. Jackson no doubt placed the Stonewall Brigade in winter quarters in Winchester not because of favoritism but because he intended to call upon them to reinforce Johnston's army against McClellan, and he wanted his best troops in the vanguard. For the charges and specifications against Loring, see *OR* I, 5, pp. 1065–1066. The War Department transferred Loring out of Virginia.
14. General Orders, No. 14, Adjt. and Insp. Gen.'s Office. 13 Mar. 1862. *OR* I, 5, p. 1099. Davis to Lee, 2 Mar. 1862. *OR* I, 5, p. 400. See Abstract from return of the Army of the Potomac for the month of February, 1862. *OR* I, 5, p. 752.
15. See Douglas Southall Freeman, *R. E. Lee: A Biography*, I, (New York: Charles Scribner's Sons, 1934), pp. 566–76, 597–98, and 602–604.
16. Fremont's command actually had approximately 28,000, although 9,000 were outside the campaign area. Lee did not know the precise size of McDowell's command but believed it to be a substantial force.

17. See Jay Luvaas, "Lee and the Operational Art: The Right Place, the Right Time." *Parameters* (Autumn, 1992), pp. 2–18, for a marvelous introduction to Lee and the operational art. For an explanation of the operational art of war, see U.S. Department of the Army, Field Manual No. 100-5, *Operations* (Washington, D.C.: U.S. Government Printing Office, 1986), p. 10.

18. For Hotchkiss's role, see Archie P. McDonald, ed., *Make Me a Map of the Valley: The Civil War Journal of Stonewall Jackson's Topographer* (Dallas: Southern Methodist University Press, 1973).

19. Jackson to Longstreet, 5 Apr. 1862. *OR* I, 12, 3, p. 844.

20. Lee to Jackson, 25 Apr. 1862. *OR* I, 12, 3, pp. 865–66. See Jackson to Ewell, 10 Apr. 1862. Lee to Jackson and Lee to Ewell, 21 Apr. 1862. *OR* I, 12, 3, pp. 845 and 858–60.

21. Lee to Jackson, 1 May 1862. *OR* I, 12, 3, p. 878. Also see Jackson to Lee, 29 Apr. 1862; Ewell to Lee, 30 Apr. 1862; Jackson to Ewell, 3 and 4 May 1862. *OR* I, 12, 3, p. 872, 876–79.

22. Quoted in Freeman, *Lee's Lieutenants*, I, p. 355; Jackson to Ewell, 18 May 1862. *OR* I, 12, 3, p. 897.

23. Lee to Jackson, 16 May 1862. *OR* I, 12, 3, pp. 892–93. Also see Taylor to Jackson, 14 May 1862. *OR* I, 12, 3, p. 889.

24. Jackson to Lee, 20 May 1862. *OR* I, 12, 3, p. 898. Also see Johnston to Ewell and then to Jackson, 17 May 1862. *OR* I, 12, 3, pp. 896–97; Douglas Southall Freeman, *Lee's Lieutenants: A Study in Command*, I (New York: Charles Scribner's Sons, 1942), p. 371.

25. See Vandiver, pp. 250–55, for a description of the battle.

26. See Vandiver, pp. 268–72 for a clear explanation of Jackson's plan and position. At Port Republic, the South Fork of the Shenandoah River splits, becoming the North River and South River.

27. See Vandiver, pp. 275–83. Also see Robert G. Tanner, *Stonewall in the Valley: Thomas J. "Stonewall" Jackson's Shenandoah Valley Campaign, Spring 1862* (New York: Doubleday & Company, Inc., 1976).

28. Lee to Jackson, 8 and 11 June 1862. *OR* I, 12, 3, pp. 908 and 910.

29. For the friendship of Stuart and Jackson, see Vandiver, pp. 409–410.

30. Quoted in Vandiver, p. 235. Also see Hill to Stuart, 14 Nov. 1862. James Ewell Brown Stuart Papers, Virginia Historical Society; Robertson, *General A. P. Hill*, p. 172.
31. One only needs to read letters from Lee's staff members to notice their inability to grasp the man.
32. See Charles Royster, *The Destructive War: William Tecumseh Sherman, Stonewall Jackson, and the Americans* (New York: Alfred A. Knopf, 1991), pp. 264–68; and Freeman, *R. E. Lee*, II, 440; III, 328, 385, 405, 423–24, 531–32; IV, 118, 194, 220, 297, 402, 483–84, 504–505.
33. Lee to Son, 19 Dec. 1861. R. E. Lee Papers, Duke University. See Royster, *The Destructive War*, Chapter 2, on Jackson's desire to invade the North.
34. Quoted in Freeman, *R. E. Lee*, II, p. 462.
35. Hill to Stuart, 14 Nov. 1862. James Ewell Brown Stuart Papers, Virginia Historical Society; Robertson, *General A. P. Hill*, p. 172.
36. Lee to Jackson, 8 and 16 June 1862. *OR* I, 12, 3, pp. 908 and 913. Also see Lee to Jackson, 11 June 1862. *OR* I, 12, 3, p. 910.
37. See Vandiver, pp. 293–303; Freeman, *Lee's Lieutenants*, pp. 496–502; General Orders, No. 75. HQ, Army of Northern Virginia. 24 June 1862. *OR* I, 11, 2, pp. 498–99.
38. See Vandiver, p. 327.
39. After Action Report (hereafter AAR) of Lee, 18 Apr. 1863. *OR* I, 12, 2, p. 176. Lee to Jackson, 25 July 1862. *OR* I, 12, 3, p. 917. See General Orders, 5, 7, and 11. Headquarters [Union] Army of Virginia. 18, 10[?], and 23, July 1862. *OR* I, 12, 2, pp. 50–52.
40. Lee to Jackson, 25 July 1862. *OR* I, 12, 3, p. 917.
41. Lee to Jackson, 25 July 1862. *OR* I, 12, 3, p. 917.
42. See AAR of Lee, 18 Apr. 1863. AAR of Jackson, 4 Apr. 1863; AAR of Pope, 13 Aug. 1862. *OR* I, 12, 2, pp. 176–85 and 133–35. For the best book on the battle, see Robert K. Krick, *Stonewall Jackson at Cedar Mountain* (Chapel Hill: University of North Carolina Press, 1991).
43. See Henderson, pp. 452–90. While Longstreet's Corps suffered greater casualties in the attack, his delays could have proven disastrous. Had McClellan pushed forward two corps, as Halleck had instructed him to do, Longstreet's delay would have enabled them to play a major role in the battle's outcome.

44. AAR of Lee, 19 Aug. 1863. *OR* I, 19, 1, p. 144. Also see Lee to Davis, 23 Aug. 1862. *OR* I, 12, 3, p. 941.
45. For the best account of Antietam, see Stephen Sears, *Landscape Turned Red: The Battle of Antietam* (New York: Tickner & Fields, 1983). See James I. Robertson, Jr., *General A. P. Hill: The Story of a Confederate Warrior* (New York: Random House, 1987), pp. 141–47, for Hill's march and attack.
46. Jackson's only reserve was Hood's Division, attached temporarily.
47. Lee shifted Walker's Division and Anderson's Brigade. The reserve was McLaw's Division.
48. Lee to Davis, 2 Oct. 1862. *OR* I, 19, 2, p. 643.
49. Lee to Randolph, 10 Nov. 1862. *OR* I, 19, 2, p. 711. See Lee to Jackson and Lee to Longstreet, 28 Oct. 1862. *OR* I, 19, 2, pp. 685–86. The two corps were announced in Special Orders, No. 234. HQ, ANV. 6 Nov. 1862. *OR* I, 19, 2, pp. 698–99.
50. Lee to Jackson, 3 May 1863. *OR* I, 25, 2, p. 769. See also Royster, *The Destructive War*, pp. 190–228 and Freeman, *Lee's Lieutenants*, 2, 563–83.
51. Freeman, *R. E. Lee*, II, p. 560: Pendelton to wife, 1 June 1863. W. N. Pendleton Papers, SHC, UNC.

Chapter 3. "You have done your best to sacrifice this army"

1. William Marvel, *Burnside* (Chapel Hill: University of North Carolina Press, 1991), pp. 159–60. Also see Stephen W. Sears, *George B. McClellan: The Young Napoleon* (New York: Ticknor & Fields, 1988), pp. 339–41.
2. See Appendix for more information on McClellan's struggles with authority figures.
3. Quoted in T. Harry Williams, *Lincoln and His Generals* (New York: Alfred A. Knopf, 1952), p. 177.
4. Scott to McClellan, 3 May 1861. *OR* I, 51, 1, 369–70.
5. McClellan to Scott, 9 May 1861. *OR* I, 51, 1, pp. 373–74; McClellan to Dennison, 25 May 1861. Stephen Sears, ed., *The Civil War Papers of George B. McClellan: Selected Correspondence, 1860–1865* (New York: Ticknor & Fields, 1989), p. 25. Also see McClellan to Cameron, 20 May 1861. *OR* I, 2, 1, p. 642; Scott to McClellan, 21 May 1861. *OR* I, 51, 1, pp.

386–87; and McClellan to Lincoln, 30 May 1861. Sears, ed., *Papers of McClellan*, pp. 28–29.

6. Scott to McClellan, 24 May 1861. *OR* I, 2, p. 648. Also see McClellan to *Soldiers of Army of the West*, 16 July 1861. *OR* I, 2, p. 236. For an excellent assessment of the campaign, see Stephen Sears, *George B. McClellan*, pp. 83–92.

7. Scott to McClellan and Thomas to McClellan, 22 July 1861; General Orders, No. 2. Adjutant General's Office. 25 July 1861; General Orders, No. 1. Headquarters, Division of the Potomac. 27 July 1861. *OR* I, 2, pp. 752–53, 763, and 766. Technically, McClellan named it the Division of the Potomac, which consisted of the Department of Washington and the Department of Northeastern Virginia.

8. Quoted in Stephen Sears, *George B. McClellan*, p. 132.

9. McClellan to Wife, 27 July 1861. Stephen Sears, ed., *Papers of McClellan*, p. 70.

10. McClellan to Wife, 30 July 1861. Stephen Sears, ed., *Papers of McClellan*, p. 71.

11. McClellan to Wife, 27 July 1861. Stephen Sears, ed., *Papers of McClellan*, p. 70.

12. McClellan to Lincoln, 4 [2] Aug. 1861. *OR* I, 5, pp. 6–8.

13. McClellan to Scott, 8 Aug. 1861. *OR* I, 11, 3, p. 3. McClellan determined the grossly inflated figure before the famed detective, Allan Pinkerton, conducted his spying efforts. As Sears has explained so well, Pinkerton's exaggerated numbers merely verified what McClellan believed to be true, that the Confederate forces vastly outnumbered his.

14. McClellan to Scott, 18 July 1861; McClellan to Wife, 2 Aug. 1861. Stephen Sears, ed., *Papers of McClellan*, pp. 60 and 75.

15. Scott to Secretary of War, 9 Aug. 1861. *OR* I, 11, 3, p. 4.

16. McClellan to Wife, 8 Aug. and 10 Aug. 1861. Stephen Sears, ed., *Papers of McClellan*, p. 81.

17. McClellan to Wife, 16 Aug. 1861; McClellan to Wife, 19 Aug. 1861; McClellan to Cameron, 13 Sep. 1861. Stephen Sears, *Papers of McClellan*, pp. 85, 87, and 100.

18. McClellan to Wife, 16 Aug. 1861; McClellan to Wife, 19 Aug. 1861; McClellan to Cameron, 13 Sep. 1861; McClellan to Wife, [11? Oct. 1861]; McClellan to Wife, [31 Oct. 1861]. Stephen Sears, *Papers of McClellan*, pp. 85, 87, 100, 107 and 114.

19. John Hay diary, undated. Tyler Dennett, ed., *Lincoln and the Civil War in the Diaries and Letters of John Hay* (New York: Dodd, Mead & Company, 1939), p. 33.
20. McClellan to Wife, 6 [Sep.] 1861. Stephen Sears, ed., *Papers of McClellan*, p. 95. Also see McClellan to Wife, 21 July [1861]. Sears, ed., *Papers of McClellan*, p. 65.
21. McClellan to Cameron, undated [31 Oct. 1861]. *OR* I, 5, pp. 9–11.
22. Hay diary, 10 Oct. 1861. Dennett, ed., *Lincoln and the Civil War*, p. 27; McClellan to Wife, [31 Oct. 1861]. Stephen Sears, ed. *Papers of McClellan*, p. 113. See also Hay diary, 13 Nov. 1861. Dennett, ed., *Lincoln and the Civil War*, pp. 34–35.
23. Quoted in T. Harry Williams. *Lincoln and His Generals*, p. 45.
24. McClellan to Wife, 17 Nov. 1861. Stephen Sears, ed., *Papers of McClellan*, p. 135.
25. See Stephen B. Oates, *With Malice Toward None: The Life of Abraham Lincoln* (New York: Harper & Row, 1977), p. 23.
26. McClellan to Lincoln, 10 Dec. 1861, with Enclosure. *OR* I, 11, pp. 6–7.
27. McClellan, *McClellan's Own Story*, p. 158; Quoted in Williams, *Lincoln and His Generals*, p. 57.
28. McClellan to Wife, 18 May [1862]. Stephen Sears, ed., *Papers of McClellan*, p. 269.
29. See McClellan to Stanton, 3 Feb. 1862. *OR* I, 5, p. 45.
30. Presidential General War Orders, No. 3. 8 Mar. 1862. *OR* I, 5, p. 50. Also see President War Order, No. 3, 11 Mar. 1862; and Stanton to McClellan, 13 Mar. 1862. *OR* I, 5, pp. 54 and 56.
31. Theodore C. Pease and James G. Randall, ed., *The Diary of Orville Hickman Browning*, I (Springfield: The Trustees of the Illinois State Historical Library, 1925), p. 537.
32. See *OR* I, 11, 3, pp. 57–62 for the inquiry.
33. Lincoln to McClellan, 25 May 1862. *OR* I, 11, 1, p. 32.
34. Lincoln to McClellan, 6 Apr. 1862 and 9 Apr. 1862. *OR* I, 11, 1, p. 14 and 15. Also see McClellan to Lincoln, 6 Apr. 1862. *OR* I, 11, 3, pp. 73–74. On manpower, see *OR* I, 11, 3, pp. 230 and 238.
35. McClellan to Wife, 8 Apr. [1862]. Stephen Sears, ed., *Papers of McClellan*, p. 243.
36. McClellan to Stanton, 5 May 1862. *OR* I, 11, 3, p. 142;

McClellan to Lincoln, 14 May 1862. *OR* I, 11, 1, pp. 26–27. McClellan to Wife, 19 Apr. [1862]. Sears, ed., *Papers of McClellan*, p. 244. Several months earlier, when he tried to sell Lincoln on a campaign in the lower Chesapeake region, McClellan had claimed that the roads "are passable at all seasons of the year," compared to those in northern Virginia, which he deemed in "unpassable condition." *OR* I, 5, p. 44. Also see Stanton to McClellan, 18 May 1862. McClellan to Lincoln, 21 May 1862. *OR* I, 11, 1, pp. 27–29; Lincoln to McClellan, 21 May 1862. *OR* I, 11, 3, p. 184.

37. Lincoln to McDowell, 28 May 1862. Roy T. Basler, ed., *The Collected Works of Abraham Lincoln*, V, p. 246.

38. McClellan to Stanton, [9 Mar. 1862]; McClellan to Stanton, 27 Apr. 1862; Stephen Sears, ed., *Papers of McClellan*, pp. 199 and 247–49; McClellan to Lincoln, 21 May 1862; McClellan to Lincoln, 26 May 1862, *OR* I, 11, 1, pp. 29 and 33.

39. McClellan to Stanton, 30 May 1862; McClellan to Stanton, 28 May 1862; Lincoln to McClellan, 28 May 1862. *OR* I, 11, 1, pp. 35–37.

40. McClellan to Stanton, 1 June 1862 and 2 June 1862. *OR* I, 11, 1, pp. 749–50. McClellan averred, "I think he is too able for that," McClellan to Stanton, 27 May 1862. *OR* I, 11, 3, p. 193.

41. Lincoln to McClellan and McClellan to Lincoln, 18 June 1862. *OR* I, 11, 3, pp. 233–34; McClellan to Wife, 22 June [1862]. Stephen Sears, ed., *Papers of McClellan*, p. 305.

42. McClellan to Stanton, 25 June 1862. *OR* I, 11, 1, p. 51; Lincoln to McClellan, 26 June 1862. *OR* I, 11, 3, p. 259.

43. McClellan to Wife, 4 and 17 July [1862]. Stephen Sears, ed. *Papers of McClellan*, p. 335 and 363.

44. McClellan to Stanton, 25 June 1862 and 27 June 1862. *OR* I, 11, 3, pp. 254 and 266; McClellan to Stanton, 28 July 1862. *OR* I, 11, 1, p. 61; McClellan to Lorenzo Thomas, 1 July 1862. *OR* I, 11, 3, p. 281. See also David Homer Bates, *Lincoln in the Telegraph Office: Recollections of the United States Military Telegraph Corps During the Civil War* (New York: The Century Company, 1907), pp. 108–111.

45. Lincoln to McClellan, 2 July 1862. *OR* I, 11, 3, p. 286.

46. McClellan to Wife [7 July 1862]; McClellan to Marcy, 4 July

1862. Stephen Sears, ed., *Papers of McClellan*, pp. 341 and 334; McClellan to Stanton, 3 July 1862. *OR* I, 11, 3, pp. 291–92. Also see McClellan to Wife, 8 July and 10 [July] 1862. Stephen Sears, ed., *Papers of McClellan*, pp. 346 and 348.

47. McClellan to Lincoln, 4 July 1862. *OR* I, 11, 1, p. 72.
48. McClellan to Wife, 9 July and 10 [July 1862]. Stephen Sears, ed. *Papers of McClellan*, p. 348. McClellan may have projected his personal inadequacies on to Lincoln.
49. McClellan to Wife, 8 July [1862]. Stephen Sears, ed., *Papers of McClellan*, p. 346; McClellan to Lincoln, 7 July 1862. *OR* I, 11, 1, pp. 73–74.
50. Halleck Memorandum to the Secretary of War, 27 July 1862. *OR* I, 11, 3, pp. 337–38.
51. See Pease and Randall, eds., *The Diary of Orville Hickman Browning*, I, p. 563.
52. McClellan to Wife, 10 and 8 Aug. [1862]. Stephen Sears, ed., *Papers of McClellan*, pp. 388–90.
53. McClellan to Lincoln, 29 Aug. 1862. *OR* I, 11, 1, p. 98.
54. John Hay diary, [1] and 5 Sep. 1862, Tyler Dennett, ed., *Lincoln in the Civil War*, pp. 45 and 47.
55. McClellan to Wife, 5 Sep. [1862]. Stephen Sears, ed., *Papers of McClellan*, p. 435.
56. McClellan to Wife, 15 Sep. [1862]. Stephen Sears, ed., *Papers of McClellan*, p. 463.
57. Lincoln to McClellan, 15 Sep. 1862. *OR* I, 19, 1, p. 53.
58. McClellan also received reinforcements, but the benefits to Lee outweighed those to McClellan.
59. McClellan to Wife, 18 Sep. 1862. Stephen Sears, ed., *Papers of McClellan*, p. 469; McClellan to Halleck, 19 Sep. 1862. *OR* I, 19, 2, p. 330; McClellan to Wife, 22 Sep. [1862]. Stephen Sears, ed., *Papers of McClellan*, p. 477. Also see McClellan to Wife, 20 Sep. [1862], in Sears, ed., *Papers of McClellan*, pp. 473 and 476.
60. John Hay diary, 14 July 1863. Tyler Dennett, ed., *Lincoln in the Civil War*, p. 67.
61. General Orders, No. 163. Army of the Potomac. 7 Oct. 1862. *OR* I, 19, 2, pp. 395–96.
62. Quoted in Williams, *Lincoln and His Generals*, p. 173.
63. Lincoln to McClellan, 13 Oct. 1862. *OR* I, 19, 1, pp. 13–14.

64. Halleck to McClellan, 14 Oct. 1862. *OR* I, 19, 2, p. 421; McClellan to Halleck, 21 Oct. 1862; Halleck to McClellan, 21 Oct. 1862. *OR* I, 19, 1, p. 81.
65. Lincoln to McClellan, 24 [25] Oct. 1862; McClellan to Lincoln, 27 Oct. 1862; Lincoln to McClellan, 27 Oct. 1862. *OR* I, 19, 2, pp. 485 and 496–97.
66. McClellan to Wife, [c. 29] Oct. [1862]. Stephen Sears, ed., *Papers of McClellan*, p. 515.
67. McClellan to Wife, 4 [Nov. 1862]; McClellan to Wife, 7 Nov. [1862]. Stephen Sears, ed., *Papers of McClellan*, pp. 518 and 520.
68. McClellan to Wife, 9 [10] August [1861], [31 Oct. 1861], [30 Oct. 1861], 10 [July 1862]. Stephen Sears, ed., *Papers of McClellan*, pp. 81–82, 114, 113, and 349.
69. *Diagnostic and Statistical Manual of Mental Disorders*, Third Edition—Revised (Washington, DC: American Psychiatric Association, 1987), pp. 337–39 and 349–51. See also the Appendix of this book.
70. McClellan to Wife, 7 Nov. 1862. Stephen Sears, ed., *Papers of McClellan*, p. 520.

Chapter 4. "I cannot direct both parts of my command at once"

1. William C. Davis, *Jefferson Davis: The Man and His Hour* (New York: HarperCollins, Publishers, 1991) is the best biography of Davis. See also Davis, *Jefferson Davis*, pp. 303–304.
2. Quoted in Eric Walther, *The Fire-Eaters* (Baton Rouge: Louisiana State University Press, 1992), p. 79. For information on Montgomery, see Cameron Freeman Napier, *The First Confederate White House* (Montgomery: The First Confederate White House, 1986); William Howard Russell, *Pictures of Southern Life, Social, Political, and Military* (New York: James G. Gregory, 1861), pp. 20–21; William Howard Russell, *My Diary North and South* (Boston: T.O.H.P. Burnham, 1863), pp. 172–74; T.C. DeLeon, *Four Years in Rebel Capitals* (Mobile: The Gossip Printing Company, 1890), pp. 37–39; Henry D. Capers, *The Life and Times of C. G. Memminger* (Richmond: Everett Waddey Co., 1893), pp. 310–11 and 329–30. Thanks to my friends Lynda Crist, Mary Dix, and Ken Williams for their help here and throughout the chapter.

3. Martin Crawford, ed., *William Howard Russell's Civil War: Private Diaries and Letters, 1861–1862* (Athens: University of Georgia Press, 1992), p. 52.
4. For the best biography of Johnston, see Craig L. Symonds, *Joseph E. Johnston: A Civil War Biography*. New York: W. W. Norton & Company, 1992. A pro-Johnston biography is Gilbert Govan and James W. Livingood, *A Different Valor: The Story of General Joseph E. Johnston, C.S.A.*. Indianapolis: Bobbs-Merrill Company, 1956. A forthcoming volume with some keen insights is Steven Harvey Newton, "Joseph E. Johnston and the Defense of Richmond," Ph.D. dissertation at the College of William and Mary, 1989.
5. Johnston to Col. R. S. Garnett, 26 May 1861. Memorandum in relation to Harper's Ferry by Johnston, [26 May 1861]. *OR* I, 2, p. 881. Also see Geo. Deas to Garnett, 23 May 1861. *OR* I, 2, pp. 867–70. Johnston claims a smaller number of "effectives."
6. Lee to Johnston, 1 June 1861. *OR* I, 2, p. 897.
7. Lee to Johnston, 3 June 1861 and Johnston to Lee, 6 June 1861. *OR* I, 2, pp. 901 and 907–908.
8. Lee to Johnston, 7 June 1861. *OR* I, 2, p. 910.
9. Cooper to Johnston, 13 June 1861. *OR* I, 2, pp. 923–25. Also see Johnston to Cooper, 15 June 1861 and Cooper to Johnston, 18 June 1861. *OR* I, 2, pp. 929–30 and 934–35.
10. Cooper to Johnston, 18 June 1861; Davis to Johnston, 22 June 1861. *OR* I, 2, pp. 934 and 945.
11. Beauregard to Davis, 9 July 1861, Cooper to Johnston, 17 July 1861. *OR* I, 2, pp. 969 and 478.
12. Davis to Johnston, 20 July 1861. *OR* I, 2, p. 985. For Davis and Johnston at First Manassas, see Davis, *Jefferson Davis*, pp. 347–53 and Symonds, *Joseph E. Johnston*, pp. 112–24.
13. Quoted in Symonds, *Joseph E. Johnston*, p. 121.
14. Quoted in Davis, *Jefferson Davis*, p. 357; Johnston to Cooper, 29 July 1861. *OR* I, 2, p. 1007.
15. For the best discussion of the rank order, see Steven Harvey Newton, "Joseph E. Johnston and the Defense of Richmond." Ph.D. dissertation at the College of William and Mary, 1989, pp. 13–19.
16. Johnston to [Davis], 12 Sep. 1861. *OR* IV, 1, pp. 605–608.
17. Davis to Johnston, 14 Sep. 1861. *OR* IV, 1, p. 611.

18. See G. W. Smith Memorandum on Council of War, 31 Jan. 1862. *OR* I, 5, pp. 884–87. Also see Davis, *Jefferson Davis*, pp. 364–65.
19. Quoted in Davis, *Jefferson Davis*, pp. 97 and 366.
20. Johnston to Benjamin, 18 Jan. 1862; Benjamin to Johnston, 25 Jan. 1862. *OR* I, 5, pp. 1036–37 and 1045–46.
21. Johnston to Whiting, 9 Nov. 1861, Johnston to Benjamin, 1 Feb. 1862. *OR* I, 5, pp. 944 and 1057.
22. Davis to Johnston, 4 March 1862, Johnston to Davis, 1 Mar. 1862. *OR* I, 5, pp. 1086–87 and 1089. A good discussion of the affair exists in Newton, "Joseph E. Johnston and the Defense of Richmond [note 5 above]," pp. 56–61.
23. Benjamin to Johnston, 26 January 1862. Also see Taliaferro et al. to Loring, 25 Jan. 1862. *OR* I, 5, pp. 1046–49.
24. On strategy, see Frank E. Vandiver, "Jefferson Davis and Confederate Strategy," in Bernard Mayo, ed., *The American Tragedy: The Civil War in Retrospect.* Hampden-Sydney, VA: Hampden-Sydney College, 1959; and Archer Jones, *Civil War Command and Strategy: The Process of Victory and Defeat* (New York: The Free Press, 1992).
25. Johnston to Jackson, 28 Jan. 1862, Johnston to Davis, 5 Feb. 1862. *OR* I, 5, pp. 1050 and 1062. As his leading biographer has noted, "The essence of Johnston's strategic vision can be stated in a single phrase: concentration of force." Symonds, *Joseph E. Johnston,* p. 140.
26. Thos. S. Preston to Wife, 13 Mar. 1862. Preston–Davis Papers, University of Virginia. Also see Johnston to Davis, 13 Mar. 1862. *OR* I, 51, pt. 2, pp. 1073–74.
27. Davis to Johnston, 28 Feb. 1862. *OR* I, 5, pp. 1083–84. Johnston to Davis, 13 Mar. 1862. *OR* I, 51, pt. 2, p. 1073.
28. Davis to Johnston, 15 Mar. 1862. *OR* I, 5, p. 527.
29. Quoted in Symonds, *Joseph E. Johnston,* p. 158. Also see Symonds, *Joseph E. Johnston,* pp. 156–57; Johnston to Lee and Lee to Johnston, 8 May 1862; Davis to Johnston, 11 May 1862. *OR* I, 11, 3, pp. 499–501 and 507–508.
30. Davis to Winnie, 2 June 1862. Jefferson Davis Papers, Museum of the Confederacy. See also Symonds, *Joseph E. Johnston,* pp. 163–74, and Davis, *Jefferson Davis,* pp. 423–25.
31. Davis to Varina, 23 June 1862. Jefferson Davis Papers, Museum of the Confederacy.

32. Davis to Speaker of the House, 14 Mar. 1862. *OR* IV, 1, p. 997. Perhaps the best description of Johnston's position would be an army group commander.
33. See Davis to Seddon, 15 Dec. 1862. *OR* I, 20, 2, pp. 449–50.
34. Johnston to Davis, 22 Dec. 1862. *OR* I, 20, 2, pp. 459–60.
35. Johnston to Davis, 6 Jan. 1863. *OR* I, 17, 2, p. 827; Johnston to Wigfall, 4 and 8 Mar. 1863. Wigfall Papers, Library of Congress.
36. Johnston to Wigfall, 4 Mar. 1863. Wigfall Papers, Library of Congress.
37. Johnston to Wigfall, 15 Dec. 1862 and 8 Mar. 1863. Wigfall Papers, Library of Congress.
38. Johnston to Cooper, 1 May 1863. *OR* I, 24, 1, p. 214.
39. Davis to Pemberton, 7 May 1863. *OR* I, 24, 3, p. 842.
40. Seddon to Johnston, 9 May 1863. *OR* I, 24, 1, p. 215.
41. Johnston to Pemberton, 29 May 1863. *OR* I, 24, 1, p. 279.
42. Johnston to Wigfall, 8 Mar. 1863. Wigfall Papers, Library of Congress; Johnston to Seddon, 10, and 12 June 1863. *OR* I, 24, 1, p. 226.
43. Johnston to Seddon, 15 June 1863 and Seddon to Johnston, 16 June 1863. *OR* I, 24, 1, p. 227. Also see AAR of Pemberton, *OR* I, 24, 1, p. 281.
44. See Davis to Johnston, 15 July 1863, Johnston to Davis, 8 Aug. 1863. *OR* I, 24, 1, pp. 202–207 and 209–213.
45. Johnston to Davis, 16 June 1863. *OR* I, 24, 1, p. 196. See also Cooper to Johnston, 22 July 1863. *OR* I, 24, 1, p. 232.
46. See Symonds, *Joseph E. Johnston*, p. 248.
47. Hardee to Cooper, 17 Dec. 1863; Hardee to Ives, 24 Dec. 1863. *OR* I, 31, 3, pp. 840 and 860.
48. Seddon to Johnston, 18 Dec. 1863; Davis to Johnston, 23 Dec. 1863. *OR* I, 31, 3, pp. 842 and 856–57.
49. Johnston to Wigfall, 23 Apr. and 30 Apr. 1864. Wigfall Papers, Library of Congress. Also see Castel, *Decision in the West*, for a good analysis of Johnston's conduct of the Atlanta Campaign.
50. Actually the increase is greater, because of those killed, wounded, and captured during the campaign. In Johnston to Bragg, 27 June 1864, Johnston estimates his killed and wounded at 9,000. *OR* I, 38, 4, pp. 795–96.
51. Johnston to Bragg, 27 June 1864. *OR* I, 38, 4, pp. 795–96. Also see Davis to Bragg, 23 June 1864. *OR* I, 39, 2, p. 658; numerous

requests by Johnston are in *OR* I, 38, 4. Sherman's massive numerical superiority, Johnston later contended, compelled him to use cavalry on the line.

52. Sources for the different calculations are: Circular. Artillery Headquarters, Army of the Mississippi. 7 July 1864. Maj. George S. Storrs Papers, Kenesaw Mountain National Battlefield Park (copy in possession of author); Special Field Orders, No. 29. HDQRS. Mil. Div. of the Miss. 26 June 1864. *OR* I, 38, 4, pp. 601–602. Braxton Bragg estimated the 7 percent difference. My thanks to Archer Jones for pointing this out to me. For the number of men detached to protect the railroad, see John Bigelow, *The Principles of Strategy: Illustrated Mainly from American Campaigns* (New York: Greenwood Press, 1968), pp. 118–19. Reprinted from original by J. B. Lippincott Company, 1894.

53. Davis to Johnston, 7 July 1864. *OR* I, 38, 5, p. 867. For the Hood letters, see Richard M. McMurry, *John Bell Hood and the War for Southern Independence* (Lexington: University Press of Kentucky, 1982), pp. 95–97, 110, and 114.

54. Bragg to Davis, 15 July 1864. *OR* I, 38, 5, p. 881. Also see Hood to Bragg, 14 July 1864. *OR* I, 38, 5, pp. 879–80.

55. Davis to Johnston and Johnston to Davis, 16 July 1864. *OR* I, 38, 5, pp. 882–83.

56. Cooper to Johnston, 17 July 1864; Johnston to Cooper, 18 July 1864. *OR* I, 38, 5, pp. 885 and 888.

57. Lee to Johnston and Johnston to Lee, 22 Feb. 1865. *OR* I, 47, 2, p. 1247.

58. See Symonds, *Joseph E. Johnston*, pp. 354–55.

59. Of course, in this case Grant and Sherman had the same weakness as Lee and Jackson.

Chapter 5. "If I got in a tight place you would come—if alive"

1. Quoted in T. Harry Williams, *McClellan, Sherman and Grant* (New Brunswick: Rutgers University Press, 1962), p. 46.

2. Grant, *Personal Memoirs of Ulysses S. Grant* (New York: Da Capo Press, Inc., 1982, originally published in 1885), p. 11.

3. William Tecumseh Sherman, *Memoirs of General William T. Sherman* (New York: Charles L. Webster & Company, 1891), Vol.

I, p. 14. For a good biography of Sherman, see John F. Marszalek, *Sherman: A Soldier's Passion for Order* (New York: The Free Press, 1993).

4. Theodore Lyman to Wife, 29 Mar. 1865. George R. Agassiz, ed., *Meade's Headquarters, 1863–1865: Letters of Colonel Theodore Lyman from The Wilderness to Appomattox* (Freeport, New York: Books for Libraries Press, 1970), p. 327. Originally published in 1922.

5. James Harrison Wilson, *Under the Old Flag*, Vol. II, p. 17.

6. See Sherman to Editor, 13 Mar. 1885. "Sherman on Grant," *North American Review*, 142, p. 112.

7. Grant to sister, 9 Feb. 1862. John Y. Simon, ed., *The Papers of Ulysses S. Grant*, Vol. 4, p. 179.

8. Grant to S. B. Buckner, 16 Feb. 1862. John Y. Simon, ed., *The Papers of Ulysses S. Grant*, Vol. 4, p. 218.

9. Sherman to Grant, 15 Feb. 1862, Sherman to Grant, 15 Feb. 1862. John Y. Simon, ed., *The Papers of Ulysses S. Grant*, Vol. 5, pp. 215–216.

10. Grant to Sherman, 19 Feb. 1862. *OR* I, 7, p. 638. Perhaps Grant realized what many Civil War generals failed to understand, that promotions follow victories and that if a general concentrates on victories, promotions will follow.

11. Grant to Julia, 9 June 1862. John Y. Simon, ed., *The Papers of Ulysses S. Grant*, 5, pp. 140–41.

12. Sherman to Brother, 4 Jan. 1862. Reel 5. Sherman Papers, Library of Congress.

13. Sherman to Grant, 10 Mar. 1864. Sherman, *Memoirs*, I, p. 400.

14. Grant to Halleck, 11 May 1862. John Y. Simon, ed., *The Papers of Ulysses S. Grant*, Vol. 5, p. 114.

15. Sherman to Ellen, 6 Jun. 1862. M. A. DeWolfe Howe, ed., *Home Letters of General Sherman* (New York: Charles Scribner's Sons, 1909), p. 228; Grant to Julia, 4 May 1862. John Y. Simon, ed., *The Papers of Ulysses S. Grant*, Vol. 5, p. 111; Sherman, *Memoirs*, Vol. I, p. 283.

16. The letter from Grant to Sherman, 4 Aug. 1862, apparently did not survive. In Sherman to Grant, 17 Aug. 1862, Sherman opens his letter by repeating Grant's offer and accepting it. *OR* I, 17, pt. 2, p. 178.

17. Oliver Otis Howard, "Grant at Chattanooga," *Personal Recollections of the War of the Rebellion, Military Order of the Loyal Legion of the United States, New York Commandery* (New York: Published by the Commandery, 1891), p. 249.
18. Sherman to Grant, 10 Mar. 1864. Sherman, *Memoirs*, I, p. 400.
19. Sherman to Grant, 17 Aug. and 4 Oct. 1862. *OR* I, 17, Pt. 2, p. 178 and 260–61.
20. Grant to Halleck, 14 Dec. 1862. John Y. Simon, ed., *The Papers of Ulysses S. Grant*, Vol. 7, p. 29.
21. Grant to Julia, 27 Mar. 1863. John Y. Simon, ed., *The Papers of Ulysses S. Grant*, Vol. 7, pp. 479–80.
22. See Grant to Banks, 23 [22] Mar. 1863. *OR* I, 15, pp. 300–301; Grant to Halleck, 2 Apr. 1863. *OR* I, 24, 1, p. 24.
23. See Grant to Sherman, 21 Feb. 1863 and Sherman to Grant, 21 Feb. 1863. John Y. Simon, ed., *The Papers of Ulysses S. Grant*, Vol. 7, pp. 345–46.
24. Quoted in Bruce Catton, *Grant Takes Command* (Boston: Little, Brown and Company, 1968), p. 160.
25. Sherman, *Memoirs*, pp. 343–44.
26. Grant to Sherman, 27 Apr. 1863 and Sherman to Grant, 28 Apr. 1863. *OR* I, 24, pt. 3, pp. 240 and 243.
27. Armies regularly took fodder and food from the enemy country-side as they advanced. What made Grant's efforts so risky was his decision to take very little food with him. His army relied almost exclusively on the Mississippi population for its food until it opened a supply line in late May. Grant to Sherman, 9 May 1863. *OR* I, 24, 3, pp. 285–86.
28. Theodore Lyman to Wife, 18 May 1864. George R. Agassiz, ed., *Meade's Headquarters, 1863–1865*, p. 102.
29. Grant, *Personal Memoirs*, pp. 282–83.
30. *OR* I, 24, 3, 450–42. Grant recommended that McPherson receive a promotion to brigadier general also.
31. Sherman to Grant, 10 March 1864. Sherman, *Memoirs*, I, p. 400.
32. Howard, "Grant at Chattanooga," p. 248; William S. McFeely, *Grant: A Biography* (New York: W. W. Norton & Company, 1981), pp. 118–19.
33. Sherman to Thomas, 20 Oct. 1864. *OR* I, 39, 3, p. 378. See Sherman to Halleck, 24 Dec. 1864. *OR* I, 44, p. 799.
34. Sherman to Halleck, 25 Dec. 1863. *OR* I, 31, pp. 497–98.

35. Grant to Halleck, 15 Jan. 1864. John Y. Simon, ed., *The Papers of Ulysses S. Grant*, 10, pp. 14–16. In January 1864 the Red River and other waterways west of the Mississippi were too low for navigation. Banks later conducted a raid up the Red River, with near-disastrous results. Grant also proposed a massive raid into North Carolina, which Halleck rejected. Grant to Halleck, 19 Jan. 1864 and Halleck to Grant, 17 Feb. 1864. John Y. Simon, ed., *The Papers of Ulysses S. Grant*, 10, pp. 39–41 and 110–12. On the Meridian Expedition, Sherman's troops neglected to twist the rails, which enabled the Confederates to repair them readily. On the Savannah and Carolinas Campaigns, Sherman's troops seldom committed such an error.

36. Grant to Sherman, 4 Mar. 1864. Sherman to Grant, 10 Mar. 1864. Sherman, *Memoirs*, I, pp. 399–400.

37. Grant to Sherman, 4 Apr. 1864. *OR* I, 39, 3, pp. 245–46.

38. For the best account of the Atlanta Campaign see Albert Castel, *Decision in the West: The Atlanta Campaign of 1864* (Lawrence: University Press of Kansas, 1992). Castel, however, is excessively critical of Sherman.

39. National Thanks from Lincoln to Sherman, 3 Sep. 1864, Grant to Sherman, 4 Sep. 1864. Sherman, *Memoirs*, II, p. 110.

40. Sherman, *Memoirs*, II, pp. 31–32. Sherman's Meridian Campaign in early 1864, as well as his pursuit of Hood in October, provided valuable experience for the massive raid through Georgia.

41. Sherman to Grant, 1 Oct. 1864. *OR* I, 39, 3, p. 3.

42. Sherman to Grant, 9 Oct. 1864. *OR* I, 38, 3, p. 162.

43. Grant to Sherman and Sherman to Grant, 11 Oct. 1864. *OR* I, 39, 3, p. 202.

44. Grant to Julia, 1 Jan. 1865. John Y. Simon, ed., *The Papers of Ulysses S. Grant*, 13, p. 203.

45. See Grant to Sherman, 6 Dec. 1864; Grant to Sherman, 18 Dec. 1864; Grant to Sherman, 27 Dec. 1864. *OR* I, 44, pp. 636–37, 740–41, and 820–21.

46. Quoted in Joseph T. Glatthaar, *The March to the Sea and Beyond: Sherman's Troops in the Savannah and Carolinas Campaigns* (New York: New York University Press, 1985), p. 175.

47. Sherman, *Memoirs*, II, pp. 355–57.

48. Sherman, *Memoirs*, II, p. 377.

Chapter 6. "I am ready to cooperate with anybody and everybody"

1. See Richard S. West, Jr., *The Second Admiral: A Life of David Dixon Porter, 1813–1891* (New York: Coward-McCann, Inc., 1937), p. 181.
2. Porter journal, pp. 429–30. David Dixon Porter Papers, Library of Congress [LC].
3. Porter journal, pp. 424–26. David Dixon Porter Papers, LC; Porter to Fox, 12 Nov. 1863. R. M. Thompson and Wainwright R. Thompson. eds., *Confidential Correspondence of Gustavus Vasa Fox, Assistant Secretary of the Navy, 1861–1865*, (New York: 1919) Vol. 2, p. 150.
4. See Grant to Sherman, 8 Dec, 1862. John Y. Simon, ed., *The Papers of Ulysses S. Grant*, 6, pp. 406–407; Sherman to Porter, 8 Dec. 1862. *OR* I, 17, 2, p. 392; Porter, *Incidents and Anecdotes of the Civil War* (New York: D. Appleton and Co., 1886), pp. 125–26.
5. Gideon Welles diary, 21 Sep. 1863 and 13 July 1863. Howard K. Beale, ed., *Diary of Gideon Welles: Secretary of the Navy Under Lincoln and Johnson* (New York: W. W. Norton & Company, 1960), Vol. I, p. 440. See West, p. 31; Beale, ed., *Diary of Gideon Welles*, I, pp. 128–29 and 157; James Russell Soley, *Admiral Porter* (New York: D. Appleton and Company, 1903), pp. 62–63.
6. Sherman to Porter, 8 Dec. 1862. *OR* I, 17, 2, p. 392.
7. Porter to Sherman, 12 Nov. 1862. *Official Records of the Union and Confederate Navies* (Washington, DC: U.S. Government Printing Office, 1990 [hereafter *ORN*]), I, 23, p. 479; Sherman to Porter, 16 Nov. 1862. *OR* I, 17, 2, pp. 867–68; Porter to Sherman, 24 Nov. 1862. *ORN* I, 23, p. 500.
8. Porter journal, p. 435. David Dixon Porter Papers, LC.
9. Porter journal, pp. 436–38. David Dixon Porter Papers, LC; Porter, *Incidents*, pp. 126–27.
10. See AAR of Sherman, 3 Jan. 1863. *OR* I, 17, 1, pp. 605–10; Porter to Welles, 27 and 31 Dec. 1862 and 3 Jan. 1863. *OR* I, 17, 2, pp. 883–88.
11. Porter to Welles, 31 Dec. 1862. *OR* I, 17, 2, p. 886. Also see *OR* I, 17, 1, p. 625.
12. Porter journal, p. 415. David Dixon Porter Papers, LC.
13. Sherman to Porter, 3 Jan. 1863. *ORN* I, 23, p. 606. Also see Sherman to Rawlins, 4 Jan. 1863. *OR* I, 17, 1, p. 612.

14. Porter to Welles, 28 Jan. 1863. *ORN* I, 24, p. 127. See also Sherman, *Memoirs*, I, pp. 296–303.

15. Grant to Halleck, 20 Jan. 1863. *OR* I, 24, 1, pp. 8–9; Porter to Fox, 16 Jan. 1863. See also R. M. and W. R. Thompson, eds., *Confidential Correspondence*, 2, p. 154.

16. See Sherman to Rawlins, 29 Mar. 1863, unidentified naval officer's diary, 22 Mar. 1863. *ORN* I, 24, pp. 491 and 495; Sherman to Porter, 1 and 4 Feb. 1863; Porter to Sherman, 3 Feb. 1863; Porter to Welles, 27 and 31 Dec. 1862 and 3 and 18 Jan. 1863. *OR* I, 17, 2, pp. 882–89.

17. Porter, *Incidents*, pp. 168–69; Porter journal, pp. 562–63. David Dixon Porter Papers, LC.

18. See Grant to Sherman, 22 Mar. 1863. John Y. Simon, ed., *The Papers of Ulysses S. Grant*, Vol. 7, pp. 455–56.

19. See Grant to Sherman, 22 Mar. 1863, Grant to Farragut, 23 Mar. and 23 Mar. 1863; Grant to Porter, 23 and 26 Mar. 1863. John Y. Simon, ed., *The Papers of Ulysses S. Grant*, Vol. 7, pp. 455–61 and 475; Grant to Porter, 29 Mar. and 2 Apr. 1863. *OR* I, 24, 3, pp. 151–52 and 186.

20. Grant to Porter and Porter to Grant, 29 Mar. 1863, Grant to Porter, 2 Apr. 1863. *OR* I, 24, 3, pp. 151–52 and 168.

21. Porter to Welles, 13 July 1863. *ORN* I, 25, pp. 279–80. Also see Grant, *Personal Memoirs*, pp. 240–41; Porter to Fox, 25 Apr. 1863. R. M. and W. R. Thompson, eds., *Confidential Correspondence*, 2, p. 172.

22. Welles to Porter, 2 Apr. 1863, Porter to Welles, 11 Apr. 1863. *ORN* I, 24, p. 522 and 541; Porter to Grant. 11 Apr. 1863. *OR* I, 24, 3, p. 186.

23. See Porter to Welles, 17 and 19 Apr. 1863, Porter to Commanders of *Benton* et al., 10 Apr. 1863. *ORN* I, 24, pp. 552–55.

24. Porter, *Incidents*, p. 177.

25. Porter to Grant, 20 Apr. 1863. *OR* I, 24, 3, p. 211; Porter to Fox, 25 Apr. 1863. R. M. and W. R. Thompson, eds., *Confidential Correspondence*, 2, p. 176.

26. Porter to Grant, 20 Apr. 1863. *OR* I, 24, 3, p. 211.

27. Quoted in West, *The Second Admiral*, pp. 182–83. Also see Sherman to Grant, 2 June 1863. *OR* I, 24, 3, p. 372.

28. AAR of Grant, 6 July 1863. *OR* I, 24, 1, p. 58.

29. Sherman to Porter, 4 and 19 July 1863. *OR* I, 24, 3, pp. 473 and 531.

30. Porter to Fox, 28 Mar. 1862 and 3 Mar. 1863. R. M. and W. R. Thompson, eds., *Confidential Correspondence*, p. 94 and 161.

31. Porter to Welles, 13 July 1863. *ORN* I, 25, pp. 279–80.

32. Porter journal, pp. 439–41. David Dixon Porter Papers, LC; Porter to Fox, 25 Apr. 1863. R. M. and W. R. Thompson, eds., *Confidential Correspondence*, 2, pp. 172–73.

33. Sherman to Porter, 16 Nov. 1862. *OR* I, 17, 2, p. 868; Porter to Sherman, 24 Nov. 1862. *ORN* I, 23, pp. 501–502. Also see Sherman to Grant, 17 Aug. and 4 Oct. 1862. *OR* I, 17, 2, pp. 178 and 260–61.

34. Porter journal, pp. 436–38 and 430. David Dixon Porter Papers, LC. The quotation on 430, Porter asserted, was from a wartime letter to Welles. In fact, Grant possessed an inordinate ability to master details.

35. Quoted in Soley, *Admiral Porter*, pp. 478–79.

36. Sherman to Porter, 14 Oct. 1863. *ORN* I, 25, p. 469.

37. Porter to Sherman, 29 Oct. 1863. *ORN* I, 25, p. 524.

38. Porter to Grant, 15 Dec. 1863. *ORN* I, 25, p. 636; Porter to Grant, 26 Dec. 1863. *OR* I, 31, 3, p. 498.

39. Porter to Grant, 14 and 16 Apr. 1864. *OR* I, 34, 4, pp. 153–54 and 172.

40. Porter to Sherman, 29 Dec. 1864. *OR* I, 44, p. 832. Also see Porter to Welles, 27, 28, and 29 Dec. 1864. *ORN* I, 11, pp. 261–67.

41. Grant to Stanton, 1 Jan. 1865. *OR* I, 46, 2, p. 3.

42. Grant to Terry and Grant to Porter, 3 Jan. 1865. *ORN* I, 11, pp. 404–405.

43. See Terry to Rawlins, 15 Jan. 1865, Porter to Welles, 17 Jan. 1865. *OR* I, 46, 2, pp. 140 and 165–66; Porter to Welles, 14 Jan. 1865. *ORN* I, 11, pp. 432–33.

44. Porter to Welles, 15 Jan. 1865. *OR* I, 46, 2, p. 140.

45. Sherman to Porter, 17 Jan. 1865. *OR* I, 47, 2, pp. 68–69.

46. Porter to Welles, 24 Jan. 1865. Benjamin F. Butler, *Butler's Book* (Boston: A. M. Thayer & Co., 1892), pp. 88–90. Letter printed in its entirety.

47. Quotations in West, *The Second Admiral*, pp. 239 and 335.

Chapter 7. "I cannot spare this man. He fights."

1. Lincoln to Grant, 13 July 1863. *OR* I, 52, 1, p. 406.
2. Quoted in Stephen B. Oates, *With Malice Toward None: The Life of Abraham Lincoln* (New York: Harper & Row, Publishers, 1977), p. 300; Stanton to Halleck, 23 Apr. 1862. *OR* I, 10, 1, pp. 98–99.
3. Quoted in T. Harry Williams, *Lincoln and His Generals*, pp. 85–86; Salmon P. Chase diary, 1 Aug. 1862. David Donald, ed., *Inside Lincoln's Cabinet: The Civil War Diaries of Salmon P. Chase* (New York: Longmans, Green and Co., 1954), p. 103. Lincoln's personal congratulations to Grant for a victory at Corinth, Mississippi, in early October, may have indicated this transformation of attitude. See Lincoln to Grant, 8 Oct. 1862. *OR* I, 17, 1, p. 160.
4. See Welles diary, 5 Jan. 1863. Howard K. Beale, ed., *Diary of Gideon Welles*, I, p. 217.
5. See Dana to Stanton, 20 Mar. to 4 July 1863. *OR* I, 24, 1, pp. 63–117.
6. Lincoln to Hon. I. N. Arnold, 26 May 1863. Roy T. Basler, ed., *The Collected Works of Abraham Lincoln*, VI, p. 230; story in Oates, *With Malice Toward None*, p. 354.
7. Grant to Lincoln, 20 July 1863. *OR* I, 52, 1, p. 416. Also see Gideon Welles diary, 31 July 1863. Howard K. Beale, ed., *Diary of Gideon Welles*, I, pp. 386–87.
8. Grant to Hon. E. B. Washburn, 22 Mar. 1862. John Y. Simon, ed., *The Papers of Ulysses S. Grant*, 5, p. 408; Grant to Father, 21 Apr. 1861. John Y. Simon, ed., *The Papers of Ulysses S. Grant*, Vol. 2, p. 7.
9. See Brooks D. Simpson, *Let Us Have Peace: Ulysses S. Grant and the Politics of War and Reconstruction, 1861–1868* (Chapel Hill: University of North Carolina Press, 1991), pp. 2–5.
10. Grant to Father, 27 Nov. 1861. John Y. Simon, ed., *The Papers of Ulysses S. Grant*, Vol. 3, p. 227; Lincoln to Greeley, 22 Aug. 1862. Roy T. Basler, ed., *The Collected Works of Abraham Lincoln*, Vol. V, p. 388.
11. Grant to Father, 3 Aug. 1862. John Y. Simon, ed., *The Papers of Ulysses S. Grant*, 5, p. 264.
12. See Lincoln to Grant, 9 Aug. 1863. *OR* I, 24, 3, p. 584.

13. Lincoln to Grant, 9 Aug. 1863. *OR* I, 24, 3, p. 584; Grant to Lincoln, 23 Aug. 1863. John Y. Simon, ed., *The Papers of Ulysses S. Grant*, 9, pp. 196–97. Initially, emancipation caused quite a stir, but soldiers acquiesced to the policy much faster than they did to black enlistment.

14. Grant to Washburne, 2 Dec. 1863. John Y. Simon, ed., *The Papers of Ulysses S. Grant*, Vol. 9, p. 491; Lincoln to Grant, 8 Dec. 1863. *OR* I, 31, 2, p. 51.

15. See Grant to Halleck, 18 July 1863, Lincoln to Grant, 9 Aug. 1863. *OR* I, 24, 3, pp. 529–30 and 585.

16. Grant to Halleck, 7 Dec. 1863. *OR* I, 31, 3, pp. 349–50.

17. See Halleck to Grant, 17 and 21 Dec. 1863, Dana to Grant, 21 Dec. 1863. *OR* I, 31, 3, pp. 454 and 457–58; Grant to Halleck, 15 Jan. 1864. *OR* I, 32, 2, pp. 100–101.

18. Halleck to Grant, 8 Jan. 1864. *OR* I, 32, 2, p. 41. The campaign up the Red River turned out disastrously and deprived the Army of the Tennessee of 10,000 veterans at a critical moment in the Atlanta Campaign. If McPherson had had 10,000 more men with his army during its turning movement at Resaca, he might have been more willing to assail the defenders, seize the Western & Atlantic Railroad—Johnston's supply line—and trap the Confederate Army of Tennessee between his and Sherman's main command. Of course, Lincoln had no way of predicting the repercussions.

19. Grant to Halleck, 19 Jan. 1864. *OR* I, 33, pp. 394–95.

20. Halleck to Grant, 17 Feb. 1864. *OR* I, 32, 2, pp. 411–13.

21. Grant and Sherman confronted these problems in force after Halleck left the Mississippi River Valley for Washington.

22. For the best biography of Stanton, see Benjamin P. Thomas and Harold M. Hyman, *Stanton: The Life and Times of Lincoln's Secretary of War* (New York: Alfred A. Knopf, 1962).

23. John Hay diary, 28 Apr. 1864. Tyler Dennett, ed., *Lincoln and the Civil War*, p. 176.

24. Porter could not wait for the complete accumulation of transports and supplies. The second time they ran the batteries, Grant and Porter had lost the element of surprise.

25. Sherman to Halleck, 26 Dec. 1863. *OR* I, 31, 3, p. 498.

26. See Sherman to Halleck, 26 Dec. 1863. *OR* I, 31, 3, p. 498.

27. Sherman to Halleck, 24 Dec. 1864. *OR* I, 44, p. 799.
28. Grant to B. Burns, Esq., 17 Dec. 1863, Rawlins to Washburne, 20 Jan. 1864. John Y. Simon, ed., *The Papers of Ulysses S. Grant*, Vol. 9, pp. 541 and 543.
29. Quoted in McFeely, *Grant*, p. 153; Welles diary, 9 Mar. 1864. Howard K. Beale, *Diary of Gideon Welles*, I, pp. 538–39.
30. The thesis, first proposed by T. Harry Williams in *Lincoln and His Generals* and accepted by many scholars, that Grant created a modern command structure is a weak one. The situation early in the war with Winfield Scott as commanding general, stationed in Washington, with subordinates commanding the field armies, more closely resembles a modern command structure. But that system, too, is quite different from that of the chief of staff as created by Elihu Root and as it evolved during the twentieth century. Brig. Gen. John A. Rawlins was Grant's chief of staff.
31. See Grant to Banks, 15 Mar. 1864; Grant to Ord, 29 Mar. 1864; Grant to Sigel, 29 Mar. 1864; Grant to Butler, 2 Apr. 1864; Grant to Sherman, 4 Apr. 1864. John Y. Simon, ed., *The Papers of Ulysses S. Grant*, Vol. 10, pp. 200–201, 233–34, 236–37, 245–47, and 251–53.
32. Sherman to Banks, 24 Apr. 1864. *OR* I, 34, 3, p. 274.
33. Townsend to Meade et al., 30 Apr. 1864. *OR* III, 4, p. 250. Thanks to Jay Luvaas and BG Hal Nelson for mentioning this order to me.
34. Hay diary, 30 Apr. 1864. Tyler Dennett, ed., *Lincoln and the Civil War*, pp. 178–79.
35. Roy T. Basler, ed., *Collected Works*, Vol. VII, p. 324.
36. Grant to Lincoln, 1 May 1864. John Y. Simon, ed., *The Papers of Ulysses S. Grant*, Vol. 10, p. 380.
37. Hay diary, 9 May 1864. Tyler Dennett, ed., *Lincoln and the Civil War*, p. 180.
38. See Meade to Grant, 16 July 1864, with enclosure from H. J. Hunt to Humphreys, 16 July 1864. *OR* I, 40, 2, pp. 276–77. The division from the Nineteenth Corps was coming from New Orleans to reinforce Grant's forces.
39. Grant to Halleck, 9 July 1864, Lincoln to Grant, 10 July 1864. *OR* I, 37, 2, pp. 134 and 155.
40. Grant to Lincoln, 10 July 1864, Lincoln to Grant, 11 July 1864.

OR I, 37, 2, pp. 155–56 and 191; Hay diary, 14 July 1864. Tyler Dennett, ed., *Lincoln in the Civil War*, p. 210.

41. See Halleck to Grant, 19 and 23 July 1864, Grant to Halleck, 22 and 24 July 1864. *OR* I, 37, 2, at pp. 384–85, 413, 422, and 426.

42. Halleck to Grant, 21 July 1864. *OR* I, 37, 2, p. 408. Also see Grant to Halleck, 18 July 1864. *OR* I, 37, 2, p. 374. Grant's three departments were Susquehanna, West Virginia, and Washington. He omitted the Middle Department, which extended from New Jersey down to the Eastern Shore of Maryland and Virginia, with its heart at Baltimore.

43. Grant to Lincoln, 25 July 1864. *OR* I, 37, 2, pp. 433–34.

44. Stanton to Halleck, 27 July 1864. *OR* I, 37, 2, p. 463. Also see Grant to Halleck, 26 July 1864. *OR* I, 37, 2, p. 445.

45. Grant to Halleck, 1 Aug. 1864. *OR* I, 37, 2, p. 558.

46. See related correspondence in John Y. Simon, ed., *The Papers of Ulysses S. Grant*, 11, pp. 359–61.

47. Lincoln to Grant, 3 Aug. 1864. *OR* I, 37, 2, p. 582.

48. Grant to Sheridan, 7 Aug. 1864. *OR* I, 43, 1, p. 719.

49. Grant to Sheridan, 26 Aug. 1864. *OR* I, 43, 1, p. 917.

50. Grant, *Memoirs*, p. 580.

51. Grant to Lincoln, 19 July 1864. *OR* I, 37, 3, p. 384.

52. Lincoln to Grant, 20 July 1864. *OR* I, 37, 2, p. 400.

53. Halleck to Grant, 11 Aug. 1864, Grant to Halleck, 15 Aug. 1864, Lincoln to Grant, 17 Aug. 1864. *OR* I, 42, 2, pp. 111–12, 193–94, and 243.

54. See Lincoln to Grant, 29 Mar. 1864 and reply. Roy T. Basler, ed., *Collected Works*, Vol. VII, p. 272; Lincoln to Grant, 19 Jan. 1865, Grant to Lincoln, 21 Jan. 1865. John Y. Simon, ed., *The Papers of Ulysses S. Grant*, 13, pp. 281–82.

55. Grant to Sherman, 16 July 1864. *OR* I, 38, 5, p. 149; Lincoln to Grant, 17 July 1864. *OR* I, 40, 3, p. 289.

56. Stanton to Grant, 12 Oct. 1864, Grant to Stanton, 13 Oct. 1864. *OR* I, 39, 3, pp. 222 and 239; Lincoln to Sherman, 26 Dec. 1864. *OR* I, 44, p. 809. Also see Sherman to Grant, 1 and 11 Oct. 1864; Halleck to Grant, 2 Oct. 1864; Grant to Sherman, 11 and 12 Oct. 1864; Grant to Stanton, 14 Oct. 1864. *OR* I, 39, 3, pp. 3, 25–6, 202, 222, and 266.

57. For other examples, see Lincoln–Grant correspondence, *OR* I, 46, 2, pp. 473–74 and 668.

58. Lincoln to Grant, 25 and 27 Feb. 1865, Grant to Lincoln, 26 Feb. 1865. *OR* I, 46, 2, pp. 685, 704, and 717.
59. Stanton to Grant, 3 Mar. 1865. *OR* I, 46, 2, p. 802. Also see Grant to Stanton, 3 Mar. 1865; Lee to Grant, 2 Mar. 1865; Grant to Lee, 4 Mar. 1865. *OR* I, 46, 2, pp. 801–802 and 824–25; McFeely, *Grant*, pp. 199–208.
60. Grant to Lincoln, 20 Mar. 1865. *OR* I, 46, 3, p. 50; Quoted in Oates, *With Malice Toward None*, p. 418.
61. Lincoln to Stanton, 30 Mar. 1865, Stanton to Lincoln, 31 Mar. 1865. *OR* I, 46, 3, at pp. 280 and 332.
62. See Grant to Bowers, 2 Apr. 1865. *OR* I, 46, 3, p. 450; Grant, *Memoirs*, p. 541.
63. See Oates, *With Malice Toward None*, pp. 420–21.
64. Sheridan to Grant, 6 Apr. 1865. *OR* I, 46, 3, p. 610; Lincoln to Grant, 7 Apr. 1865. Roy T. Basler, ed., *Collected Works*, Vol. VIII, p. 392.
65. Gideon Welles diary, 14 Apr. 1865, Howard K. Beale, ed., *Diary of Gideon Welles*, II, pp. 282–83.

Chapter 8. Partners in Command

1. See Michael Fellman, *Inside War: The Guerrilla Conflict in Missouri During the American Civil War* (New York: Oxford University Press, 1989).
2. See Gary Gallagher, " 'Upon Their Success Hang Momentous Interests': Generals," in Gabor Boritt, ed., *Why the Confederacy Lost* (New York: Oxford University Press, 1992), pp. 79–109. The two men shared approaches to the war on the strategic level, and contrary to widespread belief, Davis could leave well enough alone.
3. See "Lincoln and the Strategy of Unconditional Surrender" in James M. McPherson, *Abraham Lincoln and the Second American Revolution*, pp. 65–91.
4. Quoted in Thomas and Hyman, *Stanton*, p. 124.
5. Howard commanded the Department and Army of the Tennessee, the same one that McPherson had led. Schofield commanded the Department of the Ohio and Tenth Corps in the Atlanta Campaign and eventually headed the Department of North Carolina and two corps in the final weeks of the North

Carolina Campaign. Sheridan headed the Cavalry Corps for the Army of the Potomac and the Middle Military Division.

6. See Grant to Halleck, 28 June 1864. *OR* I, 40, 2, p. 475; Halleck to Sherman, 28 June 1864. *OR* I, 38, 4, p. 629.

Appendix. McClellan's Tragic Flaws in the Light of Modern Psychology

1. *Diagnostic and Statistical Manual of Mental Disorders.* Third Edition, Revised (Washington, DC: American Psychiatric Association, 1987).
2. *Diagnostic and Statistical Manual of Mental Disorders.* Third Edition, Revised, p. 338.
3. Michael J. Goldstein, Bruce L. Baker, and Kay R. Jamison, *Abnormal Psychology: Experiences, Origins, and Interventions* (Boston: Little, Brown and Company, 1986), p. 389.
4. *Diagnostic and Statistical Manual of Mental Disorders.* Third Edition, Revised. p. 196.
5. Samuel George Morton, *Biographical Notice of the Late George McClellan, M.D., 4 Sep. 1849* (Philadelphia: William F. Geddes, 1849), pp. 9–10.
6. For McClellan's early life, see Stephen Sear's excellent biography, *George B. McClellan: The Young Napoleon.*
7. Quoted in Sears, *George B. McClellan,* p. 1.
8. Quoted in Sears, *George B. McClellan.* p. 29. Also see Sears, *George B. McClellan,* p. 4.
9. [McClellan] to Major, undated [late Dec. 1850]. Reel 2, McClellan Papers, LC.
10. All quotations in Sears, *George B. McClellan,* p. 39.
11. Quoted in Sears, *George B. McClellan,* p. 45.
12. Quoted in Sears, *George B. McClellan,* p. 54.

BIBLIOGRAPHICAL ESSAY

This project began as a course, with a compilation of documents as its text. Among published primary materials, the single best sources for the study of command relationships in the Civil War are *The War of the Rebellion: Official Records of the Union and Confederate Armies* (Washington, DC, 1880–1901) and *Official Records of the Union and Confederate Navies* (Washington, DC, 1900).

Two splendid presidential-papers projects have offered untold opportunities for the study of a wide range of Civil War topics including command relationships. The *Papers of Jefferson Davis* (Baton Rouge, 1971–Present), edited by Lynda Crist and Mary Dix, are superbly prepared volumes. Although publications have only extended up to the second year of the war, the editors have accumulated and organized the Davis materials and have been exceedingly kind in providing access to scholars. *The Papers of Ulysses S. Grant* (Carbondale, IL, 1967–Present), edited by John Y. Simon, already includes all the war years and provides readers with a wealth of previously inaccessible correspondence from Grant. In both presidential-papers projects, the footnotes are nearly as valuable as the documents themselves. The older and incomplete *Collected Works of Abraham Lincoln* (New Brunswick, NJ, 1953), edited by Roy T. Basler, still serves as the starting place for Lincoln materials that are not in the *OR* or *ORN*.

Manuscript sources on the other primary figures in this book abound. Although Robert E. Lee papers are scattered everywhere, the Virginia Historical Society holds the largest collection. Clifford

Dowdey and Louis Manarin, eds., *The Wartime Papers of Robert E. Lee* (Boston, 1961) and Douglas Southall Freeman, ed., *Lee's Dispatches* (New York, 1957), are good starting places. Thomas J. Jackson papers also appear in a variety of locations, including the Library of Congress, Virginia Military Institute, Virginia Historical Society, and Virginia State Library. George B. McClellan papers and David Dixon Porter papers reside at the Library of Congress. Stephen Sears has published a volume entitled *The Civil War Papers of George B. McClellan* (New York, 1989) with selected correspondence. The largest holdings of Joseph E. Johnston materials exist at the College of William and Mary, and valuable letters of Johnston's are part of the Wigfall Family Papers at the Library of Congress. The bulk of Sherman's papers are on microfilm from the Library of Congress and the University of Notre Dame. In addition to all of these, a host of manuscript collections contain relevant information on each one of these individuals. The most important are George Gordon Meade papers at the Historical Society of Pennsylvania and Henry Wager Halleck papers at several locations, including the U.S. Military Academy at West Point and the Huntington Library. Official materials are housed at the National Archives.

After perusing manuscript materials by these individuals, one cannot help but be disappointed in their memoirs. Easily the best of the lot is the *Memoirs of William T. Sherman*, 2 vols. (New York, 1875). It has a timeless quality and offers more military insights than any other reminiscence of the period. Studded with documents that interrupt the flow but lend credibility to arguments, Sherman's *Memoirs* has not received the public acclaim that it deserves. Like all memoirs, it is one-sided—Sherman, after all, was opinionated—yet it is chock full of interesting information, and the reader emerges from the volume having caught a glimpse of that fascinating Sherman mind.

A bit overrated but nonetheless extremely good is Grant's *Personal Memoirs*, 2 vols. (New York, 1885). Written in an extraordinarily simple and clear style, Grant's recollections make for delightful reading. But assertions of its extreme accuracy are not justified. *The Papers of Ulysses S. Grant* unequivocally disprove some of Grant's claims, particularly regarding the Vicksburg Campaign. Grant was racing against the Grim Reaper while he wrote the memoirs, dying just days after their completion, and the portion on the campaign of 1864 provides little more data than his after-action report.

Other Civil War memoirs pale in comparison to the labors of Sherman and Grant. Most are more valuable as testimony to their personalities than anything else. Joseph E. Johnston's *Narrative of Military Operations* (New York, 1874), is wholly unbalanced. Johnston spits venom at Davis and glosses over his personal failures. In response, Davis prepared a reminiscence—actually ghostwritten, with Davis as editor—*The Rise and Fall of the Confederate Government*, 2 vols. (New York, 1881), which shrewdly dodges the Davis–Johnston feud. The recollection is excessively legalistic and therefore tiresome to read. David Dixon Porter prepared a memoir, *Incidents and Anecdotes of the Civil War* (New York, 1885), that is colorful, unstructured, and embellished. George B. McClellan in *McClellan's Own Story* fails to camouflage his inadequacies as a commander, despite all his efforts.

Among the recollections and musings of the supporting cast, the best for the Union are Oliver Otis Howard, *Autobiography of Oliver Otis Howard*, 2 vols. (New York, 1907), John M. Schofield's *Forty-six Years in the Army* (New York, 1897), James Harrison Wilson's *Under the Old Flag* (New York, 1912), and Philip H. Sheridan, *Personal Memoirs*, 2 vols. (New York, 1888).

For the Confederacy, the reader must wade through a political minefield. The most important recollections are John Bell Hood's, *Advance and Retreat* (New Orleans, 1880), Jubal Early's *Autobiographical Sketch and Narrative of the War Between the States*, James Longstreet's *From Manassas to Appomattox* (Philadelphia, 1896), and Richard Taylor, *Destruction and Reconstruction* (New York, 1879). Invaluable as a thought-provoking volume is Gary Gallagher, ed., *Fighting for the Confederacy: The Personal Recollections of General Edward Porter Alexander* (Chapel Hill, 1989). Many of these soldiers contributed to Robert Underwood Johnston and Clarence Clough Buell, eds., *Battles and Leaders of the Civil War*, 4 vols. (New York, 1887).

For the theoretical aspects of warfare, the starting place is Karl von Clausewitz's *On War*, edited and translated from the German by Peter Paret and Michael Howard (Princeton, 1976). Clausewitz does not provide the reader with answers; he enables an individual to pose the proper questions. Baron de Jomini's *Art of War* (Philadelphia, 1862) provides insights into the training and mind-set of nineteenth-century military figures. Invaluable in the study of strategy are Henry E. Eccles, *Military Concepts and Philosophy* (New Brunswick, 1965) and Arthur F. Lykke, Jr., *Military Strategy* (Carlisle Barracks, 1984). Students of warfare should see Peter Paret, ed., *Makers of Modern Strategy from Machiavelli to the Nuclear Age* (Princeton, 1986), to place matters in context. Also worth reading is Headquarters, Department of the Army. *Field Manual No. 100-5. Operations* (Washington, DC, 1986). Headquarters, Department of the Army. *Field Manual No. 22-100. Military Leadership* (Washington, DC, 1990) and *Field Manual No. 22-103. Leadership and Command at Senior Levels* (Washington, DC, 1987) are also useful.

For Civil War strategy, see Archer Jones, *Civil War Command and Strategy* (New York, 1992), which provides a sound overview. More thorough treatment is available in Herman Hattaway and Archer Jones, *How the North Won* (Urbana, 1983). Readers should also examine *The Politics of Command* (Baton Rouge, 1973) by Thomas L. Connolly and Archer Jones and Jones's own *Confederate Strategy from Shiloh to Vicksburg* (Baton Rouge, 1961). J. F. C. Fuller offers some excellent insights in *Grant and Lee* (Bloomington, 1957), although he is too critical of Lee.

Perhaps the most famous volume on the command relationships in the Union is T. Harry Williams's *Lincoln and His Generals* (New York, 1952), which argues that Lincoln emerged from the war as a great strategist and established a modern command structure. A loose definition of "strategy" and a confused understanding of a "modern command structure" mar an eminently readable volume.

On the Confederate side, Frank E. Vandiver's *Rebel Brass* (Baton Rouge, 1956), an exploration into the Confederate command system, has withstood the test of time much better. To augment this fine volume, there are considerably more books on the interactions of Confederate leaders. A book entitled *West Point in the Confederacy* by Ellsworth Eliot, Jr. surprisingly includes excellent information on Confederate command relationships.

The best volume on the Confederate East is still *Lee's*

Lieutenants, 3 vols., (New York, 1942–44) by Douglas Southall Freeman. Both this book and his four-volume *R. E. Lee*, 4 vols., (New York, 1934–35) have fallen under criticism for presenting a sanitized version of Lee. Scholars and buffs, as they are want to do, have piled on their objections en masse. But the bottom line is that time after time, Freeman has arrived at the right conclusions, and has analyzed military situations carefully. Sometimes he does not discriminate among his sources well. Even so, both sets of tomes are still exceedingly valuable.

In the West, Tom Connolly's *Army of the Heartland* (Baton Rouge, 1967) and *Autumn of Glory* (Baton Rouge, 1971) are thorough yet highly critical volumes on high command in the Army of Tennessee. Virtually no one escapes Connolly's wrath. Steven Woodworth's *Jefferson Davis and his Generals* (Lawrence, 1990) rehashes much of what Connolly has done, but has injected a touch of compassion for the difficult positions which some of these ranking Rebel officers had to maintain.

The best studies on the Confederacy as a whole are Emory Thomas's *The Confederate Nation, 1861–1865* (New York, 1979) and Frank E. Vandiver's *Their Tattered Flags* (New York, 1970). *Why the Confederacy Lost The Civil War* (Athens, 1986), by Richard Beringer, Herman Hattaway, Archer Jones, and William Sill, relate home-front failures to Confederate military actions and defeat. Much older, but still worth examining, is E. Merton Coulter's *The Confederate States of America, 1861–1865* (Baton Rouge, 1950). Phillip Paludan's *"A People's Contest"* (New York, 1988), fills a comparable role for the North.

Freeman's *R. E. Lee* is still the starting point for reading on the great Confederate commander. Thomas L. Connolly overextended his argument in *The Marble Man* (New York, 1977) in an attempt to shatter the crystal image of Lee. Alan Nolan in *Lee Considered* (Chapel Hill, 1991) draws on the Connolly thesis and pushes beyond it in an unconvincing fashion.

The two best books on "Stonewall" Jackson are Vandiver's *Mighty Stonewall* (New York, 1957) and G. F. R. Henderson's *Stonewall Jackson and the American Civil War* (London, 1919). Marvelous character analyses of Jackson and William T. Sherman are found in Charles Royster's *The Destructive War* (New York, 1991). Also of value for the primary documents they include are Thomas Jackson Arnold, *Early Life and Letters of General Thomas J. Jackson* (London, 1916) and Mary Anna Jackson, *Memoirs of "Stonewall" Jackson* (1895).

Stephen Sears has written the premier biography of the Little Napoleon in his book *George B. McClellan* (New York, 1988). The best one-volume biographies of Lincoln are Stephen Oates's *With Malice Toward None* (New York, 1977) and Benjamin Thomas's *Abraham Lincoln* (New York, 1952). Also worth reading are James M. McPherson's *Abraham Lincoln and the Second American Revolution* (New York, 1991) and Gabor Boritt, ed., *Lincoln the War President* (New York, 1992). The Lincoln reader should not omit the following published primary sources on Lincoln: Tyler Dennett, ed., *Lincoln and the Civil War* (New York, 1939), the letters and diaries of Thomas Hay; David Donald, ed., *Inside Lincoln's War Cabinet* (New York, 1954), the diaries of Salmon P. Chase; Howard K. Beale, *Diary of Gideon Welles*, 3 vols. (New York, 1960); Howard K. Beale, ed., *Diary of Edward Bates, 1859–1866* (1933); and Theodore Calvin Pease and James G. Randall, eds., *Diary of Orville Hickman Browning*, 2 vols., (Springfield, 1927, 1933).

Craig Symonds's *Joseph E. Johnston* (New York, 1991) is the most worthwhile biography of the Confederate general. Easily the best biography of the Rebel president is William C. Davis, *Jefferson Davis* (New York, 1991). William S. McFeely's *Grant* (New York, 1981) is the finest biography of the general, although the author's interest in the military aspects of his life are limited. For political–military affairs, see Brooks D. Simpson, *Let Us Have Peace* (Chapel Hill, 1991). Bruce Catton's two volumes, *Grant Moves South* (Boston, 1966) and *Grant Takes Command* (Boston, 1969), are good, despite too much reliance on Grant's memoirs. Kenneth P. Williams, *Lincoln Finds a General*, 5 vols., (New York, 1949–1959) is still worth reading. The best single volume on Sherman is *Sherman: A Soldier's Passion for Order* (New York, 1993), by John F. Marszalek. B. H. Liddell Hart, *Sherman* (1929) still provokes thought. Also interesting are T. Harry Williams, *McClellan, Sherman and Grant* (New Brunswick, 1962), Grady McWhiney, ed., *Grant, Lee, Lincoln and the Radicals* (Evanston, IL, 1964), and Warren W. Hassler, Jr., *Commanders of the Army of the Potomac* (Baton Rouge,

1962). The best biographies of Porter are Richard S. West, Jr., *The Second Admiral: A Life of David Dixon Porter, 1813–1891* (New York, 1937) and James Russell Soley, *Admiral Porter* (New York, 1903).

Benjamin P. Thomas and Harold M. Hyman have written the best biography of Lincoln's secretary of war in *Stanton* (New York, 1962). They include a fascinating chapter on the Lincoln–Stanton relationship. Stephen E. Ambrose's book *Halleck* (Baton Rouge, 1962) has come under fire by Hattaway and Jones, among others. T. Harry Williams's *Beauregard, Napoleon in Gray* (Baton Rouge, 1955) is good and entertaining. Grady McWhiney prepared the first volume of *Braxton Bragg and Confederate Defeat* (New York, 1969) and Judith Lee Hallock wrote the second volume (Tuscaloosa, 1991). Charles Roland's *Albert Sidney Johnston* (Austin, 1964) ranks among the best Civil War biographies. Other fine biographies are Emory Thomas, *Bold Dragoon: The Life of J. E. B. Stuart* (New York, 1986), James I. Robertson, Jr., *General A. P. Hill* (New York, 1987), and William G. Piston, *Lee's Tarnished Lieutenant: James Longstreet and His Place in Southern History* (Athens, 1987).

Of the campaign and battle studies, the best are William C. Davis, *Battle at Bull Run* (Baton Rouge, 1977), B. F. Cooling, *Forts Henry and Donelson* (Knoxville, 1987), Robert K. Krick, *Stonewall Jackson at Cedar Mountain* (Chapel Hill, 1990), Edwin C. Bearss, *The Campaign for Vicksburg*, 3 vols. (Dayton, 1985–1986), Albert Castel, *Decision in the West* (Lawrence, 1992), Frank E. Vandiver, *Jubal's Raid* (New York, 1960), John G. Barrett, *Sherman's March Through the Carolinas* (Chapel Hill, 1956).

The best single volume on the war and its coming is James M. McPherson's *Battle Cry of Freedom* (New York, 1988). Excellent brief accounts are Charles P. Roland, *The American Iliad* (Lexington, 1991) and Frank E. Vandiver, *Blood Brothers* (College Station, 1992).

INDEX